SEEDS OF CHANGE

Tim L. Adsit

SEEDS OF CHANGE

Beacons for the Coming of His Light

TATE PUBLISHING
AND ENTERPRISES, LLC

Published by Tate Publishing & Enterprises, LLC
127 E. Trade Center Terrace | Mustang, Oklahoma 73064 USA
1.888.361.9473 | www.tatepublishing.com

Tate Publishing is committed to excellence in the publishing industry. The company reflects the philosophy established by the founders, based on Psalm 68:11,
"The Lord gave the word and great was the company of those who published it."

Book design copyright © 2012 by Tate Publishing, LLC. All rights reserved.
Cover design by Joel Uber
Interior design by Nathan Harmony

Published in the United States of America

ISBN: 978-1-61862-768-1
1. Biography & Autobiography / Religious
2. Biography & Autobiography / General
12.03.14

Dedication

This book is dedicated to the loving memory of Reverends Glyn B. and Alice Jean Adsit and all those they served with on the rural mission field in and around Hofei (Anwhei Province), China between 1947 and 1949 and those eight hundred souls they helped bring to Christ while serving there.

I would also like to dedicate the following poem to Glyn and Jean, which further helps to explain the book's title and will hopefully inspire those who choose to read the book.

Like the ripples on a quiet lake, set free,
That are caused by skipping stones and rocks,
A teacher, missionary, or minister affects eternity;
You can never tell where their influence stops.

Glyn and Jean were such teachers, missionaries, ministers, and friends;
They planted many seeds.
When seeds are planted in adults and children,
Their lives begin to change indeed.

Yes, Glyn and Jean touched the future; they taught,
And thousands of people benefited from the
seeds they planted, nourished, and grew.

We are unable to comprehend the
kind of multiplication wrought
When Jesus blesses lives that are
turned over to Him anew.

Anyone can count the seeds in an apple,
But only God can count all the apples in one seed.
May He nourish and multiply the good
in Glyn and Jean's life example
And many grow and benefit by their good deeds.

Acknowledgments

Since Reverend Glyn and Jean Adsit had no idea that a book about their missionary work, their sermons preached on the mission field, letters home while serving in China, articles written while in the field, and historical photographs would ever be published, the manuscripts and diaries that they left behind were not always completely annotated. Often, Glyn gave informal oral credit to others from the pulpit. Such statements were not always incorporated in his manuscripts. Thus, the task of uncovering all sources of indebtedness to others has been a difficult one.

In preparing this book and because of its historical significance, I have undertaken the most careful and conscientious research and, in endnotes throughout the book, have given proper credit in each instance in which I was able to discover that quoted material had been used. It is possible, however, that I have not been able to identify every single instance of this kind. If, therefore, there should remain any unacknowledged quotation in the sermons, prayers, poems, letters, reports, diaries, or articles in this book, I shall welcome information to that effect and shall be glad to credit such material to the proper source in future editions of the book.

I would also like to acknowledge the contributions of my sister, Jan Adsit Morrison, who lives in Yarmouth, Maine, who helped to edit initial drafts of the manuscript; Doris Spencer, who lives in Prineville, Oregon, an administrative assistant who helped to word process portions of the chapter outlining the history of the Disciples of Christ in China; and Claude Sandell, who lives in Bend, Oregon, who restored and scanned the color and black-and-white historical photographs appearing in the book.

All photographs of China appearing in the book are copyrighted, owned by the author, and taken by either Reverend Glyn B. or Alice Jean Adsit, both deceased. Many of the original photos were on glass slides and had to be preserved and restored for use in this book and publications to come. Special acknowledgement is given to Claude Sandell Photography, Bend, Oregon, for restoring and preserving the photographs used in this book. Mr. Sandell can be reached at 541-350-3511 or sandell@ykwc.net should you wish to contact him.

Table of Contents

Foreword **13**

Preface **15**

Introduction **17**

Chapter 1: The Story Begins **21**

Jean's Story 24

Glyn on Meeting His Future Wife 25

God speaks to Glyn 26

Men are drafted for the Army 28

**Chapter 2: What was Glyn and Jean's Experience
at Phillips University, 1941-1945?** **31**

Why did Glyn and Jean become Missionaries
and Why did they choose China? 34

Chapter 3: Cornell (1945-46) and Yale (1946-47) **39**

A Brief History of the Disciples of Christ Missionary Service in
China from 1886 to 1951 Glyn and Jean Adsit's Memoirs of Their
Missionary Experiences in Hofei, China, from 1947 to 1949 40

**Chapter 4 Speaker for the United Christian
Missionary Society, 1951** **307**

Phillips University, 1950-52—Honing the edge,
the finishing touches 309

Chapter 5: Summary. 313

Appendix: A Map of China showing
Hofei and Anwhei Province 315

Endnotes. 337

Bibliography 353

About the Author and Contact Information 367

Foreword

We live in a world driven by self-interest. Instant gratification reigns. Shallow commitments, inconsistency, and the pursuit of the next cool thing have become major themes in the lives of most Americans.

But here we have a story that began in a simpler, more generous time. It's a story about a couple who struggled like the rest of us with the common, debilitating issues of life and yet made lifelong decisions flowing *not* from self-interest but from compassion for others. Deferred gratification. Deep, eternal commitments. Sacrificial constancy. Pursuit of timeless, God-built, everlasting things. Decisions that sowed seeds of God's life and love and bore fruit a hundredfold and then some.

It's a love story not only of the deep, selfless love that Glyn and Jean had for each other but the preeminent love they both had for Jesus Christ. The first love cemented the souls of these two saints of God into a bond of unity that kept their partnership as spouses and co-laborers solid for almost fifty years. The second love compelled them to sacrifice their own comfort and ambitions for the cause of the gospel. We don't get to read stories like this much anymore.

Both loves resulted in eternal benefits for the people of Hofei, China, and hundreds in Glyn and Jean's American congregations over the decades of their service. Glyn and Jean were not Superman and Wonder Woman with lofty, superhuman goals; they were simple, humble followers of Christ through whom God worked to accomplish *His* lofty goals. They are an example to us all of God's strength made perfect in weakness. If God can use them, He can use me.

As you read this book, you will get a glimpse into Christian service both foreign and domestic, the unique difficulties of being missionaries during the communist takeover of China and the trials and triumphs of continuing their missionary passion in churches on this side of the Pacific. It was my honor, privilege, and benefit to know them personally as their nephew and to know their son, Tim, the author, since our days in the fifties hanging out at Grandma Reecie's house in Topeka.

May God use these pages to inspire you by the life of Jesus Christ that shined through these two faithful servants of God.

—Chris Adsit, April 1, 2011, Eugene, Oregon
Campus Crusade for Christ Missionary, thirty-seven years
Director of Disciplemakers International
Director of Resource Initiatives, Military Ministry

Preface

The title, *Seeds of Change*, reflects the evangelism work Reverend Glyn and Jean Adsit helped do as missionaries in the rural Hofei (Anhwei Province), China, area from 1947-49. They shared the gospel of Christ and planted many seeds. They witnessed to, converted, and baptized many Chinese people, helping bring eight hundred souls to Christ while serving in the Hofei area.

It is estimated by one of the children of a couple Glyn and Jean baptized while serving there whom, many years later visited with Glyn in America, that those initial eight hundred souls were nourished and multiplied by local Chinese Christian pastors and God into a group of growing Christians in the Hofei area estimated at eight thousand plus today.

Many Chinese came to Christ and sustained the Christian religion in small churches started by meeting in their living rooms and dens through the cultural revolution period that followed.

Not only did their Christian religion survive, but today, sixty-four years later, it is thriving. "It is estimated that there are conservatively over 65 million Protestants and 12 million Catholics in China" (http://www.thestandjournal.org/successful-evangelism-requires-political-and-cultural-sensitivity pp.2-3).

Glyn and Jean's mission ministry with the Christian Rural Service Union and, more specifically, in the Hofei Rural Center that consisted of a church, school, and hospital and focused on rural evangelism, had a small part in helping that growth to happen.

Dr. Robert A. Schuller, Sr., senior pastor and founder of the Crystal Cathedral in Garden Grove, California, once asked, "How many seeds are there in an apple, and how many apples are there in just one seed?" Obviously, almost an infinite number of apples could grow from just one seed that is planted, watered, nourished, and allowed to grow until it bears fruit and the seeds are replanted once again.

One of the greatest contributions of this book is that it traces the general history of the Christian Church, Disciples of Christ missionary movement in China from 1886 to 1951 and specifically details the never-before-published memoirs, diaries, correspondence, reports, journal articles, and selected photos Glyn and Jean kept and sent home while serving in Hofei, China, Anhwei Province from 1947-49. The book uses primary sources found in Glyn and Jean's files and adds to the history of this era. Never-before-published pictures of Chiang-Kai-Shek and Madame Chaing Kai-Shek on their way to church during a chance meeting in the mountains around Kuling, China, and descriptions of what day-to-day missionary life is really like are included.

The memoirs describe harrowing experiences when Glyn and/or Jean were shot at, arrested, incarcerated, and had to flee for their lives when caught in the middle of two advancing armies during the civil war for control of mainland China.

It was during this time that the author was born in Hofei, China, on April 26, 1948, and he plans to return there in the near future to see the country of his birth and to retrace the steps of his parents' missionary work comparing the before pictures found in this book with the after pictures to be taken on this trip and following up this story with a sequel discussing what he found there since the time his parents were forced to flee the country in 1949.

Introduction

This is the true story of two warmly human personalities who served for forty-seven years together as friends, lovers, parents, teachers, missionaries, and ordained pastors, helping fulfill God's Great Commission, which is found in Matthew 28:19-20, KJV.

The opportunity to relive the missionary portion of the lives and service of Reverend Glyn B. Carter Adsit and Alice Jean Dowd Adsit through this book—which is focused primary on the time just prior to, during their mission field experience and service, and the time just after this experience—provides a rare and unforgettable glimpse into day-to-day missionary life, service, and their riveting adventures.

Glyn and Jean were truly unusual and memorable people. They were followers of a Master who claims everything and loyal members of a church that sets no limits to its expansion. When God's call came, they were ready to take their part in the un-resting and unending movement to go "forward into all the world." Their walk of faith, their complete confidence and trust in God, and their inspirational leadership has made its mark on countless thousands of people.

Personal disciple-making became their main mission not only on the mission field in Hofei, China, but also later in life's journey during their forty-four-year ministry together after returning from China. Glyn and Jean led, invited, and nurtured people into a deeper personal relationship and walk with God. They helped equip and train people as disciples of Jesus Christ and send them into ministries as the Holy Spirit called them.

Glyn was inspired by the Holy Spirit, and God gave him strengths in stewardship; leadership; time management; pulpit ministry; evangelism; ministering to the dying and comforting those who lost loved ones; grief therapy; and planning, organizing, directing, and inspiring people through speaking, prayer, and poetry. Jean was a supportive pastor's wife and ministered very effectively to the women in the churches they served in together. In the mission field, Jean was the wind beneath Glyn's wings, and God gave her strengths in relating to people, an affable personality, caring about others, teaching, planning, organizing, and in serving and loving others in the mission field's well-baby clinic.

The reader will note that all of Glyn B. and Jean Adsit's journal entries, autobiographical materials, sermons, and letters in this book are presented in an unusual manner; they are printed exactly as their original manuscripts were typed or handwritten.

You can almost hear Glyn and Jean's voices on the printed page as you read their God-inspired sermons, letters, articles, and journal entries.

Likewise, both Glyn and Jean wrote some unpublished autobiographical material. This author has used excerpts from these original materials and left the manuscripts in the first person as they were written, except for minor spelling, grammatical, and punctuation corrections. Any additions to the original text appear in parenthesis.

Following the publication of this book, a complete version of Glyn and Jean's biography will also be published. This next book will span their entire lives from birth to death.

(The reader should note that, due to space limitations from the publisher concerning word count and number of photographs to be included, some materials had to be edited out of the book; however, they may be examined in the missionary society collection mentioned below.

The letters are on paper that is very fragile and thin, located in Glyn's old, four-drawer file cabinet; thus, they have been organized chronologically and re-word processed here as they were originally typed and/or handwritten. After the first publication of this book focused on their missionary work in China and a planned second book focused on Glyn and Jean's entire life, it is the author's intention that this collection of letters, memoirs, documents, papers, reports, manuscripts, and pictures, etc., will be given to, preserved, and housed in the Historical Society Library and Museum of the United Christian Missionary Society located in Knoxville, Tennessee, for future church historians or other scholars to use if they wish to do further research.)

Chapter 1
The story begins

Glyn was eighteen years old when he graduated from Topeka High School, Topeka, Kansas, in 1936. The family was in the midst of the Great Depression. Most of the high school students were not thinking of going to college. Glyn had no thought of it whatsoever. His one aim was to get a job of some type to take the financial burden off of his mother. His mother's family had grown to include her own three sons; two children left by her sister who died, Carl Lawayne Wells Adsit and Billie Jean Wells Adsit Eckstein; and her father, B.W. Dawson. She was just barely managing to squeeze by.

Glyn found a job with the Western Union Telegraph Company while he was still attending Topeka High School. Upon graduating from high school in the spring of 1936, the job proved to be a connecting link with the Santa Fe Railroad. Glyn applied for and secured a job with their telegraph department. Beginners were placed on the extra board until a permanent position opened up for them. Glyn worked most of the time, but the nature of his job kept him moving from one state to another; wherever a man might take off for a vacation, or wherever business increased enough to put on an extra man. Glyn started working in Topeka, Kansas, but soon found himself in the following places: Newton, Kansas; Kansas City, Kansas; Amarillo, Texas; Albuquerque, New Mexico; Las

Vegas, New Mexico; LaJunta, Colorado; Chicago, Illinois; and then Amarillo, Texas, again.

About this period of his life, Glyn writes:

> One does not have to strain very hard to realize what such a transient experience might do to my religious life. I found my interest in the church waning away. I sometimes went to church on Sunday; more often, I did not. When I was in a town for six weeks or longer, I usually got around to going to church. But I did not grow spiritually during this time; rather, I went the other way. Most of the friends I made were among railroad men. They drank a lot and cussed more. I started smoking heavily cigarettes, cigars, and a pipe, whichever were the more convenient at the time. Whenever we went on dates, which was about twice a week, we would drink about a pint between four people. That was not considered heavy drinking at all. It became the rule rather than the exception that I would be drinking on Saturday night, unless I was to work early on Sunday morning. Drinking and association with others who drank and frequenting dubious dance halls led to further transgressions along sex lines…
>
> —*My Spiritual Pilgrimage* (p. 9-11; 1952)

Glyn writes parenthetically to his professor, Dr. W.E. Powell, about this time period in his life:

> I will not parade my sins here in this paper but only mention them so that you might see and understand my spiritual pilgrimage. But in spite of such sin in my life, I still went to church occasionally. I never completely considered myself as evil. I became an expert at rationalizing because some of those with whom I was a partner in sin were the leading lights in their towns and churches.
>
> —*My Spiritual Pilgrimage* (an unpublished paper, written in partial fulfillment for the course entitled Psychology of Religion; January 2, 1952; p.11.)

The author includes this information about Glyn not to denigrate his memory but simply to show that God can take the life of a sinning, heavily drinking and smoking railroad man and telegraph operator and channel it into good for His purposes and glory here on earth.

About this period of his life, Glyn goes on to say:

> After about two years of such an existence, I was assigned to a permanent job in Amarillo, Texas. I began to search around for friends and dropped into the Baptist church one Sunday morning. They were very friendly and invited me to their Baptist Youth Fellowship that evening. They have classes for all ages. I met several nice girls and boys there and began to get back on the right religious trail again. I began to go with a girl who went to the Christian church. Naturally, I went there too. This was the first time I had actually become aware of the Disciples of Christ. I was fortunate in that Dr. Roy Snodgrass challenged my mind by his preaching. I became active in the young people's department and Sunday school class. I began to understand something of the doctrinal position of the disciples and at first did not or could not accept the freedom found in their position. I had eaten too long at the Calvinistic table, I know now. At any rate, I began to clean up my habits a bit and sinning to an occasional drink or so. I did smoke constantly, however.
>
> Dr. Snodgrass saw me on the street one day and asked, "Glyn, have you ever thought about going into the ministry?"
>
> I said, "No. Why?"
>
> "Well, I think maybe you might make a preacher if you tried."
>
> Well, I didn't think much about that conversation at the time, but by way of observation, it is interesting to me that two preachers saw something in me that I did not know was there. I attended services at First Christian

Church, Amarillo, Texas, both morning and evening unless I was working…

—*My Spiritual Pilgrimage* (p. 11-12; 1952)

Jean's Story

Alice Jean Dowd came from a different background than Glyn. Her story begins while in junior high, high school, and junior college.

Jean's father, Eirth, was a rancher and mechanic and owned a grass seed business in Stratford, Texas, and Garden City, Kansas. Jean graduated from junior high school in Stratford, Texas, where she played on the girls' basketball team, and then moved to Amarillo, Texas, where she graduated from high school and attended Amarillo Junior College.

Jean's mother died at forty-three years of age on May 5, 1940, in Saint Anthony's Hospital, Amarillo, Texas, but she taught all the girls to sew and cook before her death. Jean loved to sew.

In her scrapbook, Jean wrote, "All I am, and all I hope to be, I owe to my mother" (Dowd, Jean; on her twentieth birthday, April 3, 1939).

Jean was twenty-one years old at the time of her mother's death, and she left home to attend Phillips University in Enid, Oklahoma. She attended Phillips for one and one half years and then came home to Amarillo, Texas, in 1940.

As mentioned earlier, she met Glyn B. Adsit in the Amarillo First Christian Church one Sunday morning. He was working for the Santa Fe Railroad as a telegraph operator in Amarillo. Mrs. Briscoe, the young adult Sunday school teacher, introduced Jean to Glyn while she was home from college for Christmas vacation.

After Glyn had a religious experience, a call from God to become a minister, he said yes to God and called Jean and told her all about it.

Glyn said, "I know you thought you were going to marry a telegraph operator, and now I'm going to be a preacher. I ask you to still marry me, but if you can't, give me back the ring…"

To this, Jean replied that she would think about it overnight. The next day, she handed Glyn a note that said, "My answer is in this scripture from the book of Ruth in the Old Testament. Ruth said, 'Entreat me not to leave thee, or to return from following after thee; for wither thou goest, I will go, and where thou lodgest, I will lodge; thy people shall be my people, and thy God, my God. Where thou diest, I will die; and there will I be buried…' (Ruth 1:16-17, kjv)."

Glyn and Jean were married June 15, 1941, in the Amarillo First Christian Church, and they decided to return to Phillips University in the fall of 1941. (Unpublished manuscript information written by Glyn as dictated by Jean on March 13, 1991, to be used at her graveside and memorial service upon her death, p. 1.)

Glyn on Meeting His Future Wife

With respect to his future wife, Glyn writes:

A certain Miss Jean Dowd came home from Phillips University, Enid, Oklahoma, for Christmas vacation in 1940. Mrs. J.B. Briscoe, my Sunday school teacher, had been telling me of the students who were away from her class in college. She mentioned that Jean would be coming home from Enid and that she hoped I would get to meet her while she was there. Jean's first impression of me, so she says, is that I was that young man who knew so much about the Bible in Sunday school class and who didn't mind letting the rest of the class know that he knew it. I met her after class and went on to sing in the choir…

Romance had its way, and Jean and I fell in love. She decided not to return to Phillips and was content to be the wife of a telegraph operator. Our wedding date was set for the next June 15, 1941. Becoming engaged to Miss Dowd necessitated my life being cleaned up. I no longer drank or ran around. Our courtship was strictly on a Christian basis, and I rather enjoyed that. It makes one feel good to know that he can love someone without having to resort to cheap petting and sexual activity. I, of course, was not conscious of the religious growth along these lines at the time. But I can clearly see the growth now. Life took on a new meaning for me. I had found a family again. I was often invited to the Dowd home for meals. Jean was the cook since her mother had died some two years before I met her…

—My Spiritual Pilgrimage (p.12-13; 1952)

God Speaks to Glyn

One never knows what produces the drives that are within oneself. In Glyn's case, it was perhaps poverty, or it might have been the teaching of his mother. At any rate, what happened next in his spiritual pilgrimage changed his life and the lives of hundreds of others for all eternity. Read Glyn's own words as he tells the story about God speaking to him. He writes:

> I do know that I have always been ambitious to get ahead. My working at the telegraph office in Amarillo was not completely satisfactory to me. I could see that my progress in that department was limited. I had resolved to become the president of the Santa Fe Railroad, if that was within my power. I reasoned that others had done it and so could I if I got the necessary education and experience and made the right contacts. I decided to get a night shift with the railroad and go to business college during the day. That way, I could get the necessary shorthand and business English that would land me another job in a different department. Advancement in that department would come much quicker…
>
> I relate all of this to show that I had the idea of change and growth in my mind. I was not happy where I was and wanted to do better. I do not attribute this to any religious fact in my life at the time but rather to the desire to get ahead on a monetary basis…

It was on a Thursday that I was walking out to the business college. I had reached a point about thirty feet from a corner. I heard a voice speak to me. It said, "If you are going to change, why don't you change and do the thing you ought to do". I turned around to see who had spoken to me. There was no one within one half a block of me. I thought or said to myself, "What had I ought to do?" Immediately, the voice came in answer, "You should prepare yourself for the ministry of the Gospel of Christ." Without argument or debate, I said, "I will."

I arrived at the business college. I told my teacher what had happened. She said that that was wonderful. She was very happy for me. She too was a Christian…I finished my lessons for that day and returned to my hotel room. I called Jean and asked her if she would come to my room that night after work and told her that I had something I wanted to tell her. She was rather surprised that I would ask her to my room, but she agreed to come at midnight when I got off from work. I then went to work at four that afternoon. I told my boss, Mr. Mize, what had happened. He listened with great interest. He advised me to think a long time before I did anything definite, such as resigning from the railroad.

He said, "Be sure and count the cost. Once you burn your bridges behind you, you cannot return to the railroad."

I thanked him for his interest. I remember that I could hardly keep my mind on my work that evening…

Jean came to my room at midnight and said, "What on earth do you want to talk to me about?"

I told her what had happened. She says I said, "That's the way it is, honey. I'm going to be a preacher. If you want to be a preacher's wife, okay. If not, you can return my ring anytime." I don't think I was that abrupt, but the conversation did run something like that. She was overjoyed at my experience and said that that was all right with her…

We began to plan that very night about what we would do in the future. We knew that an education would be necessary. Jean suggested that we should go to Phillips since she knew we could work our way through there. I agreed to that. When we called to tell Dr. Snodgrass the next day, he was out of town. We talked with the assistant pastor, a Mr. Meeker. He suggested that Phillips University would be the place to go. When Reverend Snodgrass returned, he was a little disappointed that we did not decide for Texas Christian University but encouraged us to go ahead…

The next day, I turned in my resignation to the railroad, to be effective the following August 1. They tried to persuade me to stay, but finally, they saw that my mind was made up and encouraged me in my intention…

I make no attempt to explain what happened on that street corner. I know what happened to me. I know what I heard and what I answered. I also know what the years afterward have meant and done to me. I say it was God's voice speaking to me. It may have been God's voice speaking within me, using my senses as an avenue. I cannot say. I only know that I have felt peculiarly led since that day. I believe God had a hand in my affairs. After that hour, I no longer cursed. I quit drinking. I became more zealous in religious matters. My personality changed. I felt that I had a mission which I alone could fulfill…

—*My Spiritual Pilgrimage* (p. 13-16; 1952)

Men Are Drafted for the Army

In the late summer of 1940, the US Army began to draft men for the first time in many years. Glyn's number came up. The army discovered that he had a left elbow that had been injured in a car-bicycle accident some five years before while working delivering telegraphs. This injury left him with one arm slightly shorter than the other because he couldn't straighten it completely out. Glyn was placed in draft class 1-B, which allowed him to perform limited service-secretarial preferred.

Jean and Glyn were married June 15, 1941. They entered Phillips University in Enid, Oklahoma, the next September. Pearl Harbor occurred on December 7, 1941, and Glyn's draft board called him to report. He advised them that he was in school. They gave him a deferment on the basis of his limited classification and later on changed it to a 4-D status. Thus, Glyn never served in the military.

Chapter 2

What was Glyn and Jean's Experience at Phillips University, 1941-1945?

Glyn had his first experience at Phillips University between 1941 and 1945.

He writes about that experience with fond memories:

> When I told my mother that I was going to be a minister, she did not seem too surprised. She said, "I have always prayed that one of my sons would be a preacher." She also advised, "It doesn't matter to me what work my boys do, but do the best you can in whatever job you choose. If you are going to be a preacher, be a good one." I resolved that I would try to heed that advice. My grandfather, who lived with my mother, had very few things to say to me. I remember one thing he always insisted upon. It was, "If a thing is worth doing, it is worth doing right." He encouraged me to remember that as I prepared for the ministry...
>
> —*My Spiritual Pilgrimage (p.16-17; 1952)*

Glyn goes on to say:

> My religious pilgrimage at Phillips University was a wonderful experience. I have been wonderfully blessed to have

had the opportunity to study under truly great Christian gentlemen and scholars. The lives they have lived during my some ten years on this campus has not failed to have its effect upon my life. This is particularly true of any student who comes to this campus, but I have felt it particularly true in my case. I came to Phillips relatively ignorant of the Disciples of Christ. I have learned almost all I know about them while here. I have not always agreed with all of my professors, but I have always admired them. I found myself in special disagreement with two of them: Dr. C.C. Taylor and Dr. R.W. Nelson, the first on the basis of theology and missions, and the later on the basis of philosophy. But I also know that these two men have caused me to grow in those fields faster than would have been the case if they had not challenged me to do some thinking in order to meet their arguments…

I began in my freshman year to read my Bible. This was the first time that I really read it. I marked in it and memorized it. I enjoyed it for the first time in my life. This reading and marking was not occasioned by any assignments in class but was carried on from 4:30 to 5:00 a.m., when I had my personal devotions. I venture to say that I made more progress in that first year than I had made in all my previous twenty-four years and since also. I had a burning desire to know and preach what I knew. I was convinced that God had entered into my life and had changed me, and I wanted to see that others knew what he could do for them…

It was soon evident that I could make grades in my courses. It was not that it came easy but that I studied hard. This has always been the case in my studies. I really learn very slowly, but I give the necessary time to get my lessons. This fact, that I could stand at the head of my class in academic ability, was not lost on me. I knew what a miserable mess I had made of my high school opportunity along this line. I had seldom made above a C. In my senior year, I had flunked two courses. One of them was physics, and this was necessary for passing. A certain Mr. Chambers (blessed be his name forever) taught that course, and he gave me an opportunity to write an extra paper so that I could pass that course. With all this in mind, I knew that something had happened to me or to my mind. I am now convinced of that fact. Up until now, I have not made below a B in any college course. I credit the inspiration of the Holy Spirit for that ability. I was motivated by a worthy cause and found that I had abilities that I did not dream existed. It was in my sophomore year that I promised God that if He would stay with me, I would work to the limit of my ability while in school. I realize the folly of such a promise now, for I realize that it was I that was likely to go away from Him, and not Him from me...

I made several wonderful friends at Phillips in those years. Outstanding among these was Robert Carl Bowers. Bob and I hit it off right from the start. He was interested in being a medical missionary to Africa. He kept after me to consider missions. I did become interested in missions, but not in Africa. I was strangely drawn to China. My wife and I decided in 1943 to become volunteers for the China field. We were accepted and began our counseling with the United Christian Missionary Society...

While at Phillips, I learned about the disciples. I learned to pray and wait. But it was only after I had been preaching for about two years that I really felt that I belonged in the ministry. I rather felt like my time at the student churches was more or less wasted since my real work was to be in a foreign field. How little did I know what was in the future. [After returning from the mission field, Glyn and Jean served various local church congregations as ordained ministers for forty-two years.] I now see that such training will stand me in good stead since I am no longer in a foreign field...

It was while I was at Westside Christian Church in Tulsa, Oklahoma, that I began to understand people. We had a lovely group in that church. They helped me grow in

my love and appreciation for people. We had many problems to overcome, but in the process, we all grew to greater
spiritual stature…

—*My Spiritual Pilgrimage* (p. 16-19; 1952)

Jean described the experience at Phillips University in the following
passages from unpublished manuscript information written by Glyn
as dictated by Jean on March 13, 1991, to be used at her graveside
and memorial service upon her death. Jean states:

> We didn't have much money, but we knew with God's
> help, we would make it. I worked in the dime store for
> about one and one half years, and Glyn worked in Lerner's
> women's clothing and did odd jobs at the college, work-
> ing in the cafeteria and doing clean-up work. I enrolled
> in college again, and we both were ordained and received
> our BS degrees in Bible in 1945. I was elected to Cardinal
> Key and Glyn to Blue Key, an honor for being outstand-
> ing students for the four years…At first, I felt I was not a
> good student, but with Glyn's encouragement, I became
> an excellent student. In our last year at Phillips, Glyn
> decided he was called to be a missionary to China. I again
> gave him that note from Ruth 1:16-17. We were accepted
> as missionary candidates and sent to Cornell University in
> Ithaca, New York…
>
> —Unpublished manuscript information written by Glyn
> as dictated by Jean on March 13, 1991, to be used at her
> graveside and memorial service upon her death (p. 1)

Why did Glyn and Jean become missionaries and why did they choose China?

While serving as a student minister at Westside Christian Church,
Tulsa, Oklahoma, in 1943, Glyn and Jean answered these questions
using Westside Christian Church stationary as they applied for and
were accepted to the mission field. Glyn writes:

There were several reasons for my becoming a candidate for the mission field. Foremost in my thinking is the training I received at home. I was taught by a Christian mother that I owed my life to God and must serve Him by serving my fellowman. This idea never allowed me to escape into aimless living except for short periods of time…At the age of twenty-four, I decided, because of various and accumulated reasons, to enter the Christian ministry. I went to Phillips University in Enid, Oklahoma, to educate myself for the task…It was during my sophomore year that I made the decision to enter foreign missionary work. I had been preaching for almost two years and was settling down to the routine of American pulpit preaching. I saw the needs here at home and was trying by my ministering to meet these needs. Several missionaries visited our university during my sophomore year and told their stories. Every time I heard the missionary telling of the great need and opportunity among those whom they were serving, my heart would respond and speak to my mind, insisting that they were my responsibility. Finally, after months had passed, this idea possessed me and I surrendered to what I now consider God's leading…Therefore, I say it was the consciousness of the great need in other parts of the world of Jesus Christ and the influence of missionaries and, lastly, the feeling that it was God's will that caused me to decide for foreign missionary service…

I think of this decision first, as one of Christian politics and influence. I mean by Christian politics the policies and methods Christianity uses to change the culture of the countries to which they are applied…I decided that China was the key nation of the future. Four hundred and fifty million people live in China (which was the population at the time). This is one-fifth of the total population of the earth. Furthermore, China has become the religious melting-pot of the world. If such a great people could be won for Christ, they would make a tremendous impact for good upon the world. If they are not won for Christ, no one knows what influence they might exert…It is my personal conviction that Christian leadership shifts from one country to another. America is fast losing her grip. What country will become the Christian leader of tomorrow? I believe that China is ready to assume this role. Therefore, I feel we must work hard in China to prepare that field for leadership…Personalities were also a contributing factor in my decision to go to China. The missionaries from China seemed to appeal to me more than the missionaries from other countries. Their problems seemed more vital. They seemed more excited about their work and prospects…Finally, it was the type of people to whom I might go that made me decide on China. I felt that I would not be satisfied to go to Africa and work with the type of person found there. The people of China, with their heritage of culture, beckoned me on…

—Primary Source: Adsit, Glyn B. and Adsit, Alice Jean, Letter of application sent to the United Christian Missionary Society, written on stationary from the Westside Christian Church, Tulsa, Oklahoma, 1943 (p. 1-2)

Likewise, Jean writes:

My husband planned or thought missions several months before I became aware of his thoughts. One evening, he came into the store where I was working and asked if I would like to hear a speaker who was visiting the campus. We heard the speaker who was Alexander Paul from China. He presented a need in China for all those who might be willing to give themselves for work there. Upon leaving the meeting, my husband said, "That's what I want to do." Somewhere in my thinking, I had visualized missionaries as white-winged persons with a halo around their heads and could not see myself as a missionary. I had not stopped to realize that they too were human beings and subject to mistakes, needing always to watch and pray and seek God's guidance. Through the prayer, "Lord, take my life and use it as you will"; through the influence of many missionaries such as Alexander Paul, Mrs. O.J. Goulter, C. Manly Morton, Walter Haskell, Mr. And Mrs. H. G. Russell, Malcom Norment, and others; through reading books; and through talking and thinking missions, I feel that with God's help and my further training in college work, I too will be able to help the Chinese people by starting with them where they are and bringing them to where they should be as Christians...

—Primary Source: Adsit, Glyn B. and Adsit, Alice Jean; letter of application sent to the United Christian Missionary Society, written on stationary from the Westside Christian Church, Tulsa, Oklahoma, 1943

As mentioned earlier, both Glyn and Jean graduated from Phillips University with BS degrees in Bible and were ordained as pastors in 1945. They had decided to go to China as missionaries for the reasons stated above, and the United Christian Missionary Society wanted them to get some more education relating to the work in China. They were accepted as missionary candidates and sent to Cornell University in Ithaca, New York, where they both attended school and Glyn earned his Master of Science degree in sociology and rural education in 1946.

Chapter 3
Cornell (1945-46) and Yale (1946-47)

Glyn and Jean's training in Cornell and later Yale, where they studied special courses designed for missionaries, was a valuable experience. Concerning this time period, Glyn writes:

> We became acquainted with other churches. I preached in two Presbyterian churches and also attended a Lutheran and Northern Baptist church. We took communion at both places. I feel that I became more tolerant and liberal in my feelings toward other communions at that time. I realized that all of us must be partly right, and at any rate, we were all Christians…
>
> It was while we were at Yale [University in New Haven, Connecticut, in the spring of 1946-47] that I had several "low" periods. I began to wonder if I should really go to China. The grind was long and hard. We studied until we thought we could not go another hour and then went on more and more. But when a period of depression would come, always the answer for my prayers would come. Our strength was sustained and my doubts removed. I had the impression that there was a job in China for me to do, and if I did not do it, it would not be done. I still believe that to be true. I was truly tried in the furnace that year. I think it was a natural feeling resulting from the fact that I was leaving my country, home, and friends. There was a

slight rebellion, but once that was overcome in prayer and devotional thinking, it ceased to be a problem…

—*My Spiritual Pilgrimage* (p.19-20; 1952)

When Glyn and Jean went to Yale University, they studied courses relating to China with Chinese teachers and studied the language. Glyn states, "We studied Chinese language about twelve hours a day for one year, and also courses in Chinese religions and culture. Jean and I received our certificate for the two terms in Chinese studies. We did not work for any degree at that time. This was in the spring of 1946-47" (Unpublished manuscript information written by Glyn as dictated by Jean on March 13, 1991, to be used at her graveside and memorial service upon her death, p. 1).

The United Christian Missionary Society held a commissioning service in Indianapolis, Indiana, and Glyn and Jean then set sail for China in the summer of 1947. Since this aspect of their lives and work together is so potentially significant historically, the author has collected all the never-before-published rare photographs, documents, diaries, letters, communications, reports, and articles Glyn and Jean wrote and received regarding their time in China. Great care has been taken to document all primary sources, present them either in this chapter or in the appendices, and simply narrate the story letting the documents speak for themselves exactly as they were written in the first person. The author has tried to present the materials chronologically since most of the material is dated. But before the reader launches into Glyn and Jean's memoirs, a brief overview of the historical work of the Disciples of Christ in China is in order.

A Brief History of the Disciples of Christ Missionary Service in China from 1886 to 1951

What follows is a brief historical overview of the Disciples of Christ missionary work in China up to and including Glyn and Jean's time of service there.

Later in her life, after her return from China, Jean Adsit was contacted by Marilynne Hill, director of adult work for the United Christian Missionary Society. In a letter from Marilynne to Jean dated September 1, 1961, she encloses a manuscript, a rough draft copy of the group study packet that she proposes to use in Christian Women's Fellowship (CWF) groups during January to June 1962 when the mission study theme will be the Christian Mission on the Rim of East Asia. She asks, "Would you be willing to review the manuscript for next year's mission study programs and let me have any suggestions you care to make toward improving the sessions?" (Hill, Marilynne; director of adult work, the United Christian Missionary society, to Mrs. Glyn Adsit, September 1, 1961, p.1).

In a portion of her manuscript for the mission study program to be used by Christian Women's Fellowship Groups during January to June 1962 entitled, *Lest We Forget China Sixty-Five Years of Ups and Downs,"* Lois Anna Ely writes in the introduction:

Introduction

From 1886 to 1951 is a long time-span for one program. That covers more than half a century in China and means the work of 175 missionaries, some of whom served for long terms and some for short, and most of whom cannot be mentioned by name because of the limitations of time and space.

The five areas where disciples served in the lower Yangtze Valley are all in the far eastern part of China, although not on the coast. The Yangtze is one of China's great rivers that empties into the ocean north of Shanghai.

The resource material in this booklet is broken up by years in which major incidents in China itself disturbed the ongoing mission from abroad. Work was disrupted repeatedly. In 1900 came the Boxer Uprising, a period when no foreigner was safe. In 1910 came the revolution, a time when the whole country was in chaos. In 1927, the armies of Chiang Kai Shek created havoc as they took the country by force. In 1937, the Japanese began to overrun China. Finally, in 1949, the Communists took over. Each time one of these major upheavals occurred, the missionaries were forced to flee to safety, usually to some other part of China, until this last occurrence drove [almost] all Westerners out of China

For your information, a historical chart is included.

The Boxer Uprising was an attempt on the part of the Chinese to oust foreigners. The word *Boxer* is a loose translation of the Chinese name for the village militia who were called out by the government in an effort to provide for the national defense. The boxers went to rampage, attacking all "foreign devils" and Christians as "secondary foreign devils."

It might help to present this series of events in a time line.

Historical Chart/Timeline, Disciples of Christ in China

1886	Disciples of Christ send their first missionary to China. Dr. Macklin opened medical work in Nanking.
1900	Withdrawal of missionaries because of Boxer Uprising (anti-foreign demonstrations)
1910	Revolution in China; emperor dethroned, republic established. University of Nanking opened, first union venture.
1919	Emphasis on developing Chinese leadership.
1922	National Christian Council of China organized.
1924	Constitution completed of the Chinese Christian Churches (eighteen organized churches)
1925	Missionaries and Chinese share administrative responsibility for work of stations*, eighteen outstations (twenty-three day schools, seven boarding high schools, three hospitals, and two training schools for nurses)

1927	Missionaries evacuated when Chinese nationalist armies sweep through the country.
1931	Chinese churches hold first youth conference.
1937	Japanese occupation begins; missionaries either go west with refugees or evacuate.
1945	Goulter and Bates returned to China, emphasis on rural work
1947	[Adsits join team]
Oct. 1, 1949	Birthday of the People's Republic of China, beginning of Communist control.
1952	The last of Disciples of Christ missionaries leave China.

* Nanking, Luchow Fu (later known as Hofei), Chuchow (later known as Chuhsien), Wuhu, Natungchow (later known as Nantung).

Pioneers Who Served Until Retirement

Dr. William Macklin

Dr. William Macklin is honored as the first missionary Disciple of Christ sent to China. He reached Shanghai in January 1886. For a few weeks, he remained there, studying the language and culture of the people and considering a place to begin permanent work. Nanking was his choice. He moved there in April. His first residence was an old Buddhist temple. There, in January 1889, he took Dorothy DeLany as his bride.

Dr. Macklin had begun medical work in a dispensary soon after his arrival in Nanking. By 1893, land had been leased and a hospital built and opened. Beside it stood the new home where the Macklins were to live most of their years in China.

Dr. Macklin was much more than a doctor. He translated books and pamphlets on public health. He fought the drug habit. In tea houses and in the homes of the people, he was a busy evangelist, telling the gospel story to eager listeners. In June of 1888, Dr. Macklin baptized his first convert, Shi Kwei-piao, a professional storyteller who throughout his long, full, Christian life, up and down the Yangtze River, told the gospel story he had come to love.

Dr. Macklin worked in every way he could to help the people's livelihood. He was loved by the common people both inside the city and in the villages nearby, where he often rode on horseback. Dr. and Mrs. Macklin were among the seven hardy souls who began work in China before the end of the nineteenth century and carried on until regular retirement.

William Remfry Hunt, Linguist and Storyteller

William Remfry Hunt arrived in China in 1889 and served until furlough in 1920. He was one of the pioneer resident missionaries at Chuchow. There, his rare skill with the Chinese language, his interest in manners and customs, his acquaintance with temple worship and ritual, and his grasp of Chinese literature won for him the appreciation of the educated Chinese and supplied him with a wealth of illustrations that he used in sermons and addresses to the delight of all the people. Mr. Hunt married in 1893 a woman of winning personality and deep consecration. The Hunt home was open for the training sessions of the evangelists, a special work of Mr. Hunt's.

Miss Emma Lyon, Pioneer School Woman

Emma Lyon went to China in the autumn of 1892. Not long after her arrival, she started the Christian Girls' School just below the Nanking Drum Tower. There, she spent forty-two years except for furloughs, a long continued piece of work well done. By September 1896, land was purchased for the school and the first building erected. The building ultimately became a missionary residence, but in those first years, in addition to housing the missionary, it supplied classrooms, school dormitory rooms, and an assembly hall. Miss Lyon lived for church and school, yet she took time for many friendly calls on people inside the city and beyond the city gates.

Frank Garrett, Evangelist, Builder

Frank Garrett was another who served until retirement. He with his wife arrived in China in 1896. Death took Mrs. Garrett after seventeen years of fine service. Mr. Garrett's work was largely evangelistic, but during his long and fruitful ministry, he accomplished many significant things both in evangelism and education. Besides, many mission buildings were the outcome of his efficient planning and oversight. At the mission convention in July of 1900, Mr. Garrett reported the completion of the chapel that, through all the years of mission life, was known as the Drum Tower Christian church. He modestly reported in 1900 that while certain aspects of the structure were disappointing, the "important parts" were strong and that the building was large enough for many years to come.

Mary Kelly, Evangelist, Counselor

Mary Kelly also began work in 1896. She taught some, but her primary interest was evangelism, and she was soon at work among the women at Drum Tower; South Gate; and Hsiakwan, the customs port of Nanking. In addition, she itinerated outside the city walls. All of this was a fitting preparation for the many years of work she was to do in residence at South Gate, Nanking. Miss Kelly was a woman of broad sympathies, an excellent co-worker, and a valuable counselor.

Dr. Elliott Osgood, Versatile Pioneer

Dr. and Mrs. Osgood went to China in 1898 and soon moved to Chuchow. In the two short years before the Boxer Uprising, Dr. Osgood and his wife made many friends both among the common people and the prominent and influential. He did medical work in a little dispensary. He preached, taught, and continued his work in Chuchow until retirement except for furloughs and short periods when he supplied for absentees in other stations. Mrs. Osgood returned to America some years ahead of her husband to help see their children through school.

We Began Work in Old China

Ups and Downs, 1889 to 1900

Protestant Christian missionary work began in China in 1807 with the arrival of Robert Morrison of the London Missionary Society. The first American Protestant missionary was Peter Parker, a medical man and appointee of the American Board of Commissioners (congregational) who arrived in 1834.

In those early years, missionary work was scarce and fitful. China most reluctantly admitted anyone from the West. Not until treaties in the mid-nineteenth century forced open the way for foreign residence and commerce, established diplomatic relations, and legalized the propagation of Christianity by foreigners and Chinese did missionary expansion speed up.

The first missionaries of the Disciples of Christ served amid opposition, antagonism, and aloofness from a China clinging to old ways, a China gradually waking from medieval sleep. The anti-foreign, anti-Christian excesses of the Boxer year (1900) really marked the beginning of the end of old China.

The Disciples of Christ sent thirty-three missionaries to China before the Boxer Uprising. Dr. and Mrs. Macklin, William Remfry Hunt, Miss Emma Lyon, Frank Garrett, Miss Mary Kelly, and Dr. Elliott Osgood pioneered through those difficult years in old China and continued until retirement. They were highly esteemed for their long and fruitful service both by the growing Chinese Christian Church and by the brotherhood at home.

Length of good and effective service is a blessing, but it's not the sole measure of influence. Others who made valuable contributions despite short duration of service should be mentioned if space were available.

Death had claimed four even before the end of the century. Ill health had taken others from the field. Two had left the mission for diplomatic services. These were sad losses in those trying times, but all who left the mission helped at home to interpret China and its need for Christianity.

What did these beginners accomplish in the less than two decades of Christian work in China before the Boxer Uprising? They opened closed doors and made way for friendship and understanding in Nanking, Chuchow, Luchowfu, Wuhu, and in the outlying districts of all those walled cities. Besides medical and educational work, there were Christian churches in each of those cities, two of them in Nanking.

A Quarter Century of Growth

Ups and Downs, 1900 to 1925

Missionaries in the lower Yangtze Valley evacuated their stations and remained in Shanghai through the terrifying days of the Boxer Uprising. They exchanged ideas and experiences with those from other parts of China and spent much time on language study or translation. Every day was one of anxiety for the young churches and the Christian friends left behind. Happily, our missionaries returned to their stations to find that there had been no violence to people or property. They reported the work had been "somewhat held together by the members."

One hundred and eleven new missionaries joined the mission in the first quarter of the new century. An institute for evangelistic training was founded in Nanking. It later became part of the union Theological Seminary. A fifth station was opened at Nantungchow.

Need for Developing Chinese Leadership

Increasing staff meant increased oversight of the work. Missionaries had found that steady and systematic instruction was necessary for the making of worthy Christians. Able Chinese preachers like Li Hou-fu were developed in this period. Every day made evident the need not only for more competent ministers but also for teachers, physicians, and other Christian leaders. The training process was emphasized but never quite caught up to the need. The mission agreed that in the future, more time should be given to the education of children. From each of the stations, itinerating continued, sometimes it bore immediate fruitage. Sometimes it would be discouragingly late.

The First Union Venture

In 1910, the mission pointed with joy to the University of Nanking as an accomplished union institution for higher learning. Disciples had encouraged this union venture. They hoped this would be the first of several.

Why the Revolution?

The later Manchus (the ruling family and their supporters) were decadent. The country was full of corruption, political wiles, and social ills. Down came the Manchus! Off came the hated queues! The emperor was dethroned and a republic born, but not without bloodshed. In came revolution, bringing freedom, rebellion, disorder, and change. The revolution broke out on October 10, 1911. Most of our missionaries, taking with them some of the Chinese girl students, went to Shanghai for safety.

Dr. Macklin and Frank Garrett stayed in Nanking throughout the revolution and rebellion. The Manchu city within the Nanking walls was completely destroyed and the Manchus killed. Dr. Macklin, by heroic efforts as a neutral go-between, saved the city from complete destruction. Nanking was largely shorn of its physical glory.

Dr. Macklin and Mr. Garrett won undying gratitude for their helpful service to the wounded and needy. William Remfry Hunt worked with the Chinese Red Cross. He exclaimed over the fine caliber of the Chinese youth of the better class who worked with him.

Interestingly, at Wuhu, a flood did more damage than did the revolution.

Missionaries in those first days after the revolution were frequently called upon for speeches on popular government. Those were difficult days for the Chinese. They had many new things to learn. That was true in mission life as well as in political life.

The Chinese and missionaries had been holding separate conventions, the one in English, the other in Chinese. In the convention of 1912, the missionaries agreed that they should share all their convention minutes with the Chinese convention. This was a step forward. In that convention, there was a new emphasis on self-support and self-government in the Chinese church.

In those post-revolutionary years, promising pieces of work closed because there was no one to carry on. Due to furloughs and insufficient new appointees, there was only one Disciple representative on the faculty at the University of Nanking, although our quota was five. What was true in the university was true in other phases of work. There was a constant cry for more missionaries and more trained Christian Chinese workers. A new institution came into being to help supply the need.

Ginling College Founded

Ginling College for women was founded in 1915. Minnie Vautrin, who had arrived in China in 1912 and had served as principal of the Christian Girls' School in Lochowfu, after her first furlough, returned to serve long and faithfully as dean of the education department of Ginling.

Steps Toward a Partnership

In 1919, the missionary convention began in the China mission; the process by which the missionary was to step into the background or step aside as quickly as a Chinese Christian was able to function in his stead. The 1919 convention resolved that beginning in 1920, the advisory committee would consist of four foreigners, one of whom would be the mission secretary and act as chairman, and three would be Chinese elected in the Chinese convention.

From 1920 on, the two conventions grew closer together as they worked on a mission constitution that would be an effective document for the future. By 1924, the constitution was completed. Under it, the two conventions went out of existence, and in their stead, there came into being a convention of the Chinese Christian churches, of which both Chinese and missionaries were members. An administrative committee was elected on a fifty-fifty basis except for several members elected at large who might be either Chinese or missionaries.

The quarter of a century ended with that big step forward. It marked a change to a relationship of partners. The mission had placed upon Edwin Marx the honor, responsibility, and burden of Western administrative secretary and mission treasurer. He had filled his post well through the years of transition (1922-1924). Beginning in 1925, Mr. Marx shared administrative responsibility with the first Chinese secretary of the mission, Mr. Li Hou-fu. The 1925 convention was a great one. Chinese was the language spoken, except for guest speakers who had to use interpreters.

Note: Nearly a quarter of a century later, a document that outlined a procedure for turning over to the nationals the reins of leadership was presented to the board of trustees of the United Society. This document, the Strategy of World Mission, in 1959 was made the basic policy of the Division of World Mission. But thirty-four years earlier, exactly such steps as it outlined were being taken in China.

A Growing Partnership

Ups and Downs, 1925 to 1937

The immediate years of growing partnership seemed to face a bright future. There were eighteen organized churches and more than twenty regular meeting places. Twenty-three elementary schools were under the sponsorship of the mission and seven high schools with dormitory facilities. There were three hospitals and two training schools for nurses. Furthermore, Disciples were involved in several union colleges, including the union Theological Seminary.

Our mission was among the very first to make a change to the partnership form of organization. It was off to a very good start. Mr. Li Hou-fu was proving an able executive, as were the Chinese members of the administrative committee and the council. In all stations, most aspects of the work were encouraging. The peak number of missionaries had been reached in 1922, more than sixty. Some of these were just ready to begin full-time work in this partnership period.

Promise was high. And then came 1927.

Because of 1927

And what was 1927? It was the year in which the Chinese Nationalist armies, saturated with hate and anti-Christian propaganda, determining to rid China of unequal treaties, pushed north, committing atrocities as they marched. In Nanking, elements in the army completely out of hand brought death to several foreigners, among them Dr. John Williams, the beloved vice president of the University Nanking. Mission properties were looted and burned. Missionaries and Chinese Christians alike were threatened. It was a time of great anxiety and mutual concern.

Some Blessings to Count

What a blessing it was that the Chinese had had a short but very valuable experience in administering the work. The National Christian Council, which had come into being in 1922, was another blessing in those days. The N.C.C. headquarters in Shanghai was a sort of clearing house for mission news from all over China. One could go there for consultation and always receive careful consideration for one's problems.

Loss of Needed Missionaries

Many missionaries who went to the homeland in 1927 never returned. Why? China was unsettled. The future of mission seemed uncertain. Besides, there was a commitment to a gradual reduction in the proportion of missionary staff as the Chinese assumed responsibility. The Great Depression hit America, and some of those on furlough were unable to return. By 1928, the full roster of missionaries had dropped to forty-one, and of those, ten were on furlough. Then, happily for mission work, the animus that had been turned toward the foreigner subsided and was turned toward Communism.

Because of 1927, there was an evacuation of all our mission stations. Westerners and some Chinese sought refuge in overcrowded Shanghai. A few remained there for the duration of the trouble. Others returned to the homeland or went to Japan or to the Philippines. Wherever they were, they worked and waited with great concern for all of those they had learned to love. By the autumn of 1927, life was stable enough for missionaries to begin returning to their stations.

School Problems

People were busy with restoration of work, rehabilitation of buildings, and facing a future filled with many problems. The most immediate problems were the schools. They were required to register with the new government. Registration called for financial guarantees, a Chinese principal at the head of the schools, a majority of Chinese citizens on school boards, the adoption of prescribed minimum curriculums, and a prohibition of all required religious instruction. The union institutions led in registering, and one by one, with due care and caution, our mission schools registered also.

Some schools found that religious instruction on a voluntary basis was of more value than under the compulsory system. Out of mission schools from primary to university came some very fine Christian young people.

Young People's Summer Conferences

In 1931, the Disciples of Christ in China held their first young people's summer conference. The second was held in 1932 in spite of the Manchurian incident and the threat of war. In 1933, Mr. Li Choh-wu, pastor of the Wuhu Christian Church, in addressing the mission convention made a pleas for more lay leaders, saying, "We have depended too much upon our paid leaders…Growth and self-dependence can only come when the membership come to realize that they themselves must carry on." The young people's summer conferences in the years 1933 to 1936 had as a basic aim the starting of Christian young people in more effective ways of leadership.

Thriving Work in 1936

Schools, hospitals, and churches were thriving again in 1936, in fact right up to the vacation season in 1937. The only all-mission gathering looked forward to for that summer was the seventh young people's summer conference to be held in Nantung the third week in August. Nantung young people were looking forward to sharing with the conferees the beautiful new gymnasium on the school campus.

Note that name, Nantung. One of the changes made by the new government set up with Chiang Kai-shek as head was in geographical names. Nantugnchow, for example, became Nantung. Luchowfu became Hofei and Chuchow, Chuhsien. Peking ("northern capital") became Peiping ("northern peace"). Many names were changed and maps outdated.

That summer work was prospering, yet there was a sense of caution. The China mission newsletter for June 1937 made this statement: "Close attention is naturally paid to the change in Japanese cabinet. Statements that it is the time to settle the Sino-Japanese question are not read happily in this county, for they imply that the decision rests in Tokyo rather than in free adjustments between the interests of the two countries."

Bombs Begin to Fall

On July 7, 1937, Japan launched her all-out attack on China at the Marco Polo Bridge not far from Peiping (Peking). That was the beginning of active warfare and travel chaos. Because of the travel situation, the young people's summer conference was called off. During the third week in August, when the conference would have been in session, on August 17, bombing planes flew over Nantung and dropped eight bombs on the mission compounds. The hospital was burned to the ground, and a mission residence and the school gymnasium were completely demolished.

The Nantung hospital in 1915 had as a staff one missionary couple, one boy who wished to be a nurse, one coolie, and one woman servant. It grew to be a well-equipped and well-staffed hospital. There were more than a hundred people in the hospital at the time of the bombing. Mercifully, only seventeen were killed.

Nanking's Terrible Months

The destruction at Nanking was colossal. Bombing began in August and ended with the Japanese occupation in December. The people who could trekked to freedom in West China. The government fled. Schools fled. Ginling College and the University of Nanking fled as units.

On the Ginling campus, ten thousand women and girls found refuge. Between thirty and forty thousand people found shelter on the university grounds and in foreign compounds round about. Minnie Vautrin and a handful of colleagues kept the women and girls safe on the Ginling grounds. Searle Bates, James McCallum, and Lewis Smythe, with the several other Westerners who remained in Nanking, policed safety zones, protected people, foraged for food, and tried to protect mission property. Grace Bauer, a Disciple technician at the university hospital, valiantly stayed on the job. Dr. Brady of the hospital staff was out of the city but returned to the hospital as soon as permitted.

Attack, evacuation, occupation! So began the war years.

The War Years

Ups and Downs, 1937 to 1945

Each member of the China mission of the Disciples of Christ, Chinese and foreign, could tell a long and interesting story of personal experiences in the war years. Those who, for the sake of freedom, trekked to the west, found many places to be of service. Some were stopped midway to free China and did relief work where it was greatly needed. Dr. Luther Shao was loaned to the National Christian Council and National Committee for Christian Religious Education and did work in free China that was greatly appreciated. Mr. Li Hou-fu, the Chinese secretary of the mission, made the trek west, but strain and hardships were too much and he died in 1939. Dr. Shao took his place and carried on well. By correspondence and visitation, he knit together sundered mission ties.

Dr. and Mrs. Lewis Smythe (Mrs. Smythe a physician and daughter of pioneer Frank Garrett) as soon as possible reached the University of Nanking at its wartime campus in Chengtu. The Smythes made a contribution to administration, education, health, economics, and morale that is unforgettable. Cammie Gray, who went early to West China, did much in friendly ways to tie our scattered mission folk together. After America's entry into the war, Dr. Searle Bates, Mrs. Edna Gish, and Margaret Lawrence went to the west to strengthen the work there.

Mixed Feelings in the Mission

There were mixed feelings in the mission as to the wisdom of working under Japanese occupation. Geographically, all of our work was in occupied territory, and people needed to be served. The little handful of missionaries who were in our stations at the beginning of the occupation took heart when they saw the Chinese people regaining their morale. There were few preachers and paid workers; however, there were people needing to be served, the majority uneducated and underprivileged. One missionary wrote to his absent colleagues, "We never had a better chance to do what we came out here to do." The mission newsletter stated, "We are agreed that what we are able to do in this occupied area is tremendously worthwhile and though we realize that we can only go step by step. Every step is a great value."

Step by Step Under Occupation

Minnie Vautrin and a few Ginling colleagues opened a home craft school for young women from among those who had refugee on the Ginling campus. She started the experimental middle school for girls. The experiment was to see if such a school would be permitted to run. Gradually, other schools, all substandard because of all sorts of inadequacies, opened in the different stations. Children and young people were served and employment given to willing workers.

A sad experience of those days was to have Miss Vautrin break under the strain. Katherine Schutze accompanied her home, where she was given every care, but she died by her own hand in May of 1941.

Colleagues Called Back

People flocked to the churches, and various programs were carried on to meet their needs. Gradually, the missionaries at work in the occupied stations ventured to call back even distant colleagues. They did so reluctantly because there were many annoyances and certain dangers on the field. The dangers of travel and the whole uncertainty of the future presented problems, but there was work to be done, and by the autumn of 1940, the missionary staff was approaching the pre-war figure. The Chinese colleagues in the West China were needed, but new leaders were in the making. Victor Siao, as just one example, did as much as any one person could do to hold together the work at South Gate, Nanking 'til the end of the war years.

Then Came Consular Advice

Some of the missionaries with their children got back to their stations just in time to hear the US consular advice for women and children to leave China. Work was gradually turned over to Chinese colleagues. By the summer of 1941, Lois Ely was the only one of our missionary women in occupied China, and she, after completing two years of work in occupied Nanking, went to Shanghai on loan to the National Christian Council for editorial work.

After Pearl Harbor

A bare skeleton staff of missionaries was left in the interior stations. Pearl Harbor ended their activities. Ultimately, they were brought to Shanghai for repatriation. Folk from the interior were given preference in the matter of exchange. Oswald Goulter, because of his Australian citizenship, was not permitted to sail on either the first or second trip of the motor ship *Gripsholm*. Miss Ely, Mr. Goulter, and Mr. Marx were interned in three different camps, Mr. Goulter for the duration. Mr. Marx and Miss Ely sailed on the second exchange ship.

Partners Take up the Burden

The missionaries who left the field in 1940-41 had time to make plans with their colleagues, the partners who took up the burden. Mr. Li Chow-wu, pastor at Wuhu and evangelistic secretary for the mission, wrote at the time: "After you left here we suffered tribulation and anguish all the time. But through our God who loves us we were conquerors in all these… As for our church, all the members are zealful in loving our God and manifest this by the riches of their liberality."

'Til the Curtain Fell

Ups and Downs, 1945 to 1951

Oswald Goulter, released from internment in Shanghai, and Searle Bates, who flew down from West China, were the first of our missionaries to return to their stations at the end of World War II. Luther Shao, Chinese administrative secretary for the mission, was the first Chinese to return from West China. A slow but heartening procession of war-weary people followed him, all grateful for Christian gifts from overseas that provided for their return and partial rehabilitation. Margaret Lawrence and Edna Gish from West China were the next missionaries to arrive. They were soon joined by other folk from America. By the end of 1946, there were nineteen adults and two missionary Smith children on the field.

Property of Concern

Property was an immediate concern. Building head to be patched up; leaks attended to; crumbling walls strengthened; doors, window panes, and locks renewed. Some property had to be recovered from private occupants and from government and military occupation. Much equipment had been destroyed, pilfered, or worn out. New equipment was almost impossible to come by.

Dr. and Mrs. Corpron returned to Hofei (formerly known as Luchow-fu) and at once began repairing the hospital. There were only fifteen useable beds, and those were immediately filled. The sick poured in at a faster rate than repairs could be attended to. Doctor Corpron had to tell patients that they could be admitted only if they would bring their own beds, bedding, and food. Grace Young returned and was a welcome addition to the nursing staff.

Work on the Upgrade

By 1947, work everywhere was on the upgrade. Communists were a threat on the countryside but did not interrupt any of the work in the cities. He Hofei Christian hospital almost reached its prewar status. The Nantung hospital, without a missionary physician or nurse, could not do so well. Schools, particularly in Nanking, overflowed. Enrollment in the Nanking Theological Seminary in 1947 reached an all-time high.

The larger of the mission churches that same year, in addition to attaining self-support, raised from a third to a half of the funds necessary for repairs on church properties. It truly seemed that a new day was at hand.

New Plans for the New Day

The new plan was to add to work already well-organized and going forward a new emphasis on country work throughout the mission. Already, there were on the field four missionary families (Cherryhomes, Smiths, Reynolds, and Adsits) and one single woman trained for rural evangelism because before the war the mission had been conscious of inadequate staff for the line of work. Seven missions in the Nanking area and five large union institutions agreed to unite forces in a Christian Rural Service Union and chose Chuhsien (former Chuchow) as the first training center. Lewis Smythe was active on the planning committee. Oswald Goulter was named field director for the project. C.W. Chang, a disciple and dean of the College of Agriculture and Forestry of the University of Nanking, was chairman of the union committee.

Chuhsien was selected for the first training center for several reasons. It was essentially a market center surrounded by a populous farming district. It was easily accessible by train from Nanking, and there were ample buildings and land available without cost. The rural churches and the Chuhsien city church along with the government authorities heartily welcomed the new project.

And so Chuhsien once again had resident missionaries after years without any. An experienced Chinese agricultural worked continued in the Hofei Rural Center. New people trained for rural development added much of hope for the future of the whole program.

A Look at the Educational Programs

Many individuals in the young and middle-aged bracket who were serving China in a truly Christian spirit had come from mission schools. One of the missionaries wrote at this time, "As never before, China longs for a reformed social and political life. Let us, as Christians, give renewed attention to character building in China through Christian schools of all types."

Disciples Active in Union Work

In addition to the new venture of rural evangelism, Disciples were sharing in other union work. A Disciple missionary and a Chinese colleague had helped prepare teaching materials to be published by the National Committee for Christian Religious Education for nationwide use.

In the union institutions in this period were three Disciple couples. Two were at the University of Nanking; another couple, well-trained student workers, were assigned to the Wuhu Academy.

Administering the Work

Administering the overall work in this period were Dr. Luther Shao, Chinese executive secretary, and co-secretary with him and western secretary of evangelism James McCallum. Mr. and Mrs. McCallum, who had begun work in 1921, were devoted missionaries with heartfelt interest in the entire mission program, able planners for the tasks ahead.

The Chinese church appreciated the return of the missionaries. It rejoiced in the return of members who had been scattered throughout the west. It was proud to welcome back faithful workers who had the opportunity to study abroad and returned hoping to add momentum to a Christian program of advance.

And Then the Curtain Began to Fall

The nationalist government, in conflict with the Communists, lost the mainland of China and fled to Formosa. October 1, 1949, is celebrated as the birthday of the People's Republic of China, the Communist regime. That was the beginning of another exodus of our missionaries from work they loved. Days increasingly filled with problems. Our workers tried to stay on and work. Finally, it became obvious that they were not to be permitted to do so. One by one, all agreed that they could not carry on. On January 3, 1951, the United Christian Missionary Society received a cablegram: "All Disciple missionaries have applied for exit." They began returning home in February. The Goulters were the last to leave, returning home via Australia, where they were delayed from May to December, finally reaching home in January 1952.

The curtain fell. The Chinese Christians of ours and other brotherhoods are largely behind that curtain. Some are in other lands. Some are in our own land. Here and abroad, they have found their way into our churches and the churches of other communions. Let us remember these Chinese away from home. Let us remember our fellow Christians in China.

Glyn and Jean Adsit's Memoirs of Their Missionary Experiences in Hofei, China, from 1947 to 1949

A Quick Overview and Look Ahead in Time

Both Glyn and Jean had an abiding faith in God that He would give them the power to do what He wanted them to do while in China. They arrived in China by ship, the *SS Marine Adder*, in the fall of 1947, stopping first in Japan, which was still under US military occupation.

When they were aboard the ship going to China, Jean experienced some seasickness. When they arrived in China, she missed a menstrual period and went to a Chinese doctor named Dr. Lee, and he said she was pregnant; and that, coupled with the seasickness, made her feel miserable at times. Once they arrived in China, they got off the ship in Shanghai and made their way to Hofei, Anhwhei, a provincial capital and army headquarters. Jean and two other missionary women went by small boat to Hofei. They were Lyrel

Teagarden and Winona Wilkinson. They traveled by boat since they were afraid to have Jean travel by an old, rickety bus over roads that were in bad shape. They were afraid she would have a miscarriage or something. The women stayed hidden on the boat since there were robbers and water pirates who might have harmed them or kept them for ransom if they had been seen. Glyn went ahead to Hofei and greeted Jean, Lyrel, and Winona as they arrived. The Chinese also greeted them by popping long strings of firecrackers.

In Hofei, the Disciples had a strong missionary work already going, a local Chinese church of over six hundred and several stations around the countryside where they had work of various kinds going on. In Hofei, Glyn and Jean lived in an eight-room stone house that had little heat, outside toilets, and no running water. Glyn liked to joke that the only running water they had was a person running from the well and running back to the house carrying water. Glyn and Jean also had two servants: Ho-Yin and Shu-Yin, a young couple who worked for them. Jean did work at the baby clinic, where she encouraged Chinese mothers to bring their babies for exams and washing. Jean helped give them baby powder, powdered milk, and baby clothes when they came.

Hofei was a large, walled city, and the missionary station had a large hospital run by the mission. Most of the medical staff were Chinese under the supervision of medical missionaries sent by the United Christian Missionary Society. Since most pregnant Chinese women would not come to a hospital, except as a last resort, to have a baby, many of the younger nurses had seen very few normal births at the hospital. When Jean was ready to have her baby, this author, the hospital room was crowded with Glyn, American and Chinese doctors, other missionaries, and many of the Chinese staff to see the foreign baby born. Timothy Lee Adsit (named Timothy for the Timothy in the Bible, which means "honoring God," and Lee in honor of the Chinese doctor who told Jean she was pregnant) was born April 26, 1948. From then on, much of Jean's time was taken up in caring for the baby.

Jean worked in a nursery the mission provided for single Chinese mothers who had lost their husbands in the war with the Japanese who had occupied the area earlier. She gave nursery care and taught what she could to these small children and provided them with one or two meals a day. Their mothers worked at various jobs in Hofei to support their fatherless families. Jean said, "This nursery work gave her great satisfaction" (Unpublished manuscript information written by Glyn as dictated by Jean on March 13, 1991, to be used at her graveside and memorial service upon her death, p. 2).

Glyn was the treasurer for the mission. He visited the various churches in the area to first find out what their crucial needs were. He ran a rural center, where he had Chinese youth, all boys, coming to study many subjects: agriculture, school teaching, etc. These were taught by Chinese teachers from Nanking University. Glyn was gone from Hofei much of the time, and this left Jean alone with the small baby, Tim, and their servants. All this time, the war between Chiang Kai Shek and the Communists was going on. It was sometimes dangerous to go into the countryside because some of the farmers were farmers by day and communist workers by night.

Concerning this time period, Glyn writes:

> I was shot at one time and hidden in Chinese Christian homes many times. The military situation began to worsen, and it was apparent that our missionary area would become a major battleground within a few months. Our mission met, and it was decided that families with children should go south to Nanking. We went by bus, boats, and truck. We got caught in a skirmish near Nanking but were not injured. We went through Chiang Kai Shek's army coming toward the north as we were going south. We arrived in Nanking (just before the gates closed) and stayed there for a while, and as the military situation was getting worse by the hour as the Communists came south, the American Ambassador, J. Leighton Stuart, advised that we leave China. We went to Shanghai and we boarded a large US

troop carrier ship. The ship started north along the east coast of China and picked up Americans and others as we went. We reached Tiensin near Peking [now modern-day Beijing], and from there, we went to Japan, where we visited the missionaries working there…We set course for San Francisco, California, arriving there the week before Christmas 1948, having been in China for one and one-half years…Although we left almost everything in our eight-room house in Hofei when we left, Jean never complained about the loss of all we had. What was more important to both of us was that our family was out of China safely and with reasonably good health. We still had each other, our faith, and our education. We would trust God for the future…

> —Unpublished manuscript information written by Glyn as dictated by Jean on March 13, 1991, to be used at her graveside and memorial service upon her death, p. 1.

While in China, Glyn and Jean helped bring many souls to Christianity, but more about that portion of the story later.

Now, against this quick historical overview, let's go back in time to more fully develop and document in chronological order the details of the events leading up to their time in China, their missionary work in China, and the events coming home from China.

Primary sources used heavily in this portion of the book include the following: Glyn B. Adsit's diary from 1945-49; passports, medical records, photographs, cultural artifacts brought home from China in a steamer trunk; Glyn and Jean's letters sent home to relatives; a series of slides and photos Glyn took while in China; correspondence received by Glyn and Jean while in China; several articles Glyn wrote for a missionary magazine entitled *The World Call*; several manuscripts, papers, and documents Glyn wrote about this time period after he returned; and personal interviews conducted by the author with colleagues of Glyn and Jean on the mission field, some of whom are still alive today.

Glyn B. Adsit's Diary, 1945-49

Discovered by the author only recently in an old, four-drawer file cabinet belonging to Glyn, the following diary is written in his own, sometimes-difficult-to-read handwriting, and concerns the events that occurred between 1945 and 1949. Due to space, I have only used portions herein dealing with the 1947-49 period of Glyn and Jean's missionary service. It is presented exactly as Glyn wrote it, in a steno pad used for taking shorthand, except for any grammatical corrections or spelling changes. The author apologizes in advance if any person's names or places are misspelled, but Glyn's handwriting was often difficult to read. Glyn writes:

February 10, 1947

If we consider our lives as channels instead of reservoirs, we can think of this: God uses us as a channel. His power flows through, leaving just the right ingredients to make us healthy and powerful of spirit and taking away the sins and poisons that are wasteful and would harm us. It is like a man breathing, taking in clear, fresh air and breathing out foul, used air.

February 18, 1947

Today was one of great joy and rejoicing. We learned today that we are to go to Chuckow in Anhwei, China. It is a small farming village of some thirty thousand people. We have a church of about two hundred (there). The land is bad, and people are poor. Only 30 percent are literate. Surely, much work in the name of Christ can be done here. Winters are cold, and summers are hot. George and Marge (Margaret Kennedy) Cherryhomes will be only other missionaries there. I will be able to devote almost all my time to strengthening the churches and developing new ones. My prayer is that God might give me necessary wisdom to meet this task. Society is allowing double allotment of money and weight for shipping goods over. This means we get $1,000 and eight tons.

February 28, 1947

Our instructions for securing passports came today from Janet Holroyd. It seems that this incident has brought into sharp focus the fact that we will be leaving our beloved United States. Although time for departure is six months away, the tug at my heart is causing a strange feeling, and there is no thought of not wanting to go, but that's thoughts of all those I love, those in Topeka, Enid, Great Bend, Tulsa, Colorado, Lawrence, and California.
How long will it be before we will feel at home in China? Jean is a little upset over the prospects of having a baby in Chuckow, where there is no doctor. I feel sure that some way can be worked out to have it here in Hofei, or Nanking, or someplace when and if she has a child.

March 12, 1947

God indeed still speaks to men. It was some six years ago that God told me to prepare myself for Christian service. Yesterday, He again spoke with such force that I had to obey. I received, at that time, spiritual strength to settle a quarrel of some months standing between me and Verla Elliot. These were the words God said to me: "You are treating her wrong. Admit your guilt and resolve from this day on to be a better man of God. Tell her, 'I hold nothing against you, and if forgiveness is needed, I ask for it. As far as I am concerned, you have at no time wronged me. I was merely to weak to meet the issues as they came. From this day on let us be friends.'" I told Verla what God said to me. We are friends again. "Dear God, I again give myself unreservedly to Thee. May nothing stand between me and Thee. Prepare me, oh Lord, to do Thy will, for I know that anything outside Thy will is of no avail. Amen."

March 15, 1947

For the past few weeks, I have been doing serious thinking as to what kind of a program I would try to follow in my missionary work in China. Several ideas have come, but one that expells most of the others is that it would be useless for me to try and figure out a pre-arranged plan; this would surely fail. I think it best to keep in touch with God day by day, trying hard to find the answers to problems as they arise day by day. I hope to be a channel through which God can work. That is my desire to remove all obstacles, to make an unreserved surrender to Him. Today, I am praying for humility. I know I need it. The past few days have been full of spiritual joy. Everything has seemed in tune.

July 24, 1947

The sorrow at parting is not easy. One must cry to release the tension that grips the heart. We left Lakin, Kansas, today. Mr. Dowd, Goldie, Ralph Dowd, Phil Wilson, Beverly Adsit, Beth Wilson, and Gladys and Bill Burns saw us off. Lakin is not much of a town. An oil and gas boom is now on. Ralph wants to give us a typewriter. It was very hard for Jean to leave. She cried.

July 29, 1947

We are on the train to San Francisco via Grand Canyon. Mother, Duane, and Pat saw us off at Topeka. Mom did her best to be brave. She did not cry. Duane and Pat said that their baby would be five when we saw it for the first time. My feelings today are mixed. I am a little afraid and also very humble, as I realize the great task we are embarking upon. Only the knowledge that Jesus is going with us makes it possible for me to go. Mother is in good health, and I fully expect to see her in five and one half years. God willing, our health is perfect, and I only have one desire. "God give us a child, we are now beginning to try to have one, and we have tried for six years to keep from having one. I hope it is not too late. God, grant my deep desire."

August 13, 1947

We reached Honolulu at 3:00 p.m. The Garcias met us, along with several church members from the First Christian Church. They gave each of us some leis. It is a beautiful Hawaiian custom. The giver kisses the recipient as the lei is put on the shoulders. We visited this beautiful island and had a short swim in Waikiki beach. At 6:00 p.m., we went to the First Christian Church for a dinner. This church has the most beautiful baptistery I have ever seen. Friends we have met on board are Dr. Djan of Peking Christian College, Kiang Wen Har and family, Mr. Kung the army man, Mr. Ding, Don Flaherty, Syracuse in China, West China Union University, Aberigti, Szechwan, China. There are about three hundred missionaries on board, counting children and Mr. And Mrs. Lelek going to Nanking as ambassadors from Czechoslovakia. We reached Yokohama, Japan, where Sharrocks debarked. We met Hendricks. Sharrocks had no trouble getting through customs. Missionaries were exempt from custom inspections. We were not allowed to get off the ship at this place. People did not look too hungry, but they scrambled for food that was thrown from ships. We could see no sign of their city being destroyed. We were in port from 7:00 a.m. to 2:00 p.m. Next, we reached Kobe. This is a beautiful port, but they were very cautious not to let us see any of it. We were there one and one half hours. This morning, we are seeing the water change color from blue to yellow. We will see land of the China coast within two hours. We are excited and ready for customs. Jean missed her monthly period. Can it be that she is pregnant?

August 26, 1947

Today, we are to land in China. How long we have waited for this day. Our visit to the Canyon was thrilling. We expected to see a great wonder, but we cannot explain how we felt when we saw the mile-deep canyon with its varied changing colors. We felt very close to God. San Francisco is one of the most beautiful towns I have seen. The great amount of water and sloping hills add to its beauty. But I felt the godlessness of the city. We stayed from August 1 to 8, 1947 at the Franciscan Hotel. On August 8, 1947, we were up early to be sure everything was in order, to catch the boat. We were expecting some trouble in trying to take some large suitcases aboard, but they did not object. Our accommodations are crowded but adequate. Fourteen men are in my room, twelve women in Jean's. We are sleeping in the officers' quarters of *Marine Adder*. [P.L.] Disciples aboard ship are Chatfields (John and Jean); Hallam and Helen Shorrock; Grace Young; Verla Elliot; and one independent family, the Taylors; and ourselves. This ship is not too fast, making only about seventeen knots on the average (per hour). The food is good, and there is quite a choice.

September 5, 1947

Today, the *General Meigs* sails from America. Missionaries, Doctor and Mrs. [Oswald] Goulter and Mrs. [Douglas] Corporan and Edna Gish are on board sailing for China. It is almost impossible to describe what inconvenience going through customs is. We had no trouble getting our baggage through, but our freight has been slower. The Chinese system is cumbersome and involved in too much paperwork. A person is sent all over town trying to find a proper address only to discover that the address is wrong.

September 28, 1947

We had some trouble with a pedi-cabbie who tried to rob two ladies, Verla Elliot and Grace Young, in our party. Doctor Corporan and I were in the midst of a good fight with fists for a few minutes. We went to jail but were released two hours later. Shanghai is the noisiest, dirtiest, smelliest place I was ever in. My first impression is that these people don't know God or Christ, and most of them are too busy eeking out a living to worry about it. "Yells, smells, and a lot of little hells" describes this place.

It is hard to get used to seeing children with such awful sores in their heads and limbs. Many of them have the itch. We have been told that Shanghai does not present a true picture of China. We hope not. The people here are discourteous and almost act like animals at some times, but I must never forget that they too are made in the image of God. We are staying in the Lutheran Center, 310 Hart Road, until we move to Chuchow. We met Chandler of O.M.S., who is trying to start a school in Nanking. Both Jean and I have been sick with colds for a few days. We took sulfa-diazine to knock it out. We are having fun trying to use our Mandarin [dialect] here among the Shanghai Chinese dialect people. Most of them speak some Mandarin. We received word from home that Mr. Holder, a negro friend of mine, had died of a heart attack. He was seventy-one years old.

October 30, 1947

Nanking, the capital of China, is much better than Shanghai. Jean likes it here better. We went to Chuhsien, a good place to work. Our future home is all run down and will need much repair. [It was formerly occupied by Cherryhomes.] [There] is plenty of work to do in and around Chuhsien; sixteen small villages with no pastors. I hope to help train men for these places. [We had] trouble with soldiers who want to move in our property.

There is a great deal of confusion here among our missionary organizations. It is hard to plan a program very far ahead. But the desire and intention to serve Christ is evident in lives of missionaries here.

It is surprising how many problems arise about money out here. Temptation, I know from whence you come. You are devil sent. I will not be discouraged when problems arise day by day. It is my hope that I will never turn back from this great task of trying to turn China Christward.

There is a possibility that we might be sent to Hofei to work with Goulter. This is more likely to be true if Goulter accepts the opportunity to head up Kiangon, Anhwei, rural work. There is a definite clash of opinions about how our work should be done out here. I have already been accused of being too impatient.

[The] best news of all: Jean is to have a baby in April 1948. We are very thankful that God is entrusting us with this life. We are finding it difficult to get J. McCallum to do things quickly. He moves too slowly for me. We still have no language teacher, and we have been here two months.

February 14, 1948; Valentine's Day

We left Nanking for Hofei late in November. Jean went ahead with Lyrel and Winona. They traveled by river boat, and Jean had her first taste of crude traveling. We have found how to travel in more comfort on these river boats. You bribe the boat captain, and he lets you stay in his private quarters. I did not go with Jean because I had to stay in Nanking to see that our freight moved from Shanghai. Ju Shoa San took care of the moving details. Our two servants and I left Pukow by bus the day before Thanksgiving and traveled over the bumpiest road in my experience. We arrived in Hofei around 4:00 p.m. Jean, Dr. Corporan, and Grace Young met us at the station.

We walked back through town, and they suggested that I visit the church. As we went in the gate, they shot two strings of firecrackers as a sign of welcome. Since Thanksgiving, I have been studying Chinese and making trips into the countryside. Oswald Goulter, Pastor Wang, and I went to San Ho, thirty miles from Hofei. We rode our bikes up and got caught in a snowstorm and had to wait five days before we could walk back. We walked one-third of the way and then hired chairs to carry us on in. [The author wishes the reader to note parenthetically that Glyn commented many times while recalling this story in later interviews: "This was one of the most humiliating experiences of my life, to be carried on the backs and shoulders of other human beings trudging through the snow and mud. Our feet were frozen, and our bikes would not go through the snow and mud. We had little choice but to hire the chair carriers." [Adsit, Glyn B., interviewed by Timothy Lee Adsit and Janice Lynn (Adsit) Morrison, Brookings, Oregon, 7:00 p.m., during a slideshow of he and Jean's experiences in China, shortly before his death, circa 1998. The interview was recorded on audio tape, and Glyn narrated for the historical record what people, places, and things were depicted in each slide shown.]

We have been to Sha Li Tan, where we have a school and want room to start a church. Er Shr Pu is about sixteen miles from here, and we went there to visit a family who had asked us to come and see them. They are interested in becoming Christians. Oswald wants me to take over this place and see what I can do with it. Mrs. Yang, our first English teacher, and I are going out to instruct this family in Christian doctrine. The family also wants us to introduce Western medicine and agricultural methods. These past few months have been ones of great tension. We are constantly wondering if and when the Communists are coming. It has worried me more because Jean is pregnant and cannot be moved very easy. But our older missionaries are very helpful and encourage us greatly. Jean is having a very difficult time in adjusting to these Chinese people. Will this cause us to stay home after our first term?

I am to preach my first sermon in China next Friday. I will preach in English, and Mr. Tan will interpret for me. I have been teaching a Bible class for English-speaking students. These men and young men are very much interested in Christianity. We have enjoyed, very much, our experience of moving into our home. We even have electric lights. What a blessing light is! Seeing our bright lights in this dark country town makes me appreciate what Jesus said, "You are the light of the world!" I like Hofei and see great prospects for our Christian efforts here. We are getting a great hearing, and many are accepting Christ's way of life.

No date given

Address in Shanghai: China Bible House, Mr. Mortensen, Secretary, Hong Kong Road. China Sunday School Union, 152 Peking Road (East) (J.N. Montgomery). Maffet Presbyterian Hospital, Chunkiang Ku. Kiangsu.

—Adsit Diary and Letters, 1945-49, 51 pages, Glyn B. Adsit Unpublished Materials Collection in possession of Timothy L. Adsit, 1635 SE Jonathan Avenue, Dallas, Oregon 97338.

Glyn's diary ended at this point, and no further entries were made. However, the author located and is in possession of a number of never-before-published photographs and letters that both Glyn and Jean sent and received during this same time period that verify many of the entries in the diary and further expand upon the details of their work for God while in China.

Selected Missionary Memoirs: Unpublished Letters, Certificates, Correspondence, Papers, and Photographs

The story continues…

- From Glyn Bemister Carter Adsit, Amarillo, Texas, July 25, 1941, to Mize, F.V., Manager, "A" Telegraph Office, Santa Fe Railroad, Amarillo, Texas (letter of resignation). The letter reads: "Please accept this as my resignation, effective August 26, 1941. I want to thank you for the fine cooperation I have had from you and all the employees in this office. Thank you and God bless all of you. Signed, Glyn B. Adsit."

- Mize, F.V., Manager, "A" Telegraph Office, Santa Fe Railroad, Amarillo, Texas, Personal letter accepting resignation to Mr. G.B. Adsit, July 26, 1941. The letter reads, "Dear, sir, I regret very much that you are leaving us. However, I congratulate you very much that you are going to school and entering the ministry. The world needs men that have religious convictions, with the courage to live it and support it to the fullest extent. Your work has been highly satisfactory, and I have asked that a service letter be furnished you. If at any time I can be of any service to you, please do not fail to call on me. Yours sincerely, F.V. Mize, Manager and Wire Chief."

- Davis, John L., Editor, "Classroom and Campus," *World Call*, February, 1945. p. 24.

"Phillips University, Enid, Oklahoma. Recently four Philippians, Mr. and Mrs. Robert Fink, and Mr. and Mrs. Glyn Adsit, having visited in Chicago and Indianapolis, where they passed qualifying examinations, were accepted for missionary service on the foreign fields. They will attend Cornell next year. The Adsits plan to specialize in evangelistic work and the Finks in rural evangelism in China and India, respectively…"

- "Bible College Students Ordained," *Christian Evangelist*, July 4, 1945, p. 655.

"Five students from the Bible College of Phillips University were ordained at a union ordination service held at the University Place Church, Enid, Oklahoma, on Wednesday evening, May 22. The Christian churches of Enid and the home churches of those ordained participated in the service.

Those ordained were Muriel Watkins, Uniontown, Pennsylvania, who will enter the mission field; Mrs. Glyn Adsit, Amarillo, Texas, and Glyn Adsit, Topeka, Kansas, minister of West Side Church, Tulsa, and living link missionary of Central Church (in a student relationship), who will become missionaries to China; James Otis Pearce, Armory, Mississippi, pastor of the church at Walter, Oklahoma; and Onan Yale, Grinnell, Kansas, minister of the church at Lovell, Oklahoma.

Ray Snodgrass, minister of Central Church, Enid, gave the ordination sermon, 'Prior to All'; Dean Stephen J. England presented the credentials to the candidates for ordination; Carl Covey, executive secretary of the Oklahoma Christian Missionary Society, Oklahoma City, conducted the examination of the candidates; and F. H. Marshall, dean emeritus of the Bible College, gave the charge…"

(Re-printed by permission, White, Cyrus N., President and Publisher, Christian Board of Publications, 1221 Locust Street, Suite 1200, St. Louis, MO 63103)

- Adsit, Glyn B., Graduate Student in Sociology and Rural Education, Cornell University, Ithaca, New York, to Editor, Letter and picture to World Call Magazine, Indianapolis, Indiana, October 11, 1945.

"Dear, sir, I am not sure you will be interested in the following, but you might find something in it. I am not much of a writer, but some of the facts are here for you to use if you see fit.

If you go 'far Above Cayuga's waters' and stop in room 201, Warren Hall on the beautiful campus of Cornell University, you will find forty-seven missionaries hard at work.

These missionaries are participating in a short course of 'Relief and Rehabilitation of the Far Eastern Countries.' Thirty-six of these missionaries either have been or soon will be in China. Burma claims four; Philippine Islands five; Korea two; India and the Netherland East Indies one each.

Church unity is being practiced. Ten different church groups are represented in this meeting. These churches are Southern Baptist, Disciples of Christ, Episcopalian,

National Holiness, United Brethern, Dutch Reform, Methodist and Presbyterians.

Five of these missionaries were recently released from the Japanese prison camps in the Philippine Islands. Among these were our own Allen and Daisy Huber. Several of this group arrived in the United States abroad the Gripsholm during recent years.

Their day is a busy one, starting at 8:15 a.m. and lasting until 4:00 p.m. The subjects are taught by specialists and fit the needs that the missionary expects to find when he returns to his field in the near future. (China had just been occupied by the Japanese.) The course includes home and family life; nutrition; health and sanitation; visual aids; cooperatives; seeds and plants; village reconstruction; re-forestation; religious education; child care; emergency relief; and education.

Men and women who have faced famine, flood, bombs, and Japanese are eager to share their experiences with others in order that all may hear a better witness for Christ in the days ahead. Several of this group have left during the course to take up their work in the mission field. It encourages those remaining because they feel that soon, the planes and ships will be taking them to the field also.

Disciples of Christ participating in the Relief and Rehabilitation Course are: Lewis Smythe, Miss Stella Tremaine, Miss Lyrel Teagarden, Miss Verla Elliot, Mr. And Mrs. Allen Huber, and Mr. And Mrs. Glyn Adsit.

The enclosed picture is one I snapped of the group. I can't remember all the names. The X's mark Stella Tremaine and Lyrel Teagarden. Verla Elliot is directly behind Lyrel, and Jean Adsit is directly behind Stella. Sincerely yours, Glyn B. Adsit."

- Goulter, Oswald J., "You in Heaven" Democracy Can Win in China, If—, *The Christian-Evangelist*, July 10, 1946, pp. 679-680. Article sent to Glyn B. Adsit. Concerning the new Christian Church, Disciples of Christ mission program opening up in China, Oswald J. Goulter writes:

"The Christian Church has a particularly favorable position for carrying the Christian message to China. Our people are vigorous, democratic, open minded, and untrammeled by ecclesiasticism and rigid orthodoxy. The area which has been set aside for our missionary work is most strategically situated in the lower Yangtze Valley in the neighborhood of the nation's capital. Our China mission is just in the process of initiating a great forward evangelistic program for this vast territory. We have a task here in what is the most strategic and yet the most neglected area in any of the great mission fields, which might well challenge the finest brains and the most adventurous spirits in our entire brotherhood.

I have had the privilege of working in this field almost continuously for twenty-five years. Every year of this period we have seen wars or social upheavels and revolutions of the most alarming kind in our own neighborhood. I was with the Chinese Christians when they were going through the agony of seeing their country literally looted and torn to shreds by the invaders. In that hour of dire need, a few missionaries and Christian leaders were able to demonstrate that in the moment of utter despair, the Christian faith could afford a foundation for freedom, honor, and democracy. Over and over again, people told me, 'The only decent thing on which we can depend that remains in our wretched country is the Christian Church.'

After Pearl Harbor, my Chinese friends wept when they saw the Japanese military police standing guard in my own study. When the police demanded to know for what they were weeping they went away with sad hearts, but with an unshakable determination that after the war when freedom returned, they would work for a Christian society. I was compelled to leave them for a period of more than three years of internment, but on my return, I found them eager for leadership and for a more effective program of Christian work in the unevangelized countryside. But the task now is so enormous that it not merely challenges the small group of Chinese Christians, but presents a gigantic task to our entire brotherhood. 'You in heaven,' 'Instruct me,' say our Chinese friends…" (Goulter, Oswald J., "You in Heaven" Democracy Can Win in China, If—, *The Christian-Evangelist*, July 10, 1946, pp. 679-680.)

- The United Christian Missionary Society, "China Mission Descriptive Report," Indianapolis, Indiana, Report contained in a letter to Glyn and Jean Adsit, 1946, pp. 1-3. The report states:

"1946, the first post-war year in China, has been a year of recovery. Early in the year, missionary personnel began returning to their stations. Mr. Goulter, released from his Shanghai internment camp, and Searle Bates from West China were the first arrivals in Nanking. Mrs. Edna Gish and Miss Margaret Lawrence, coming from West China arrived next and these were followed by Miss Stella Tremaine and Miss Lyrel Teagarden who took up their former residence in Wuhu and Hofei respectively. As transportation became available others returned to China from the USA until at the end of the year there were nineteen adults and two children in residence. The first two of the new generation of missionaries who are so sorely needed, are included in this total.

Chinese colleagues soon began returning from West China where they had sojourned during the eight year war period. Dr. Luther Shao, the Chinese Administrative Secretary of the China Mission, came first, joining a mere handful of Chinese church and school leaders who had remained in Central China, carrying on what work they could during the Japanese occupation. He was followed by a continuing procession of preachers and their families, teachers and Christian Church members, all of whom were returning to their homes after an eight-year absence. There were a few unpleasant misunderstandings between those who had fled to West China and those who had remained in "occupied" territory, but this was inevitable.

Nowhere has the housing problem been more acute than in China's cities, so that many people returned with no place to stay. They possessed only that which they brought with them on a long trip which had taken two or even three months by foot, bus, boat, train, or sedan chair. They waited their turn for transportation in crowded terminal centers and often had to borrow, or wire and wait for additional funds. We were thankful that funds had been provided through the Mission, for their return and a partial rehabilitation. Most of these people showed the effect of the long, hard war years and we have rejoiced to see the gradual improvement in health and vitality in many cases.

Most of our buildings were standing at the close of the war, although much of the equipment was lost. We were soon able to hold services in all of our churches, and with the return of ministers from the West, by mid-year all of our larger churches had trained ministers. There was enough available equipment to start the Chung Hwa Girls School, and the Ruh Chuin Middle School in Nanking, as well as the Li Teh Primary School in Wuhu. By the fall term these three schools were able to carry on without an appropriation from the Mission for current expenses. The Tsung Ing School of Nantung was also started, but as yet has not flourished. Gradually, church boards have been reorganized, Bible Schools have been started or improved, choirs and Christian Youth Fellowships, have been resumed, and Institutes for revival and training of church membership have been promoted. There has been a systematic and continual visitation of the churches by the administrative members of the Mission, which has stimulated activity and has helped to iron out many difficulties. The first Young People's Summer Conference was held and a few Daily Vacation Bible Schools were con ducted under local leadership.

An effort has been made to locate as many of our former Church members as possible and to revise our church membership records. Three hundred and one persons were baptized during the year, and there remains a goodly number of enquirers. The largest congregation in the Mission is at San Ho, a country town near Hofei. This church baptized 180 on one day in the fall of the year.

There has been a gain in church self support during the year. The churches have contributed generously to the support of their workers and have tried to match the efforts of the Mission in an attempt to keep up with the rising cost-of living. By the end of the year, our *oldest Church, Drum tower, Nanking* was able to carry on without subsidy. Two more churches raised money to help with repairs, to buy or make pews, chairs, and other badly needed furnishings. Some members, as a thank offering for a safe return to their homes have provided hymnals or Bibles, while others, in memory of dear ones who have passed on, have contributed other needed items. It is difficult to give a statistical report of the year when figures mean so little. But, one church raised $600 (Chinese money) during the first six months of the year, and more than $10,000,000 (Chinese money) during the second half. One school had $11,000,000 (Chinese money) in receipts the first half year and $176,000,000 (Chinese money) for the fall term. Part of this is real gain in giving and receipts, but part of it is the picture of inflation. We cannot turn these figures into American dollars with any assurance of accuracy, because of exchange fluctuation.

We have had to give more than the usual amount of attention to property. First, we had to patch up the buildings for which we had the immediate need. These emergency repairs consisted of stopping leaks, patching walls which were in danger of crumbling, as well as restoring doors, window frames and panes, and locks. There still remains the job of adequate screening, painting and major reconditioning before the buildings can be considered as being even in fair shape. A constant effort has been to recover property occupied either by "squatters", or friends, or government and military organizations. In most cases, a small rental is offered and in some cases it will be easier to recover the property when we are able to expand our work enough to demand it's use, but we may have a long period of negotiation involving even law suits over a few cases. The problem of equipment has been even more difficult. That which has been destroyed or pilfered or worn out, we can forget about. Much has already been recovered, and the return of some has already been promised. Every piece of furniture and equipment is now so very expensive that we cannot even consider its purchase. We cannot afford to have any new furnishings made.

We have not done much as yet toward the recovery of our rural churches and outstations. We lack the personnel to work them. In the early part of last year they were too near, if not within, the areas controlled by the Communists. Some of our former districts are not yet considered quite safe to live in, but most of them are accessible now. One or two of the country churches are the most thriving in the Mission, but these are the exceptions. Several of the country churches have been destroyed. Even some in use are almost stripped of equipment. Here the members bring benches from their home for evening meetings. There is not one small portable organ in all of the fifteen churches of the Chuhsien district. Our attention for the next year must be directed toward the restoration and development of this area. Most of the new missionaries are to direct their major efforts toward rural work and this is certainly the direction in which our China Mission must move.

The most striking advance during these years has been the development of Chinese leadership. All of the major decisions of the past year have been made by Chinese workers. Dr. Luther Shao, acting as Chinese General Secretary, must be given credit for a good deal. He has been ably supported by Pastor Li-Cheo-wu and Miss Chen Hsi-ren as well as other of the East China group. The time of missionary domination has passed and the time of fifty-fifty leadership has also passed. Therefore,

1946 marks the beginning of missionary cooperation under Chinese leadership, and we are none too soon in reaching this stage of our Mission progress."

- Higdon, Dr. E.K., Foreign Division Application Packet, "How to Become a Foreign Missionary-Qualifications, Preparation and Procedure, The United Christian Missionary Society, Indianapolis, Indiana, Letter to Glyn and Jean Adsit, 1947.

As a part of the application process to become a foreign missionary, Glyn and Jean Adsit received an application packet from Dr. E.K. Higdon in 1947. The brochure states:

"The purpose of this folder is to outline the most important qualifications of a candidate for foreign service, to suggest areas of preparation, and to give in some detail the procedures leading to appointment. It is not intended to be an exhaustive discussion of what is involved in preparing for Christian service abroad and seeking appointment for that service.

Qualifications. The most important qualifications for a person who wishes to engage in Christian service abroad are: 1. Excellent health; 2.High scholarship; 3. Ability to get along with people; and 4. Deep, sane Christian experience and conviction.

Our medical examiner passes on all matters of health.

Transcripts of grades beginning with first year high school should accompany the preliminary information blank. (See Procedures).

Statements regarding Christian experience and convictions should be submitted in writing.

Testimony about ability to get along with people usually is given by those named by the candidate as his references.

Preparation. The training in college and in post-graduate schools should be so planned as to include: 1. A thorough background and foundation preparation in the

Old and New Testaments; 2. A mastery of the fundamental facts of Christianity and the ability to state in simple personal terms the candidate's belief about God, Christ, man, sin, salvation, etc.; 3. An adequate knowledge of the history of the church; 4. The principles and practices of Christian education; 5. The principles and methods of rural reconstruction; 6. Home and family life education; 7. The fundamental principles of first aid and, if possible, some experience in practical nursing; 8. A knowledge of the history, the culture, the religions and the psychological, economic and social aspects peculiar to the life of the people in the country to which the candidate plans to go; and 9. Courses in phonetics and linguistics.

A brief statement of the candidate's preparation, insofar as he has had it, in relation to each of the nine points listed above, should be submitted with the Preliminary Information blank.

Procedure. 1. Write to Dr. E.K. Higdon, candidate secretary, stating your desire to prepare for Christian service abroad; 2. He will send you a preliminary information blank to fill out and return; 3. If reports from references are favorable, you will be invited in due time to come to Indianapolis for interviews; 4. If you are accepted as a candidate, we help plan your further studies; and, in case you need financial assistance for post-graduate work, we arrange for scholarship loans of $400 to $600 per year; 5. Acceptance as a candidate does not guaranteed appointment as a missionary. Candidates are not appointed at the time they have their first interviews in Indianapolis. The appointment is made by the Board of Trustees usually only a few weeks before the candidate sails for his field. College and post-graduate days are testing and sifting times. But although appointment is not guaranteed, the years of preparation are profitably employed because the foreign division recommends courses of study which prepare the candidate for Christian service either at home or abroad; and 6. Candidates or "appointees in waiting" who are preparing for China during this war period are sent to Berkeley, California, for the study of Chinese language, history and culture in the California College in China. This follows the completion of seminary or other specialized courses."

- Higdon, E.K., Executive Secretary, Department of Oriental Missions, The United Christian Missionary Society, Indianapolis, Indiana, Letter to Whom It May Concern, April 10, 1947 (Certification of Ordination as Ministers for Mr. And Mrs. Glyn B. Adsit and Appointment as Missionaries of the UCMS)

"To Whom It May Concern, This is to certify that Mr. And Mrs. Glyn Bemister Adsit and Alice Jean (Dowd) Adsit are regularly ordained and appointed missionaries of The United Christian Missionary Society with headquarters in Indianapolis, Indiana. Mr. And Mrs. Adsit will be commissioned on June 25 (1947) for service in China.

The United Christian Missionary Society is bringing or registering its China Mission staff to its prewar strength. The Council of the Disciples of Christ in China voted in a meeting on December 31, 1946 to January 2, 1947, to assign Mr. and Mrs. Adsit to Chuchow, Anhwei, for rural work. The assignment is in line with a long range policy for the development of a program in Christian service in the rural area for which we are exclusively responsible.

We certify that we will be responsible for the travel expenses of Mr. And Mrs. Adsit both to and from China. They receive a regular monthly salary for their services. Sincerely yours, E.K. Higdon."

- Adsit, Glyn B., Minister, Graduate Student, Yale University, New Haven, Connecticut, Letter to Dr. E.K. Higdon, April 15, 1947.

"Dear E.K., Just received a telegram from Janet Holroyd, 'Could you sail San Francisco early June instead of August difference is between Tourist class accommodations and troop transport no definite arrangements with links as yet. Wire reply or any questions.'

I wired her as follows. 'We can sail early June. Can we count on this as definite arrangement? If so, we must leave school soon to pack, visit churches and relatives. Am writing letters to Higdon and Weesner.'

This wire came as quite a surprise. This will mean that several of our plans will have to be changed. My first question is about commissioning. What are we to do about being commissioned? Will there have to be a special one or something?

It will mean that we will have to leave school a little early in order that we can have time for packing and visiting the churches. As we have it figured, we should leave in early May at least. We will need at least three weeks to visit our living link and service link churches. It will probably take us a week to pack, maybe longer. We will also have to allow time for household goods to reach the coast before sailing.

Since we have just a few weeks of school left, and since we have covered all the essential grammar structure, it will not hurt us too much to leave school early. I feel that the board that examines us in China will request us to take a little more formal schooling and that we can pick up from where we leave off here. If you give us the go-ahead sign, we will begin immediately to prepare to leave here and tie up our loose strings.

I am writing Weesner in regards to the living link and service link churches. When I receive your answer to this letter, I will make request for travelling money.

The only real problem as I see it is, will we stop by Indianapolis for commissioning before we go on to Oklahoma and New Mexico? If so, what date? Please tell Miss Holroyd that we are arranging for our shots beginning tomorrow. Sincerely yours, Glyn and Jean Adsit."

• Adsit, Glyn B., Minister, Graduate Student, Yale University, New Haven, Connecticut, Letter to Mr. C.A. Weesner, April 15, 1947.

"Dear Mr. Weesner, It begins to look like life is very changeable. I just received a wire from Janet Holroyd which follows, 'Could you sail San Francisco early June instead of August differences in between tourist class accommodations and troop transport no definite arrangements with links as yet. Wire reply or any questions.'

I answered her as follows, 'We can sail early June. Can we count on this as definite arrangement? If so, we must leave school soon to pack, visit churches and relatives. Am writing letters to Higdon and Weesner.'

You have never seen two people as happy as Jean and I were when this telegram came. We are, of course, ready to sail at the earliest date. All that we ask is a little time to pack and visit relatives and friends. This change in plans will mean that my two previous letters to you in regards to working in conferences and visiting churches will be outdated. We will now have to make new dates to visit the churches.

I am assuming that unless we hear something definite about the Stratford, Texas church, that Jean will not plan on visiting there. Will you please clear this up in your answer to us?

We are now awaiting definite word from Miss Holroyd about sailing in June. If she says it is early June, then that will mean that we must leave here almost immediately in order to visit the three churches, pack, and see our relatives. We also have to squeeze in a commissioning somewhere.

If we leave here right away, it will only leave us six weeks at the most. If we get word from Higdon and Miss Holroyd this week, we could leave here any time next week, stopping at Indianapolis on the way to Oklahoma. But since all this is in the realm of if, I suppose nothing definite can be said. But if we leave here next week, that will mean April 27, May 4, 11, and 18 would be Sundays we could visit our churches. We would prefer to visit them as early as possible to leave the last days for packing and relatives. We must also allow some time for our freight to reach San Francisco.

Will you please confer with Miss Holroyd and Dr. Higdon and advise us soon as possible what conclusions you have reached. In the meantime, we will try to keep our minds on our Chinese. Please don't make it too long.

If we do leave next week, I will buy our tickets to Oklahoma or New Mexico, depending upon how the dates are arranged for visiting the churches. We will also have our household goods to ship from here. I will discuss this with you when we stop over at Indianapolis. Hoping to hear from you soon. Sincerely yours, Glyn B. Adsit."

- "Lincoln Terrace Assigned Glyn B. Adsit." Unsigned news article, name, specific date, page number not available, May 1947.

"Our Church received a letter from Mr. C.A. Weesner of the United Christian Missionary Society that the Lincoln Terrace Christian church was at the top of the list for the assignment of a missionary. He recommended Mr. Glyn B. Adsit, who, with Mrs. Adsit, are sailing for China this summer to do educational-evangelistic work.

The missionary committee of our church, with Mrs. Earl Taber as chairman, considered the matter and recommended that we accept Mr. Adsit as the service link missionary for our church. The board unanimously approved the committee's recommendation.

Mr. Glyn B. Adsit was born July 6, 1917. He is a graduate of Topeka High School. He attended the Strickler's Business College and a normal school in Topeka. He entered Phillips University in 1941 and received his BD degree last year. He is completing his preparation and language study in the east this semester. The Adsits will be commissioned in the United Christian Missionary Society trustee's meeting in June. He will be able to spend some time with us this summer before he sails.

Bob Bowers was a classmate and lab partner with Glyn in Phillips. He says, 'Glyn B. Adsit is a Christian in every sense. From the moment of his conversion in Amarillo he has been completely consecrated to the Lord. Feeling the call of the ministry in Christ's name, he left a well-paying job to come to Phillips University to adequately prepare himself. On campus, he was quickly established as a friendly, scholarly, sincere student. While in Phillips, he and his wife answered the call to missions and immediately entered preparation for this wider ministry.

All who know Glyn love him. He is sincerely concerned about those who know not the Christ and is utterly selfless in his service to all. He has a keen mind which he has applied to study and learning, earning the respect of all for his abilities as a scholar.

I but quote the opinion of the leaders of our brotherhood when I predict that Glyn will be one of the outstanding missionaries of this generation, that he will win many to Christ and will challenge the heart of everyone to a greater service in His name. He was student pastor in Nicoma Park and West Side Christian Church, Tulsa.'

The Service Link Missionary Relationship. In the above article, I referred to the fact that Mr. Adsit would be our service link missionary. The service link relationship requires that the church contribute $1,000 through the United Christian Missionary Society to the missionary's support. In order to have that much to apply on the missionary's support, it is necessary that $1,500 be given through the United Promotional Department. That amount is allocated to the various missionary enterprises, $500 to home missions, etc., and the $1,000 to foreign missions, that is, the support of the missionary.

The Lincoln Terrace Christian Church gave more than this amount in the missionary year ending June 30, 1946, and our offerings this year are considerably larger than last year. So we need have no concern but what we can support the missionary."

- Doan, Mrs. Mary Lediard, Presiding, Commissioning Service Bulletin for Glyn and Jean Adsit et al, June 25, 1947.

"Commissioning Service for Mr. and Mrs. Glyn B. Adsit, Dr. Donald Pettus Conwell, Miss Verla Marjorie Elliot, Miss Marilynne Hill, Mr. and Mrs. Harvey Lorl (difficult to read last name), and Mr. And Mrs. Hallam Carey Shorrock, Jr., June 25, 1947, Mrs. Mary Lediard Doan, presiding. [The Bulletin reads] Processional, Mrs. Frances Boese; Hymn 564; Scripture, Mrs. Doan; Presentation of Candidates, E.E. Higdon, Virgil A. Sly, C.M. Yocum; Commissioning and Responses, H.B. McCormick and appointees; Communion Hymn, 453; The Lord's Supper, George Oliver Taylor and Willard M. Wickizer; Consecration Prayer and Benediction, Rajah B. Manikam; Recessional, Mrs. Francis Boese. Appointees will be in Rooms 231 and 233 following the service."

- McCormick, H.B., President, Payne, Hazel Scott, Secretary, United Christian Missionary Society, Indianapolis, Indiana, to Glyn and Jean Adsit, Letters/Certificates of Appointment As Missionaries of the Society to China, Missions Building, Indianapolis, Indiana, June 25, 1947.

"Dear Mr. and Mrs. Adsit, Upon recommendation of the Division of Foreign Missions, the board of trustees of the United Christian Missionary Society is happy to appoint you as a missionary of the Society to China.

Every member of the board of trustees covets the opportunity to know you personally and expresses the deepest appreciation of your decision to enter foreign missionary service. You belong to that long line of heralds who have so wonderfully blessed the world in spreading love and light.

Through the division of foreign missions, the board of trustees will keep in closest touch with you and your work.

The board pledges you its loyal support and prays God's richest blessing upon you. Sincerely, H.B. McCormick, President, and Hazel Scott Payne, Secretary."

- McCormick, H.B., President, The United Christian Missionary Society, Indianapolis, Indiana, to Mr. And Mrs. Glyn Adsit, July 21, 1947.

"Dear Mr. and Mrs. Adsit, The Missionary Register furnished me by the foreign division lists you among those who will be departing for the field very shortly. It is always a delight to send a message bidding God-speed to our missionaries as they leave for their various fields of service, but it is an added pleasure to me to do so in the case of fine young people like yourselves, whom I have had the privilege of commissioning as *emissaries of the gospel of Christ.*

I recall the statement of high purpose which both of you made at the time you received your commission, and I know that you will fulfill this purpose. You are well equipped through your preparation to make an outstanding contribution toward the cause of Christ in China, and because of your deeply consecrated loves and your abiding faith in the missionary cause to which you have dedicated yourselves, your service will count for much in the program of kingdom advancement in China.

May God be with you and richly bless you both as you begin your first term of service as Christian ambassadors! We shall be thinking of you and praying for you in the days ahead and shall always welcome a word from you concerning your problems and your victories in the service. Sincerely yours, H.B. McCormick(President, UCMS)."

- Garcia, George and Marie, Minister, Filipino United Church, Honolulu, Hawaii, to Glyn and Jean Adsit, July 25, 1947.

"Dear Mr. and Mrs. Adsit, Marie and I are delighted to learn of your coming through Honolulu on your way to China. It shall be our greatest privilege to meet you and make your stop over here worthwhile.

It would not be possible at this time for you to meet Mrs. Cooper, for she is on the mainland, vacationing. She will not be back in Honolulu until after the month of August. We are sure she would love to meet you, for her interest has been in missionaries and mission work. In any case, we have spoken to several interested Disciples of Christ friends of your coming so that you and your party shall have a chance meeting them. They have already expressed interest in knowing you. For this reason, we are sure your brief stop in Honolulu will be pleasant.

Hoping you will recognize Maria on the pier. Very sincerely yours, George and Maria (Marie) Garcia."

- Adsit, Glyn., Minister and Missionary, *SS Marine Adder*, On the Ocean Voyage to China, Letter to Mrs. R.L. Adsit and Mr. and Mrs. Duane Adsit (Mother, Duane, and Pat), August 13, 1947.

"Dear Mother, Duane, and Pat, Greetings from the ocean deep and wide. It seems that there is no end to this big pond. I want to tell you most of what happened since we left Topeka, so here goes.

Our train accommodations were fine. We slept, or tried to, on the train Pullman but did not rest much. We reached the Grand Canyon early one morning. We could see the trees changing color and growing higher as we climbed the high mountains before reaching the canyon. We were signed up to take the all-expense tour. This proved wise since our three meals were included in this. No one can tell you how beautiful and grand the canyon is. You must experience this geographical phenomenon for yourself. But the thing that appealed to me were the changing colors. The colors reminded one of a rainbow. We left Grand Canyon 8:30 p.m. on the same day we arrived. We were tired but satisfied. We took two rolls of colored film, which we have sent to you.

San Francisco is a wonderful town but different from any I have ever seen. It is built on sloping mountains reaching down into the very ocean. The people are very aggressive and seem to be wealthy. But one can almost feel the godlessness of the city. Few churches are seen near the business district. We had a good hotel in the heart of the city. We ate at a different place each meal.

We got up early August 8 (1947). I saw to it that we did not miss our ship. Several hundred Christians from that area were at the dock to sing hymns and wish us God-speed and a safe voyage. It was rather difficult to leave hearing them sing, "God Be With You." Our first night out was rough. The weather was cool, and the waves were big. Several people were sick that first night. Jean did not get sick until the second day. She lost one meal and then made up her mind that she was all right. I, of course, did not get seasick. (Lucky me.) I did have a headache but got over that quickly.

Our cabins are crowded but adequate. Jean is in a room with twelve others, and I also am in a room with twelve men. I have to get up early to get shaved before the other men get up. We do not have to make our own beds. Cabin boys do this menial task. Our food is excellent. We have a choice of about three meats and always have some salad and fruit. We are served by waiters in the dining hall. The ship is small but reasonably fast. We have little room to have recreation. We spend most of our time reading Bibles, studying Chinese, and talking with the people on board. The ship load consists of about three hundred missionaries and children and many Chinese and Filipinos. We have had an abandon ship drill once so far. When the siren goes off, we run to our cabins, grab our life belts and put them on, and then wait for the second alarm. When this sounds, we run up stairs to our appointed stations.

We have one motion picture. It was *Two Sisters from Boston*. We have enjoyed it very much. We can see the dim outline of Hawaii this morning. We are all excited to think that before long (3:00 p.m.), we will be swimming at the famous Waikiki Beach in Honolulu. Some Christians, native friends, are meeting us and are going to show us around the island.

We found all our freight and baggage in San Francisco. Some of it was a little banged up, but we think it will stand the trip all right. The box the Yellow Cab packed was all right up to there. I think it will stand the trip fine.

We are very anxious to reach Shanghai. We have heard so much about our chosen country that we can hardly wait. We know that many days of hardship and disappointment await us, but we also feel that there will be great rewards. I will mail this from Honolulu. It will be our last chance to write until we reach China. It will take ten days from Hawaii to Shanghai, so do not expect letters for about one month after getting this one.

We are both feeling fine and eating like pigs. I am trying to get a sun tan. We did not have opportunity until now to stop and rest. We are sure enjoying having nothing to do. Mother, please investigate and see about the possibility of sending us the Topeka paper. If it is not too great a cost, send it to us at Chuchow, Anhwei, China, and write our board telling them to pay you for it from our credit account. Will write from China. Love, Glyn."

- Higdon, E.K., Executive Secretary, Department of Oriental Missions, The United Christian Missionary Society, Indianapolis, Indiana, "Some Comments On Rural Work With Special Reference To The Hofei District In China," Copy to Mr. Glyn B. Adsit, August 18, 1947.

"I. The Needs of Rural People. Any adequate program of Chinese rural reconstruction should meet the needs of the people or see to it that they are met. Some organizations or agencies, private or governmental, exist in every community for the service of the people, but too frequently, they fail to reach the "little man." In such cases it is the responsibility of the church to seek ways of helping these agencies function. But even after the private or government organizations begin to transform general theory into specific practice, the church and its auxiliaries have vast areas of untouched human need to which to minister. These needs include: 1) Health and sanitation; 2) play and recreation; 3) moral improvement; 4) general education; 5) adult education, especially the teaching of illiterates; 6) economic improvement; 7) religious education; 8) home and family life education; and 9) worship.

The Philosophy of Rural Reconstruction. The primary purpose of Christian rural reconstruction is to help people meet their daily needs. The motive is Christian love. The method adopted should be such that every activity in the program shall contribute to the development of the Christian community.

Methods of Rural Reconstruction. 1) The Demonstration Center: The place chosen for each center should be a typical rural community. If the soil is much more fertile than other communities, the demonstration will have little or no significance for the poorer places. The tools may be better than the average farmer uses, but power-driven machinery in a farming community where the tenants and the owners cannot afford to purchase such equipment becomes a hindrance rather than a help toward showing farmers how to improve their methods. The Center buildings should be made of local materials and erected by local labor under proper supervision.

The staff should consist of both Chinese and missionaries. Each missionary should have deep convictions about the necessity of rural reconstruction and be well-grounded in the philosophy of the task. He should be inspired by the conviction that God loves the rural people, that Christianity may become vital to them in their daily activities if it is interpreted in the field, in the school, in the home, in the market place, in the draining of swamps, and in all other experiences. It is not expected that any one person will be competent in all these fields, but the missionary to the rural people should have one special training in at least two of them. He should be an expert in adult education or religious education or home and family life training.

His primary responsibility will be to work with a staff, mainly nationals, who are trained to minister to one or more of the needs which he himself cannot meet as a specialist.

One couple should have primary responsibility for seeing that everyone on the staff keeps constantly in mind the purpose of the Center; another couple should be charged with making scientific surveys to determine such facts as a) the intensity and extent of each type of need, b) the facilities at hand to meet the needs, c) nearby agencies which can be called upon for service, d) methods to use to measure progress as in the case of new types of seed or new breeds of animals or crop rotation or soil fertilization; and e) one couple should have charge of the program of health and sanitation. This means three missionary couples. Each person should have two skills.

1. Chinese trained in home and family life education, the organization and operation of credit loan associations and other types of cooperative, play and recreation, and other needed services should be members of the Center staff as colleagues of the missionaries.

2. In places where the church is already organized, the rural reconstruction work should become a part of the ongoing program. This will involve a more comprehensive community organization than most churches have, but if the present membership is used as the nucleus, such an organization should strengthen the church as well as serve the non-church people.

3. The *vertical* rather than the *horizontal* approach to a community is a method suggested by Mr. Cheo (Formerly of Nanking Theological Seminary Faculty). The tendency in the past has been to

develop horizontally, to cover as much territory as possible whether or not it was well served. This has resulted in churches whose members come almost exclusively from one class, the farmer. The doctor, the merchant, the teacher, everyone with whom he and his family deals is non-Christian. The pressures on the Christian from these non-Christian or pagan sources are tremendous and sometimes he gives up his faith. The vertical approach would reach a more restricted area, but would influence every class in that area. Mr. Cheo would go into a non-Christian community of five hundred families and choose fifty with whom to cooperate in a program of rural service. Each of the fifty families would be given careful exposition of what was to be undertaken for the people. If any family refused to help, another would be chosen. There would be ten families from each pao. The members of these families would be responsible for the other ninety families in their group.

IV. Suggestions for Hofei Area. 1) Long-range objectives for rural work should be formulated at once. The period of time covered by these objectives should be from ten to twenty-five years. 2) Carefully estimated budgets should be prepared for 1948-49, and for, if possible, a ten-year period. The askings should be incorporated annually in the regular budget submitted to the UCMS by the Administrative Committee of the churches. 3) A statement of the personnel needed, missionaries and Chinese, should be prepared and plans made to employ from among those who are new, well-prepared, a few Chinese men and women, and to recruit others for training. The training should be given both in schools and in service under competent supervision. 4) The site of the Center should probably be moved from Hofei to keep city and rural work separated and to get nearer those who are to learn through demonstration. 5) Cooperate in the plan for an East

China rural program in the Nanking area. (The following is taken from the Minutes of a rural Work Conference held in China on June 11, 1947.)

Nanking Area: this area is about to organize a rural service-training union. Churches interested in the union: Presbyterian, Methodist, Christian, Friends, and others. Resources-Christian: University of Nanking, Ginling College, University Hospital, Nanking Theological Seminary, Bible Teachers Training School for Women, Ginling college Rural Service Station. Resources-Private: Child Welfare of the United Services to China. Resources-Government: Department of Agriculture with Home-Making/Public Health Department, and New Life Movement Women's Rural Center."

- Adsit, Glyn and Jean, Ministers and Missionaries, *SS Marine Adder*, Day and one half out of Japan on the ocean heading to China, Letter to Mother, Duane, and Pat, August 21, 1947.

"Dear Mother, Duane, and Pat, I still think this is a big ocean. We have not seen land nor another ship for days. We are finding great sport in watching the flying fishes. Our visit to Honolulu was a very pleasant one. It is as beautiful as they say. It is very refreshing to come all of a sudden upon the islands and see the water changing from deep blue to green. We arrived in Honolulu, which is on Oahu Island, at about 3:00 p.m. and as we reached the harbor and dock, the many Hawaiian swimmers came out to dive for money. They can really swim. As we pulled into the dock, we were anxiously searching the many faces to see if we could recognize the people who were to meet us. We did finally find them, and they threw beautiful leis around our necks. They are very sweet-smelling flowers and made from different island flowers. As the person put one around our necks, they would give us a kiss of welcome. It is a very charming custom. I had three put around my neck by a beautiful hostess, Maria Garcia. They told us that three cars were at our disposal with drivers and that we could go anywhere on the island and see anything we wished. We all wanted to see Waikiki Beach and swim there. We first mailed our letters at the post office and then started on a tour of the islands. The green plant growth is luxuriant and deep green. They have plants that I have never seen, such as bamboo, orchids, pineapple, etc. We finally ended up at the beach and had a short swim. I did not enjoy it too much because the tide was full and the waves kept knocking us off our feet. I was just a little uneasy. After the swim, we all went to the First Christian Church and had a supper meal. It is the most beautiful church. The baptistery surpasses any I have ever seen. They have planted live ferns and other plants in it and it seems that you are outside when you stand and look at it. We talked and visited with the church people and then started back for the boat and were on board again by 10:15 p.m. We sailed at midnight while the music of "Aloha" was being played and sung. I took several pictures in color, which I will eventually send to the States for development. They will then come to you, and you, in turn, please send them to me in a package or some way. Be sure to send these valuable things to our Nanking address.

None of us have suffered any more seasickness. We are eating hearty at each meal and growing (more) lazy by the hour. We have been having the smoothest water. Hardly a movement, the old hands say it is very unusual. It has rained several times, but we were glad for them since it cools off the hot air. Both Jean and I have a good sun tan. I peeled a little, but retained the color. There was a rumor that we almost hit a mine yesterday, but I am sure it was only a rumor since this ship has a mine repelling device on it. It works on the de-magnetic principle. This is Friday. We expect to be in China next Tuesday. We are already getting nervous. This will be mailed in Japan, from Tokyo, by a friend. Until our next letter, God bless and keep the three of you and the little baby. Love, Glyn and Jean."

- Adsit, Glyn and Jean, Ministers and Missionaries, Shanghai, China, Letter to Mother (R.L. Adsit), Duane, and Pat Adsit, August 26, 1947.

"Dearest Mother, Duane, and Pat, We are at long last in China. Our ocean voyage was very smooth, and we enjoyed it in spite of the hot weather and long stay on board. We arrived in Shanghai August 26 (1947), 4:15 p.m. We did not get off the ship until about 6:00 p.m. since we had to go through the customs inspectors who came on board our ship. They examined our passport and asked some questions about baggage. We took our baggage off the ship and went to a large building, where a man examined it. We had no trouble getting our baggage, which we had in our cabin on ship, through customs. But tomorrow, we must go down and try to locate all our baggage, which was placed in the ship's hold, and also our freight. This will be some job because it will be dumped into a long "Go down" amongst everybody's baggage, and we must ferret ours out and put it all in one place and then find a customs inspector to inspect it. There is an endless amount of red tape to getting things done here. Almost everyone tries to put the squeeze on you to get a little more money.

We are staying at the Lutheran Center. This is a home owned for the express purpose of housing missionaries in transit to their respective fields of work. Our room is large enough. We are sleeping on cots. This institution has a truck that we are going to rent to haul our baggage from the wharf to the train. We eat here also. We do not have to boil drinking water since the cook does it for us. We do have to be careful of what type of water we use to brush our teeth.

Dr. Corpron, our man from one of our stations, took us on a sightseeing tour of the city today. We have seen sights that you would not believe, but they are true. The streets are narrow and teeming with people. The noise is continuous, and the smells are all and more than we expected. We went through small alleys where people lived and worked, babies with huge running sores on heads and legs; six-year-old baby girl walking down street naked and unashamed; babies of both sexes and of all ages squatting in middle of street to mess; chickens and ducks hanging in shops covered with flies until you thought they still had feathers on them, but they were picked; Buddhist priest yelling his truths at you as you pass by, women with seven babies all under eight years of age; eggs years old yet sold as rare delicacies; barbers cutting hair on the sidewalk and shaving people's head scabs and all until blood ran down their necks; thousands of faces and not a white one to be seen, all yellow; people, chickens, and dogs living in the same house. I wanted to vomit twice but held it back. You cannot believe all this until you see it. And worst of all, we had only to take a rickshaw and go for about five minutes and we were among rich Chinese people dressed in spotless clean white garments and sleek and fat. Two great extremes and neither seeming to care about the other. We hated to touch anything or to sit down anywhere.

I am thankful that our faith is strong, else we would take the next boat back. The Chinese we learned has come in very handy. I have had to ask several questions in order to buy a pair of shorts, ink, paper, a belt, etc. They do not speak our dialect, but they understand what we say. It is no small job to hire a rickshaw to take you somewhere. You first yell at one and then ask him how much. He says, '$10,000.' I say, 'I'll give you $3,000.' He acts like he is insulted and says, '$8,000.' I tell him I don't want to buy his rickshaw; I only want him to take me somewhere. By this time, he is disgusted and I am too. I tell him $5,000 is my final price for both Jean and myself. He says $7,500 is his final price. I turn and start to walk away and get only about twenty feet when he yells that $5,000 will be all right. I, of course, intended to pay $5,000 all the time, and he intended to take that much. But if he could get a green horn to pay his price, he would really think he had done a great thing. We are getting about $40,000 to $1.00 US now. CN $5,000 would be about 12.5 cents US money. We have not learned yet whether we will go to Peking to continue our language study. The way our field secretary is talking, we might go. If we do not, we will go to Chuchow as soon as they finish a house they are building. We might have to stay in Nanking until this house in Chuchow is ready. Before I forget it, we will probably be in Shanghai for ten days yet. It will take some time to get all the necessary papers to take radio into country and to register with city police. We had to get some pictures made to give to city police. Today is Confucius's birthday, and the flags are really out and waving. This house is right on a busy street. It sets back about two hundred feet from the street, and right now, it's 9:00 p.m. I can hear so much noise. It sounds like I was standing in the middle of a Kansas Free Fair Crowd on the midway. I could not sleep last night, and hope that I am so exhausted tonight that I will sleep. It is quite amusing to walk around the streets with hundreds of thousands of dollars in your pockets. It is also lots of bother to count out this money. The bills are in denominations of $500 to $5,000. If we cash $25 into Chinese money, we are immediately a millionaire. Food and clothing are plentiful, but some things are too expensive. We will buy some food here in Shanghai to take with us. Send our mail to the Nanking address until further notice. Continue to pray for us, and we do for you. Will write again before leaving Shanghai. Love, Glyn and Jean."

- Turley, Hollis Lee, "The High Calling," *World Call*, September 1947, pp. 21-22. (Re-printed by permission, White, Cyrus N., President and Publisher, Christian Board of Publications, 1221 Locust Street, Suite 1200, St. Louis, MO 63103)

"These young people were commissioned recently by the United Christian Missionary Society to serve as missionaries on foreign fields. Reading from left: Mr. and

Mrs. Glyn B. Adsit and Verla M. Elliot going to China; Mr. and Mrs. C. Harvey Lord, to the Philippines; Mr. and Mrs. H.C. Shorrock, Jr., Japan; Marilynne Hill, India; and Dr. Donald Pettus Conwell, Belgian Congo, Africa."

- Adsit, Glyn and Jean, Ministers and Missionaries, Lutheran Center, Shanghai, China, to Mother, Duane, and Pat, September 1, 1947.

"Dear Mom, Duane, and Pat, This is Sunday, and I went to church in a beautiful place not far from this house. It is a community church, and most of the Americans in Shanghai go there. Jean had a little touch of the flu and could not go with me. She has taken sulfa pills and is okay now. I also have a slight cold and a headache. We managed to get all our baggage through without having to pay any duty except on the radio. We are now working on getting freight through. I have never seen such inefficiency. No one seems to know what to do. We are run all over town to get a signature on a paper and then find that it is the wrong one, etc. It is true that getting past the customs office is hard work and really tries your patience. This is a city of smells, yells, and little hells. We have had beggars follow for a block trying to get us to give them some money. But we dare not give a cent because a hundred of them would be on our backs, demanding money if we gave to one. We are eating our lunches at Chinese restaurants. There are several with picturesque names and settings. One is several hundred years old.

We had some excitement the other day. Five of us were on our way down to get our baggage examined, and we got into trouble. Two single ladies were in a rickshaw in front, and Dr. Corporon, our doctor at Hofei, was in one right behind them. Jean and I were in one trailing them. All of sudden, another rickshaw coolie tried to force the two single ladies to the curb, demanding money. He thought they were alone since the other two rickshaws were about a hundred feet behind. The doctor understands Chinese and heard his demands. He ran up and yanked the bad coolies' rickshaw and pulled part of the top off. He told him to go on and mind his own business and stop trying to rob the ladies. The coolies grabbed the doctor's shirt and tore it, and the doctor hit him in the nose and almost broke it. By this time, we were surrounded by about two hundred mad Chinese coolies and lower-class workers. All of them were spitting on the doctor and me and pulling at us and trying to hit us. I was pulling two men off the doctor to give him a fair chance to fight the coolie. I only got hit once real hard in the back, but it did not hurt.

All of a sudden, the doctor told me to go find a policeman. I tried to find one but could not. By the time I had returned, there was a policeman there and had stopped the fighting. We were accused of starting the fighting by the coolies in the crowd. The doctor demanded that we go to the police station. He wanted me to take the women and go on down to the wharf and complete the baggage inspection. But they forced me to go to the police station also. So, we got into the pedicab (rickshaw) of the coolie we had trouble with, and off we went to the police station. I was not afraid, but was thankful that they had not injured either the doctor or myself. The ladies were not molested, and their rickshaw coolies took them on down to the wharf without us. We were questioned at the police station, and the coolie told his version of the story, and we told ours. This station master did not want to make the decision, so he sent us to a higher authority. We piled into the rickshaw again, and off we went across town to the next police station. This time, we were more thoroughly questioned (no rough treatment). We proved it was the coolies fault and were released without fine. They kept him until after we left. We do not know what they did to him. And so it is when you are in a godless city. Life is very cheap, and the coolies and thieves would just as soon kill you as not. But we will be careful and not go out at night. We were detained about three hours by this incident, and you can be sure Jean was glad to see me walk into the baggage room.

I think we will be leaving Shanghai by this time next week. Our house in Chuchow is not ready for us to move into yet, so we will spend a week or so with different friends in our different stations until we are ready to settle down. We will probably go to Nanking from here. I will write you again within a week, telling of our plans.

Lest you think that China is all bad, let me tell you that we see many good things also. Some of the people are friendly. There is a place across the street from here where I buy ice cream. They are friendly (speak English) and smile each time they see me. Besides, when we reach Chuchow, where we are to live, the people will be entirely different from those here.

When you send packages, be sure to send correct weights (post office will tell you this). Also, try to keep the declared value of the packages as low as possible. We have to get a permit to import if anything is too expensive, say, above $50, so the way to do it is to send smaller packages and more of them. Do not worry about sending a paper just yet until we get located, unless you have already contracted to do so. There is a good English paper we are reading here that will prove satisfactory.

We have to register with the Shanghai police and get a permit before we can leave town. All foreigners have to do this. There is plenty of food in this city if one has money to buy it. I bought Jean a can of orange juice, and it cost $45,000, or $1.25 US. A stick of ice cream costs 12 cents. Money is quite a problem (keeping track of the high figures). The present exchange is $39,000 to $1. We have a bank account in a bank here that reaches the total of $CNC 7,000,000. So we are millionaires at last. It costs about six cents to ride the street cars and fifteen cents to ride rickshaws for twelve blocks. We are firmly convinced that what the individual Chinese needs is a personal experience of forgiveness through Christ. So pray for us that we may live lives that will encourage others to follow Jesus. Write soon. Love, Glyn and Jean."

- Adsit, Glyn B., Minister and Missionary, Shanghai, China, to Mother, Reecie Adsit, undated note, Circa September 1947.

"Dear Mother, Will you please send the enclosed changes of addresses to the proper places for me? I wanted to enclose them all in one letter to the States in order to save postage.

Jean has already gone to Hofei. I intend to be there within a week from today. She went with two older missionary ladies by river boat up to Wuhu. They stopped there all night at our mission and then started yesterday for Hofei two days further on. I notice that in your last letter, you said you had not heard from us for three weeks. I suppose our letters were delayed. If you do not hear from us, everything is all right. If anything should happen, you would be notified immediately, so don't worry. Weather is still lovely fall here. Temperature stays up around 70 (degrees) during the day and down to 45-50 (degrees) at night. No rain for a month. Will not write much this time, but will write long letter from Hofei. Love, Glyn."

- McCormick, H.B., President, The United Christian Missionary Society, Indianapolis, Indiana, Letter to Mr. And Mrs. Glyn Adsit, September 11, 1947.

"My Dear Mr. and Mrs. Adsit, Many times in these intervening weeks since you sailed for China, I have thought of you and of the high purpose to which you directed your lives during the period of your preparation for your life work. My prayers have gone up in your behalf, and it is my firm conviction that God has answered those prayers and has richly blessed your life and service.

Some years ago, our pioneer missionary leader, A. McLean, who walked so close to God that his memory is deeply revered by all who claim the honor of his acquaintance during his earthly life, wrote a book that is most helpful even today. This book, *The Primacy of the Missionary,* reflects the sentiment and aspirations of his own life and imparts a refreshing and poignant viewpoint of the missionary enterprise upon each re-reading.

It is a real pleasure to me to be able to send you a copy of this splendid book through the courtesy of Mr. C.D. Pantle, general manager of the Christian Board of Publication, of St. Louis. Last year, when I assumed my duties with The United Christian Missionary Society, the Christian Board extended this same courtesy, making available one of these books to each of our missionaries then in service. Many of my missionary friends wrote testifying to the value and inspiration of the book, and I feel sure too that you will find inspiration and help for your task and, through the reading of the book, you will come to know intimately in the spirit, if not the flesh, this man of God, Archibald McLean.

Please remember that back here in (the) Missions Building, we are interested in all that you are doing and are wishing you the Father's richest blessings on the part you are having in building a Christian world. Cordially, your co-worker in Christ, H.B. McCormick."

- Adsit, Glyn B., Minister and Missionary, Nanking, China, to Mother and family, September 15, 1947.

"Dear Mother and family: Your letter dated September 9 arrived yesterday, so connections are quite good so far. When we go to Chuhsien, it will take a couple of days longer. Nanking is a beautiful, old city. We arrived here last Wednesday and are staying with the McCallums. As you know, this is the country's capitol and is full of soldiers, consuls, etc. Some of the city is surrounded by a wall, which is supposed to be about five hundred years old. It looks it. We went up on top of the wall and surveyed the countryside. It is a little hilly around here, and there are one or two famous mountains within sight. Purple Mountain is one of these. Behind this mountain is the tomb of Sun

Yat Sen, the George Washington of China. It is next to Confucius's tomb, the most sacred spot in China. We have not visited it as yet. This country is still in turmoil. The war that is being fought is not like two great armies facing each other, but it is a hit-and-run affair. There are small pockets of communists all over China, and they roam and ravage the countryside. One of our stations, Hofei, is being besieged right now. Our missionaries have pulled out and are here with us now. The situation will quiet down, and the ladies will return. Our missionary doctor, Corpron is staying to run the hospital and treat wounded soldiers.

We visited our future home yesterday, Sunday. It is a lovely town of about forty thousand. Right now, there is much soldier activity in and around the town. There is a wall around most of the city, and soldiers stand continuous guard on this wall. They have dug slit trenches and set up machine guns and pill boxes. They are not being bothered yet with Communists but want to be ready if and when. Chuhsien is a small railroad pivot and is very valuable to the war that is being fought in the north, and they must protect it. There is no cause to worry about us being there. We learned that seven trains go through there each day toward Nanking, and if an emergency arises, we can pull out at almost any hour. We will not go to Chuhsien to live permanently for about one month yet. At that time, we will live with the Cherryholmes until our home is ready for occupancy. The church in Chuhsien is not much to look at. They have no pews to sit on. We sat on saw horses yesterday. It has one advantage. It keeps the people awake. The war left the people quite poor and discouraged. We are sure that better days are ahead for the Christians there. Eighty people turned out for Sunday school and church. Peter Cheo (Shao) preached a good sermon, I think. (Didn't understand much of it.) We ate dinner with Pastor Wu, who is to be my co-worker in the rural expansion program. He is young and enthusiastic. They served for dinner fish, chicken, cabbage, shrimp, soup, pork, bean-

and-meat mixture, eggs scrambled, soup, and cookies. We ate with chopsticks and enjoyed it a great deal. Pastor Wu has six children.

In the afternoon, we visited our home-to-be. It is a big house with about fourteen rooms. It has not been prepared (repaired) for years and looks like it. The front porch has fallen in, the windows are out, and the floors are warped and dirt is everywhere. Jean was some discouraged, but I think it can be fixed up to be a nice-looking place. The structure is solid, and the walls are made of brick. Most brick out here is a slate gray color. Not much for beauty but durable. There is a wall around our yard, which I think covers about one half a city block. Weeds shoulder high are in the yard. This will be cut down, and a yard and flowers at least encouraged. Our water supply will be a cistern filled with rain water. Out toilet facilities are outside (Japanese built a big one with five single holes) country style. There will be a small house in back for the servants; also a shack at gate for gate man. One must have a gate man, else the people just walk in and look around inside the wall. They are curious as can be about foreigners. There is usually a small crowd following us wherever we go in the countryside. We stop and say a few Chinese words and watch their mouths fall open because they didn't expect the funny people to be able to speak their language.

There is a great opportunity to do rural evangelism. Our mission is laying a good foundation, and I think you will be hearing of much activity in the near future. Of course, our first two years will be largely taken up with language study and cultural saturation. It will not be until we have been here a few years that we can develop a helpful program. But we can be pecking away at the general problem of converting individual Chinese. I forgot to mention that our one big drawback about our house is that we will have furniture to furnish only two or three rooms, scantily at that. We will have to depend upon Chinese furniture, wicker type, to fill up the rest. We will live in Chuhsien and travel out around a radius of about fifty miles. There are sixteen little churches that need supervision, and that will keep us plenty busy.

Wednesday of this week, McCallum and I are to go to Nantungchow and visit our station there. We will be gone for about two weeks, and must take our own bedding and enough clothes for that period. Jean will stay here in Nanking for that period of time.

I want to repeat again that almost everything is available out here but is too expensive to buy. Oh, yes, your letters are coming through just fine. You should be receiving a check for $25 from UCMS right away. Use this to buy vitamins and mail packages, etc. I have been asking questions about advisability of sending our colored pictures to us. We now think it will be all right for you to send them. But wrap them securely and separately and label them used. If you have two or three boxes, send them along and we will see what happens with them. Value each box at about 50 cents or so. Send these to Nanking address on this sheet of paper. Our monthly salary is $155 US money, but this only buys 50 percent of what it did before the war. We are able to live on it but cannot save anything as yet. On those colored slides, what I meant about separately is do not include them within a package; just send them by themselves. Our health is good, but dust irritates our noses and throats. Will have to adjust to this. The doctors in Nanking are good and sympathetic with our problems. We will have adequate health protection here. I notice in your letter that you are now thankful that you are alone and have opportunity to enjoy the quiet of the place. You also stated that you hoped that you had time now to work out your salvation for the next life. I think one cannot work out salvation. It is a gift free from God, and all one needs do is to receive it. If we can work out salvation, Christ died in vain. Else why did he die? Well, I don't need to preach to you. Will close for this week and will try to write each week. However, be patient with me since I might not be back home for a month once I leave for Nantungchow and Shanghai. Love from your son, Glyn."

- Adsit, Glyn B., Minister and Missionary, Chuhsien, Anhwei, China, to Mother and Family, September 23, 1947.

"Dearest Mom and family, I have been in Chuhsien for a week now. We have been having trouble with the soldiers (nationalists) here who want to move into our house. The house is right across from their drill grounds and present headquarters. It also overlooks most of the city and city wall. It is a good location for them, but it is our property. George Cherryholmes sent one of our pastors down to Nanking to get me to come up as quickly as I could. I came and moved into an upstairs room. The soldiers had said they were going to move in whether we liked it or not. George told them they would have to get a written request from their general and from the office of Ministry of Defense in Nanking, stating that this specific house and property was needed and guaranteeing that the property would not be defaced and would be repaired. Well, the nationalist soldiers have not moved in yet. We think they were bluffing. When I moved in, the house was still occupied by the general's wife and soldiers who had been living here for two years. They moved out after I was here three days.

The property is all mine and my servant's, who is a gardener and errand boy. His name is Tang Kai Wha. I pay him $14 a month, which is a good wage for coolie help. We have already began cleaning up the yard and planting our garden. We will have cabbage and chards and one other green. We also have many squash, which Mrs. Chu, the general's wife, left. Jean is in Nanking at McCallums's house. She will not come to Chuhsien until Cherryholmes's house is ready for occupancy. When I say I, I always mean we. Just my selfish nature creeping out. Jean is having a little harder time adjusting to China than I am, but she will manage it in time.

We are not sure yet, but she might be pregnant. She has missed two months already. Reason we are not sure is that sometimes a boat trip or a new climate will upset the cycle for months. Do not say a word about this in a letter to me since Jean doesn't know I have told you this. She wants to be sure first. She is taking calcium vitamins and a unicap each day. Send us some unicaps and some calcium pills.

I am camping in this one room all alone. Not much furniture, a cot with air mattress and mosquito net, a card table, two chairs, a kerosene lamp, a few clothes, and plenty of rats. I have poison out for the rats.

Many of our Chuhsien soldiers left to help fight the Communists around Hofei and Wuwei. These two places are where we have work and are about 125 miles from here. Our missionaries have left and are in Nanking. Two ladies are here with us. I am beginning to speak quite fluently. Everyone says I am very good. They don't know how hard I studied and am still studying each day. There are many possibilities for building the church here once we get settled and can be free from the burden of having to watch the house so closely. I am invited out for lunch today at Elder Wang's home. He is eighty-seven years of age, a pillar in the church. Will close for now. We are well and enjoying the cool weather. Write soon. Love, Glyn. P.S. Be sure to keep my letters. I want them later."

- Adsit, Glyn B., Minister and Missionary, Chuhsien, Anhwei, China, to Mother and Home Folks, October 1, 1947.

"Dearest Mother and homefolks, I am still sitting in this big, old, empty house. Soldiers are not bothering us anymore. Guess we convinced them I really live here. It is turning very cool, and it is a cold that penetrates. I can just see myself at a football game in the States, shivering away. I believe this civil war is a lot like ours of 1860. The soldiers ravage the countryside in search of food. They take almost everything they want. Chuhsien is under a curfew.

No one allowed outside the village wall or on the street after 10:00 p.m. I am having trouble sleeping; too much noise across the street where army headquarters is. The bugle blows at 5:30 a.m., and they are noisy up until 10:00 or 11:00 p.m.

Our yardman has almost finished clearing weeds off our compound. He has planted a small garden, which is still growing. Did I mention before that there is not even one tree in our yard? The Japanese cut them all down. Workmen are beginning within ten days to repair our wall and house. We have a small gatehouse, and a servant's house badly deteriorated. No missionary has lived here for fifteen years, and no repairs were done in all those years. The Japanese built a four (or five) hole toilet site close to the front gate. We will tear this down and re-build in back of house.

I am making friends each day that passes. Many high school students and soldiers and their wives want to improve their English. They come over, and we have tea and talk. I also get to use Chinese in this fashion. These contacts will come in handy later on, when we begin a drive for church membership. George and I are thinking about starting a young people's society. There are almost eight hundred young people of high school age for us to draw from.

Our Chinese instructor is arriving from Peking (now Beijing) within two weeks. He will be with us for one year, helping us in our study. We will spend one half of each day in language study for this next year.

Did you receive the colored slides of the sunsets at sea and of Hawaii? Did the $25 come from UCMS to you?

Jean continues in good health. It is a little hard to be separated for eight to ten days at a time, but such is the life out here. It looks like we will move into the Cherryholmes' house within three weeks. They work so very slow. When we get ready to move, I will make a trip to Shanghai to get our freight and travel back with it. I am going to Nanking today for a two-day stay. I am down every seven or eight days just to be sure she is all right.

Don't ever go to a Chinese feast! You are forced to eat so much you hurt all over. The Chinese serve so much meat. One meal will consist of pork, beef, chicken, fish, mushrooms, soup, rice, and one green vegetable. No bread, salt, or sugar on the table. Fish is considered the best meat, and it is set in front of the honored guest. They cook them with head and tail on, eyes and all. We are saying out here, that "a missionary must eat and drink to the Glory of God," and "each meal is literally Nearer My God to Thee" because we never know what little germ is waiting to pounce on us.

A special day was celebrated September 29, "Middle Autumn Festival." Everyone tries to get home, like on our Thanksgiving. Your friends send you a gift of moon cake, and pears or egg cake. We are expected to return the gift.

I visited a small farm village three miles from here. Our purpose was to survey the situation to see if we might eventually start some religious work there. They were very friendly. Next Sunday, I am going fifty miles north of here to participate in a baptism service. One of our country churches is baptizing twenty-five new converts. This is encouraging since we have no missionaries there. Only an old Chinese pastor who is doing good work.

I wish I had Chang here for a watch dog. We will have to get us a dog and cat. We also are thinking about buying a cow or some goats. You should see my moustache I have let grow for two weeks (me and Clark Gable). We found another American here, a Mr. Fried, who is an anthropologist studying our village. Good-bye and love until next time, your son and brother, Glyn."

- Adsit, Jean, Minister and Missionary, location Nanking, China, to Mother, Reecie Adsit, October 4, 1947.

"Dearest Mom, your letters are coming through nicely, and they certainly are appreciated and looked forward to.

Your letter asking for suggestions for a package arrived, and I'll give you one or two of the things we could use and would appreciate. Dried fruit, any kind, if you can pack this in some sort of tin so worms won't get into it; paper napkins; and some toothpaste.

There is no need to send the calcium pills to us. I have a prescription that lets me get some here at the hospital at Nanking. The mission will pay for them since all our medical needs are paid for.

We are going to have a baby. It will be here in April as far as the doctor can tell. We are thrilled and feel quite lucky that we got our order filled so quickly after we put the order (prayer) in. I am enclosing two copies of a poem I found that I think both Billie Jean and Pat would like to have. You can send them on whenever you like to them. Well, Grandmother, you're going to get it strong in the same year. When it rains, it pours.

Say, Mom, if it wouldn't trouble you too much, you might send the two negatives to Mrs. Joe Etheridge (Jean's sister, Lucille) in Amarillo. (The one you have the address of.) Negatives of the little girl in pigtails. She will really appreciate them. Thank you.

Must close now. Glad you're doing some painting and face lifting around the house. Don't work too hard. Love, Jean."

- Adsit, Glyn B. and Jean, Ministers and Missionaries, Nanking, China, Letter to Mr. Edwin Marx, October 18, 1947.

"Attention, Mr. Edwin Marx. We are trying to look into the future far enough to see what schooling we will desire above that which we already have. As you know, I have an AB in Bible from Phillips University, also an MS in sociology from Cornell University. I still want to take more study, whether in Bible or sociology. My mind is not made up which of these two fields I should follow more thoroughly. I am also aware that the next five years will probably change my mind to some extent. However, the purpose of this letter is to request that on our first furlough, we be granted enough time to study toward the

Ph.D. This will take a minimum of two years and maybe a semester more.

If, during the next few years, we change our minds, we will again address this committee, advising you of the change. Sincerely yours, Glyn B. Adsit and Jean Adsit."

• Adsit, Glyn B. and Jean, Ministers and Missionaries, Nanking, China, to Mr. Edwin Marx, October 18, 1947.

"Dear Mr. Marx, this letter is in reply to yours of September 18, 1947.

Both Jean and I have finished two semesters work in Chinese at the Yale Chinese Language Institute. We covered almost the same materials at Yale that they cover in Peking in the two first semesters. The following is a breakdown of the things we studied:

First Semester:

We studied grammar for five hours per week. This course was an explanatory course, taught by Mr. G. Kok, an English-speaking person. (Mr. Kok was born and raised in China.) New words and sounds were presented and explained in this class.

We were split up into two large groups of about thirty or forty each and had unison drill. This class was taught by Chinese teachers. Later, the two groups were divided into much smaller ones of about seven to eight, and in these small classes, we were drilled individually on phrases and tones. We received some individual coaching out of class if we needed it.

Comprehension classes were held from two to three times each week. At first, these were, of necessity, very simply conducted since our vocabulary was too small. Later, however, we spent fifty minutes listening to nothing but Chinese.

We received some training in translating from English into Chinese. We were held responsible for this in our small class drills.

A history and culture class was taught three times a week. This was a general survey course and covered: philosophy, geography, history, economics, religion and education of China. We also studied about Japan and her relations with China.

We had opportunity to attend many lectures given by Chinese and others, relative to China. Authors, who had written about China, came to our school and lectured.

We learned a few Chinese songs. This was extracurricular.

Chinese characters were introduced and explained. We learned about seventy-five the first semester. The emphasis was upon reading. We did not write them at all.

The entire course was centered around the idea of listening to the language as it was actually spoken. A Chinese teacher's voice was put onto records, and we listened many hours to the lessons in the afternoon and evening. We tried to imitate his tones and rhythm.

Our vocabulary was about a thousand words.

Second Semester:

We were divided into small groups of about seven and, in these, drilled for fluency in spoken Chinese and also in reading the characters.

Characters were given to us at about sixty a week. We were instructed to read. If we wrote, it was considered extracurricular. As the course was set up, we did not have time to write the characters.

New words were given in form of an actual happening. For example, we found ourselves meeting someone at the wharf, eating in a restaurant, being invited to someone's home, giving a lecture on Peking scenery, etc. We used our words in actual situations, which has enabled us to retain them. I do not know how many words they introduced this second semester.

We translated from English into Chinese. We made up stories about our home in America, our expected work in China, Bible stories, picnic stories, and many others. This was very helpful but extremely difficult.

We memorized several stories and recited them in our small drill groups.

We had comprehension talks each week. These became progressively harder as our vocabulary increased.

We continued our study of Chinese history.

We were given opportunity to ask questions about grammar if we did not understand it.

This second semester emphasized covering more material. I felt that we were going too fast and not concentrating as much as we did the first semester. They stressed characters very heavily, and we began to feel that we were losing some of our fluency in speaking.

In final summary, I think our Yale course for the first two semesters is quite similar to the courses taught at Peking. The one exception might be that at Peking, they learn to write the characters while they read them. Sincerely yours, Glyn B. Adsit and Jean Adsit."

- Marx, Edwin, Office of the Secretary-Treasurer, United Christian Missionary Society, China, Mission, Nanking, KU, Letter to Glyn B. Adsit, October 24, 1947.

"Dear Glyn, I appreciate the careful report on the language study that you have done. I am filing this for the present, but we hope soon to get some kind of tentative course prepared with suggestions for further pursuit of the language study. No doubt when that time comes, we will wish to build upon this report which you have given us.

With regard to your request for time for post graduate study on your first furlough, it is well to let us know what you are looking forward to. Just what amount of time can be granted you during furlough will no doubt depend upon circumstances at that time, but I feel sure your request will receive sympathetic consideration both from the United Society and from the China Mission. It will be necessary to make your wishes clear again when the time comes to plan definitely for your furlough. Yours cordially, Edwin Marx, Sec.-Treas."

- Adsit, Glyn B., Minister and Missionary, Hofei, China, Letter to Mother (R.L. Adsit), November 20, 1947.

"Dear Mother, I have received all your letters in which you say you have not received any mail from us. Well! I have sent a letter each week. I am afraid someone is stealing the stamps off our letters and throwing letters away. I am going to send this letter by registered mail to see if it gets through all right. We received the first box with the colored slides and the one with the Christmas candies and necktie and headscarf. In one letter, I mentioned that we were being transferred to Hofei in Anhwei, so write your letters and send packages to us there. Address is: Glyn B. Adsit, The Christian Mission, Hofei, Anhwei, China. There is no need for you to register your letters, as they arrive okay.

We are both well. Dust bothers my throat a little. Jean has already gone to Hofei. I am staying in Nanking to see that our freight gets moving. Jean has experienced no pains nor movement of the baby so far. She seems to be doing just fine. Your package, last one, arrived in about three weeks after you sent it. By the way, have you sent all the colored slides? We have never received the batch we took of San Francisco and Hawaii and some of China. I mailed a roll to you about a week ago. It will probably be a month before you get them.

It is turning cold here now, around 35 degrees. No heat and my feet get cold. Please let me know if those other three or four letters turn up. Tell Billie Jean congratulations and to let us know what she names the girl (Johnnie Rene). We are going to call our boy Samuel Lee, or Sandra Lea if a girl, or Nancy Jean, or what suggestions do you have?

In my last letter to you, I enclosed several changes of address I wanted you to notify for me. I suppose this one didn't reach you either. I also wrote several letters to our missionary society, which I am afraid they have never received. If you receive this one, let me know. I will write more news after I get to Hofei. We like China better every day. Love, your son, Glyn."

- Buckner, George Walker, Jr., Editor, *World Call International Magazine* of Disciples of Christ, Indianapolis, Indiana, Letter to Glyn B. Adsit, November 24, 1947.

  "Dear Mr. Adsit, I want to thank you for your sketch of the life of the old elder. It was well done. We shall use it within the next month or so in all likelihood.

  I urge you to continue writing, whether for publication or not. Nothing helps like constant practice. One minor suggestion is that you do not assume that your readers know too much. Assume rather that their information is limited but that their intelligence and understanding are up to par. Thus, you and I know who Mr. Hunt is, but when such a person is first mentioned in an article, his full name should be given with sometimes a parenthetical statement that has "early disciple missionary to China" in it.

  It is evident that in this article, you were deeply interested in the subject. That is one key to good writing. Write about that which interests you and you are more likely to interest someone else.

  In writing for our church publications, missionaries should always have in mind not preachers and professors but ordinary members of the churches.

  With every good wish, I am sincerely yours, George Walker Buckner, Jr. (DD, Office of the Editor). P.S. If you have a photo of the elder and can send it by airmail, we might want to use it with the story. We might be able to locate one elsewhere, though have not been successful as yet."

- Adsit, Glyn B., Minister and Missionary, *Luchowfu Christian Hospital, Hofei, Anhwei, China*, Letter to Mother (R.L. Adsit), December 4, 1947.

  "Dear Mother, well, you will have to congratulate the two kids upon their safe arrival of son and daughter. Our offspring is still growing. At least Jean is expanding week by week. I am sure Duane is about to bust his buttons he is so proud. Did Pat have a hard time? Jean has had absolutely no pains. She will not take enough exercises, and I am afraid she will pay for that later. She just won't walk as the doctor instructs her to.

No, I did not get my feelings hurt when you kidded us about the coming baby. I do not get my feelings hurt, and it seems that you should have found that out by now.

We like this city very much. We are in the midst of starting a new mission program after an interruption of seven years because of the war. The man who has headed up the rural work here for the past twenty-five years will be leaving within a few years, and then the load will fall upon my shoulders. So, I am all ears and eyes, trying to see and hear all I can.

Our house is being worked on now. It looks like we will be able to move in early spring. We are repairing the cistern so the water for washing clothes and hair will be soft. The big compound yard also has a well in it. This will be our drinking water. This is the time of the year when one does not hear about much military movement here in China. The Commies hole up for the winter in the mountains while the Kuomies hole up in the cities. Next spring, when the thaw is over, will be the dangerous time for us in this area, and we will be on our toes to leave at a moment's notice. You need not worry about our physical condition; even if the Communists capture us, they will hardly dare kill us since we are Americans. What they will do is make it so unpleasant for us that we will want to leave Hofei.

Bandits are everywhere around here. They are just plain farmers who have finished their crops for the year and are now turning to robbing to keep themselves alive for the winter. If one of these bandit bands captures us, we will have to pay ransom before we are released. This will happen only if we are attacked while making calls out in the countryside away from Hofei. Whenever one of these robbers is caught, they give him a quick trial and then either hang him or shoot him through the back of the head. Some life! Almost like the Wild West days.

Enclosed, you will find two more addresses, which I hope you will please notify of our change of address. Tell Marne Coats (a high school friend of Glyn's) he can subscribe to the Reader's Digest for us if he feels so moved. I ask you again, did that $25 ever arrive?

I observed an operation yesterday. The doctor was removing a cancerous growth from a man's armpit and back. The incision was about twenty-three inches long. The growth taken out weighed about one pound. I almost passed out once and had to go out for air. But I went back in and watched the rest of the operation. The amazing thing to me was that there is so little blood evident in the operation. Dr. Corpron used what is called a hot knife. It is electronically heated and just cuts its way through the flesh. We have many cancer cases here, also TB of the bones. I helped put a cast on a six-year-old boy with a TB spine. He is getting so weak he cannot walk. Will have to stay in cast for three months this time. His back is bowed and is uncomfortable.

We are finally getting our language study under way. We are learning to read Chinese hymns and the Bible. I will draw a rough sketch of our compound and house location on the back of this sheet. We can mail a letter to America for about 30 cents US. That is airmail registered. Your Christmas box came with the tie and two boxes of candy and other things. Our churches are sending boxes, but they are valuing the contents too highly. I am having to pay heavy duty on the stuff here. We know of eight boxes that are to come so far. Love, Glyn."

- Adsit, Glyn B., Minister and Missionary, Luchowfu Christian Hospital, Hofei, Anhwei, China, Christmas Letter to Friends in America, December 7, 1947.

"Dear friends, a small group of Chinese boys were talking. One asked the other boys, 'What would you like to be if you could be something other than yourself?' One little boy answered, 'I would like to be a missionary's dog.' This answer is so tragic that we cannot laugh at it. It reveals that the life of the Chinese boy is a hard experience. He had observed that there was something about a missionary that made him treat his dog with kindness and love. These were the things his little heart was yearning for.

Thank God for His Son this Christmastime. For, God so loved that, He gave. It was a great kindness on His part, a great work of grace. It has so moved our hearts that we are here, in this spiritually bleak land, trying to see that young boys and girls do not want to change places with our dog.

Jean and I are now in Hofei, the home of the Goulters, Corporons, Grace Young, Winona Wilkinson, Verla Elliot, and Lyrel Teegarden. This is a great group of workers, and we count ourselves fortunate to be able to serve with them. We are beginning our language study, using the morning of each day to read our Chinese Bibles and hymns. Our afternoons are filled with meeting of new people, watching Dr. Corpron operate on patients in the hospital, taking trips into the countryside on bicycles, trying to see that our house is properly repaired, teaching a Bible class, attending the missionaries' prayer service, and then some reading for relaxation. We have more than we can do.

Jean left Nanking by river boat for Hofei with Winona Wilkinson and Lyrel Teegarden. Since she is to have her baby early next spring, it was decided that she should not chance the trip by bus over that awful, bumpy road. The three left early in the morning, heading for Wuhu, hoping that they would make that city before night so that they could stay overnight with the Haskells and Reynolds of our mission. They started out with doubts as to the certainty of the time of arrival. (Travel is the most uncertain thing in China today, unless it is political and military situations.) They did reach Wuhu just as night fell. They started for Hofei the next morning on a much smaller boat. They slept on this boat all night, *were shot at by robbers or communists,* and arrived in Hofei the next afternoon. The water was so low in the small creek that runs up to Hofei that they had to be poled in.

I most certainly wish now that I had come to Hofei by boat. I still bear the marks of my trip on my body. I came by bus from Nanking to Hofei. If you were here, that statement alone would be enough. Since, in America, you can ride those wonderful Greyhound buses, I must try to describe that trip.

The bus left from Pukow, a small town across the Yangtze from Nanking. We had to be there by seven in the morning to board the bus. That meant that we (my two servants and I) had breakfast at 5:30 a.m. We crossed the river by ferry and ran to the ticket window to buy our tickets. We purchased a first-class ticket, which meant that we could have a seat and would not have to stand up all the way. We pushed our way into the bus and found our seat. We actually had to hunt for it because it was covered up with baggage. Finally, the bus was loaded with passengers and their baggage and started for Hofei. The people were all seated in a circle around the bus, and our baggage was piled in the middle. There was not an extra foot of space. We had to keep a constant vigil to see that the baggage did not fall on us. The roads were horrid, and many times, the bumps raised us a foot off the seat. This went on for seven hours. I was thankful that there was a hospital at the other end since I sure felt like I was going to need one.

We reached a section of the road that wound its way timidly through the mountains. This was bandit country. Two busses, a week before, had been robbed and burned in this spot. We all felt the hair begin to bristle on our necks. Everyone was anxiously peering out the windows, which had no glass on them, to see if they could spot a robber. Fortunately, we passed through without any mishap. I reached Hofei about four in the afternoon.

Dr. Corpron, Grace Young, and Jean met me at the bus station. They suggested that we might walk by the church on the way home. I was glad to have the opportunity to see the church as one of my first buildings in Hofei. Just as I walked in the gate, the Chinese let off a great string of firecrackers. They crackled and popped for about five minutes. Everyone in that part of town knew that another 'foreign devil' had arrived. About two hundred Christians had assembled to meet me and bid me welcome. It was a grand reception.

December in Hofei is wonderful. The weather is not too cold. The sun shines about every other day. The birds are still in our leafless trees and twittering away. The parson crow, the magpie, the dove, and sparrows are here in abundance. The country air is fresh and invigorating. We are walking a lot and enjoying our contact with the Chinese.

Oswald Goulter, Pastor Wang, Verla Elliot, and I took a short bicycle trip to a little village 10 li (approximately three miles) from Hofei. We left the city gate and started pedaling across rice paddies and old, ancestral graveyards. The paths were very narrow. They were made of dirt and had deep gulfs in them. We frequently had to dismount and carry our bikes across the gullies that the farmers had cut to irrigate their rice fields.

The people walking along the road presented a most interesting procession. A young man carrying a load of grass heavy enough for a horse was being led by a boy because he was blind. I admired him very much, for many blind people in China turn to begging. He was trying to make his own living. A woman about fifty years old was creeping along, carrying a load of grain and straw coolie fashion. Every step seemed to be one accompanied with pain. Her old, wrinkled face would be distorted into a grimace, and she would grunt. I thought to myself, *Dear God, if only the women of my country could see this poor wretch. How fortunate they would consider themselves. How devoted they would become in their support of your kingdom building in China.* A very small lad leading a huge, slow-moving water buffalo came next into our sight. That buffalo could have killed that little tyke with either of his horns or his strong hoof. The boy, however, was not afraid of his beast; he had ridden on its back for years, and the oxen obeyed him because he knew that the boy was his master.

The four of us finally reached our small village. The whole populace turned out to greet us. The small school that we had started the year before had purchased two strings of firecrackers, and they enjoyed the reception more than we did. The forty-one students, thirty-eight boys and three most fortunate girls, were lined up along the road in soldier fashion for our inspection. They were well behaved and most courteous.

Three small villages are cooperating to have this one school for their young people. There are about two thousand people in these villages, and the forty-one students are the only ones who are getting any schooling whatever. We also have a good Sunday school meeting every Sunday. The people gave us a most enthusiastic welcome. They want us to start church services there as soon as possible.

We were invited to eat in one of the better farm homes. The food was very good and hot. We had chicken, duck, fish, cabbage, and rice. While we were eating, many of the villagers crowded into the kitchen and watched us. Chickens, cats, and dogs also crowded under the table, waiting for us to drop a bone to them. We did this quite frequently, since that is the custom in China. (Now, the author knows where Glyn got this habit of feeding pets under the table during dinner. Glyn used to belch after dinner also, saying that in China belching was a sign of approval and satisfaction with the meal.)

After the noon meal, we went into the little school house. It is a bamboo, mud house with a thatched roof. The tables are very rough boards, and the seats are no more than saw horses. Pastor Wang explained why we had come to see them. Mr. Goulter then gave a short talk about China and America. Verla and I were introduced. Then Mr. Goulter gave each pupil a pencil tablet and pencil. The students were so pleased that they could hardly hold themselves. We left our little village and returned to Hofei confident that someday, we would win that place for Christ.

We are beginning to make plans for the work we hope to do next year. This month, we are inviting about twenty-five young farm men to come to our Rural Center in Hofei. Our purpose is to teach them scientific truths in order to break up their superstitions; better agricultural methods; and most of all, to introduce them to Christ's way of life. It is my personal hope that I can discover about ten boys in this group who will be material for future pastors. Our one great lack is men to take over our churches we now have and which we hope to found in future years. I want to teach these young men the content of the Bible and let them preach week by week, learning on the job. They will not be college graduates, but they will be good rural pastors.

We are going out week after week on trips into the countryside, looking at the work we used to have and making plans for future development. Next Saturday, we are going to San Ho, to talk with our leaders there. This is one of our largest churches. We are forced to take advantage of opportunities as they present themselves. The Communists and robbers and other unforeseen antagonists prohibit us from making long-range plans.

We Christians believe that Jesus was born in Bethlehem many years ago. We believe that He was the greatest personality that ever lived. We believe that through the power God gave Him, He overcame his arch-enemy, death. We say He is alive in our world today. If Christ is alive, where is He? I feel that if Jesus is alive and living with us today, there must certainly be a place where we can find him. I believe it is in our bodies, hearts, and minds that Jesus lives. As Paul was saying, "It is not I that Lives, but Christ that lives in me." My prayer for you this season is that Jesus is living in you.

Oh most wise God, open up my shriveled soul by Thy divine alchemy. Create within me that most wonderful of all miracles: a new birth. May I feel a new surge of strength that will let me know that my source of power is Thee. May I be found doing Thy will in such a way that men and women, boys and girls will be glad that I have lived in this place. May I accept the role that Thou dost want me to play on this earth without rebellion. May I at last be counted worthy, through Thy Sacrifice, to live eternally with Thee. Amen."

- Higdon, E.K., Executive Secretary, Department of Oriental Missions, The United Christian Missionary Society, Indianapolis, Indiana, Letter to Mr. And Mrs. Glyn B. Adsit, December 18, 1947.

"Dear Jean and Glyn, this letter will probably get as far as Nanking before Christmas, but it may not reach you by that day. However, I begin it by wishing you a Merry Christmas and a Happy New Year. But this is primarily a business letter, and I shall send a copy of it to Edwin Marx for his information and file.

Your Sound Scriber. In view of the fact that we are experimenting with sound scribers and putting a good deal of money into each one, I am interested in knowing whether or not you have found it possible to use the one you took. Perhaps you left it in Chuhsien but can still report on whether or not you had it in operation there. One thing that prompts this inquiry is a letter I received yesterday from Harriet Reynolds saying that the machine they took was damaged on the way and they have been unable to find anyone who can put it in running order. We have planned to have a sound scriber in each station, if the machines can be profitably used, and it is well for us to know before we go any further just how helpful these mechanical aids are proving to be..."

- Adsit, Glyn B. and Jean, Ministers and Missionaries, Luchowfu Christian Hospital, Hofei, Anhwei, China, to Mother, Duane, Pat, and Mike Adsit, December 21, 1947.

"Dearest Mother, Duane, Pat and Mike, Christmas greetings from our snow-clad countryside. We have had a good, heavy snow, and it really makes this part of the country look (like Christmas). Congratulations, Duane and Pat. I hope we can do as well. I can just see Duane walking the floor at night.

Mother, I received your letters and answered each one. Your dismal, pessimistic letter of November 10 arrived today, December 21. Do not send us registered letters. It takes too long to receive them. Send straight airmail. As I have said before, I say now; anything you can say in a letter or to our faces will not make us mad. We are not offended, we have not been offended, we will not be offended. Please do not assume or even think that we will ever be offended by any kidding about us or anything we have. If you do not receive a letter from us, it is because we have not time to write or because the mail service is bad. I do hope I have made myself clear on this point.

Jean is progressing nicely with the baby. She has no sicknesses, and the doctor says she is big enough to have the baby and should have no hard time and birth.

We are studying the language each day. Jean is studying household terms that will help her in handling the servants. The servant problem is a big one, and she must make her desires clear. My chief interest is to learn enough Bible terms to be able to preach (in Chinese). We have learned the Lord's Prayer and the Doxology, read the Christmas story, and a few things like this.

Looking after the repairs on our house is taking much of my time these days. We have to be constantly on the job to see that the workmen do as we want and not what they think we want done. One of our missionaries in Chuhsien had them make her a kitchen cabinet. She explained that she wanted the drain boards to slant so that the water would drain down into the sink. The carpenter made it so steep that the dishes could not stand on it; they rolled down into the sink. We do not want that to happen to ours. Ha!

I have just returned from San Ho. This country village is ninety li from Hofei. That is thirty miles. Mr. Goulter, Pastor Wang, and I rode our bikes to that place. We traveled over unbelievably narrow, winding, rough, hole-filled paths. It took us eight hours to go the thirty miles. We were so tired and sore upon arrival, that all we wanted to do was eat and go to bed. They had prepared two "nice" beds for us foreigners. The beds consisted of boards and straw. We took our sleeping bags and blankets. The bed was not bad after three nights. I was so tired I could have slept on a razor. The weather was fine when we left, but a big snowstorm came up while we were there and prevented our leaving for a week. It was impossible to get back to Hofei. Our feet were cold, and we could hardly keep warm. If it had not been for their generosity in providing us with a charcoal brazier to warm our feet by, we would have been truly miserable.

We had to attend several feasts given in our honor. We really enjoyed these and ate entirely too much food while there. The feasts consisted of from ten to sixteen courses of meats, fruits, fishes, and vegetables and rice. It took me a feast or two before I realized that I could only nibble a little on each dish. I started out trying to eat a good, healthy portion of each one and ended up about half way through the meal full and I could not complete the meal. I have drunk enough tea to float the battleship *Missouri*.

San Ho is the most isolated place I have been too. It has no cars. They do not have coal to burn, no Western clothes, no Western foods. They see foreigners only rarely. San Ho means 'three rivers.' It is in a beautiful setting, and their main transportation is water traffic. It sure reminded me of what the small villages in Jesus home country must have been like. I could just see Him standing down on the shore in a boat, discoursing day by day.

Our mission's biggest church is in this out-of-the-way little village. We have been working there for many years but have never had a missionary living there. We run up about six times a year to hold meetings and training institutes. The story of how this place grew to its present size (I mean the church) is really a thrilling story of Christian valor. A Dr. Soong moved to San Ho about twenty years ago and began to practice medicine. He was a Christian and started talking about the Christian religion and soon, he was teaching a class. Soon, he was preaching. Before long, several evangelistic groups were visiting homes in the city and countryside and persuading others to live this new way of life. Today, the church has about five hundred members. Their present church is too small, and they are making plans to build a church that will house between eight hundred and a thousand members. They do not even have a pastor now to lead them. They are growing by lay leadership. They have asked us to send them a minister, and we intend to do so this year. This Dr. Soong has now caused much grief in this church. He left his wife and started an affair with another Chinese woman. We are trying to persuade him to straighten up for the sake of the church. We were invited to the high school and asked to speak some English for the students who were studying English. We were also invited to preach to them and teach them some songs. We taught them simple ones, like; 'Row, Row Row Your Boat,' 'Three Blind Mice,' 'I Would Be True,' etc. In future years, this city will produce many Christians and leaders for our church in China.

As I stated before, the snow came and caused us to stay a week more than we had planned. We finally decided to walk home, leave our bikes there, and send some servants up after them. The decision had to be made as to which road we would take home. Where were the bandits and communists? Could we make it in one or two days? Were the roads too muddy? Could we find places to eat along the way? We settled these preliminary questions and started out Saturday morning at 6:30 a.m., walking along the way toward home (thirty miles away). Our plan was to walk one third of the way and try to hire *sudan-chairs* in a small village along the way. We left at daybreak and walked three hours while the ground was still frozen. We reached our village and hired the chairs to carry us on home. My feet are sore, and I am still recovering from the chilling I received while riding in the chair. (Actually, the author would add that Glyn's toes were partially frostbitten in this experience and he had slight trouble with them for the rest of his life because of this experience.) It is a real experience to ride in a chair. You feel foolish in having other men carrying you. It makes you feel they are like animals. It was very slippery and cold. They took off their cloth shoes and put on straw sandals. It was as if they were barefoot, but they kept moving, and their feet did not get cold. I got out and walked when I became so cold that I could not stand it any longer. We arrived home last night just as the sun was setting.

Our church in Hofei had the special Christmas music in church this morning. It made me think of home. Will close this letter for this time. Merry Christmas, even though this is late, and a happy, healthful new year. May God Bless You and give you your heart's desire. Your China Travelers, Glyn and Jean."

- Adsit, Glyn B., Minister and Missionary, Hofei, Anhwei, China, Letter to Mother and All the Rest, Christmas 1947.

"Dear Mom and all the rest, we had a wonderful Christmas. You never saw such eats. We all went over to the Goulters' for the evening meal, which consisted of a fresh ham roast, honey and biscuits, peas and carrots, a lettuce and gelatin salad, pickles and mayonnaise, minced pie, and coffee, and a lot more things that I cannot think of. We invited the two Catholic fathers that are here in Hofei, and that made thirteen around the table. We sang Christmas carols and hymns and then passed out the gifts that were under the tree. We all drew names and gave presents. The tie and things you sent were very pretty, and I am wearing the tie and Jean the scarf almost every day.

Jean continues to feel fine. She had a pain around her appendix the other night and woke me up, but the pain has gone, and the doctor says it was a gas pain from too much Christmas eating. Ha! She does eat twice as much as I do. I have quit losing weight and am feeling just fine. The reason I am weighing less is that I do not drink as much water as I used to.

The word got around that I wanted a dog, and one day, the hospital gate man brought us a little, five-week-old pup of doubtful heritage or vintage. We have named him Spunky. He is full of spunk and tries to chew our shoes off. He also is a messer and dirties all over the Corpron's house. She (Mrs. Corpron) is good natured about it and doesn't seem to care. We expect to be in our own house in about one more month, and then we can worry with him all ourselves. He looks like a cross between a Chow and an Alaskan Husky. He is short and squat, and his front legs are bowed.

I went into the street to buy some glass panes for our windows. I wanted about thirty panes. The price is terrific. I found enough glass, but it will cost us $40 for the thirty panes. Glass and iron are very precious here in China. The brick mason has finished his work on our house. They had to tear down a couple of walls and rebuild. They also fixed up the servants' quarters in back of our house. The painters and carpenters are now at work trying to improve the looks of the old house. I brought some electric wire and fixtures from America. I was able to buy a few more here in Hofei. Our house is already wired for electricity. This job cost us about $80. The mission will stand the expense.

Before I forget it, the check enclosed is endorsed and can be cashed and used for sending us out boxes or any other use you want to put it to, such as film development, etc.

All our freight has finally arrived. We have opened some boxes, and everything seems to be all right. We have not opened the box that has the mirror in it. We are afraid that it is smashed. Our refrigerator came through okay.

The price of stamps has gone up again. It now costs us about thirty cents to send an airmail. I am going to start sending slow mail. I will write each week. This letter will not be delayed, but the next one should arrive about a month after this one. If anything special happens, we will write by airmail.

The Corprons' two daughters are home for Christmas vacation. They go to the Shanghai High School. They are pretty girls and add a light touch to these vacation days. Jean is right now over at the baby clinic, helping wash the little, dirty, scabby babies.

We have begun an intensive language study, and we hardly have time for anything else. I am making frequent trips into the country. Our schedule runs something like this. Mr. Goulter, Mr. Wang, and I start out by bicycle early in the morning. We ride about ten miles and then arrive at our small village. We call on the man who has invited us to his village. We look over the school or prospective church site. We teach the children a few songs and then get down to the serious business of finding out just what we can expect to do in that village. Most of the villages want us to come and start a Sunday school. After this has gone on for about a year, the older ones have heard enough about Christianity that they want a church. We promise to supply one half the money to build a church and that we will send someone out to preach to them. Before long, we have another group of Christians.

Riding bikes is a tough job. The roads are indescribably rough and narrow. The time we rode thirty miles to San Ho, I was so shaken up that I was sore for a week. My wrists were very painful, to say nothing of my rear end.

The older missionaries are saying that the attitude of the Chinese people has changed. They used to be afraid of us and our message. Now they are very eager to hear about Christ. We are terribly handicapped in that we do not have enough Chinese trained to carry on this large program. As soon as I can master this language, I hope to launch a large training program.

My days are running something like this: We get up at 7:00 a.m. The sunrise is always beautiful, and we seem to get up in time to see it each morning. We hurry around to get down to breakfast at 7:30 a.m. We have a chapel for the hospital employees, doctors and nurses, at 8:00 to 8:30 a.m. We study with our Chinese teacher from 8:30 until 10:00 a.m. Then, I run over to our house to see that the workmen are doing what we want done. We have to watch them closely or they will plaster up a door or window or make one where we don't want it. We eat at 12:00 p.m. (noon). Our noon meal is Chinese food. The hospital kitchen sends us over the meal. We are enjoying this food very much. I can only eat one bowl of rice, but I enjoy the meats and green vegetables that they serve. The Corprons serve either cocoa or milk at each meal except breakfast, when we have coffee. I spend about thirty minutes a day mopping up after our pup and cleaning up his mess. I go back to the house at 1:00 p.m. and start the workmen out on their jobs. I stand around to see that they do it right. I return home and write letters, as I am now doing, or study Chinese. We eat supper at 6:00 p.m. The evenings are spent in playing some card games or listening to the radio. I am teaching a Bible class in English two nights a week. Sunday is full of church activities. We usually go to bed around 9:00 p.m.

Our Christmas tree is beautiful. It is a holly tree and all decorated with tinsel and bulbs. We also have one string of lights on it. A gold star stands at the top.

I am finding that we are not having to sacrifice in the way I thought we might. We have comfortable houses with heat and all the food we can eat. The real sacrifice is in the field of human contacts. It is very hard to adjust to the Chinese way of life. They seem so selfish and dishonest. We have to continually watch everything we own to keep it from being stolen. Almost one half of the people will steal. They are very eager to receive anything we want to give, but they have no conception of helping their neighbors.

We are going to stay up to see the New Year in. We are slowly learning to enjoy each day as if it might be our last one on earth. The situation in China makes us thankful for each day as it comes. Also, you people in America will never know how fortunate you are. You cannot begin to realize the poverty that there is among these people. The Chinese name for America is "beautiful country, *Meigwo*." It is just that, a beautiful country. So when you get down in the dumps or disgruntled, please remember the people in America are, of all people, the most favored on this earth.

Don't forget the next letter will be one month in arriving, but after that, they should come more often. Love, Glyn."

- Adsit, Jean (and Glyn), Minister and Missionary, Hofei, Anhwei, China, Letter to Mother, December 26, 1947.

"Dearest Mom, we had a good Christmas. Glyn and I did not exchange gifts this year because when we get into our house, there will be expenses of getting chests, tables, desk, etc. *made*! Thanks for the snapshots of the kids and their children. They're sweet babies, and I hope they will both get along fine. When our baby comes, we'll take some snaps of it too and send (them). We've about decided to change the names to Timothy Lee (Timmy) and Sherron Ann (Sherry).

It costs between 35 and 40 cents American money to send an airmail home at the present rate of exchange; however, it changes every day or so, and apparently, it's going up still more. Package with the suit hasn't arrived yet. When it does, I'll write you and tell you how it arrived, etc. I'll appreciate sweater sets because it's so cold here. However, I hope they'll be big enough to wear after the baby arrives; next winter, in other words.

Although we aren't settled yet, I can answer some of the questions you ask us. We eat a foreign or an American breakfast. It consists of coffee, toast, egg, rice or cereal, jam, and tangerines. Tangerines grow in China, and although they're expensive to eat, we buy them because we need vitamin C in our diet. Hofei is a chicken center, so we've lots of eggs. Coffee is almost $1 American money per pound right now, but we also afford it because we've decided we'll eat and keep warm if it takes all we make, plus having to borrow. We must stay healthy. At noon, we eat Chinese food. The hospital cooks for all the patients, and we buy from them; it's cheaper and very well cooked. This is usually a green vegetable and greens of some sort, bean sprouts, chopped up beef and chicken soup, plus the rice. We drink dried milk, one cup full at noon, and then we usually eat some fruit either tangerines or dried persimmons or maybe some dried fruit from America. One family here just came out, and they are well stocked with American food. At night, we eat a foreign or American meal again. In Shanghai, we have been able to buy rations from UN RRA: canned meats, vegetables, preserves, and lard, butter, and the like. We make all our own bread. We cook on a coal and wood stove and keep things warm on a Chinese stove made of cement and burning straw and cotton seed cake. We didn't buy a coal and wood stove, but we bought one from an older missionary that was here. We burn oil in our heating stove. In the upstairs, we have hot water chests that both heat water and the room. They work like this. Upstairs, the pipe runs through a tin barrel like tin chest, and in the top is a small gallon bucket that heats water (this is hooked to a pipe from a downstairs stove).-There will be one in our bathroom and one in the bedroom. Oil is expensive, but we have to have it. We'll have electric lights here. However, I am not sure it will be the right voltage for my iron. I'll take up the rest of the questions later. Glad that my family are writing each other some. Maybe you could exchange some of the news. Love, Jean and Glyn."

- Adsit, Glyn B., "A Prodigal Son Returns: A Story of Wang Yun Ting, Elder at Chuhsien," *World Call*, January, 1948, pp. 17-18 (Re-printed by permission, White, Cyrus N., President and Publisher, Christian Board of Publications, 1221 Locust Street, Suite 1200, St. Louis, MO 63103).

"Wang Yun Ting was born near Wuhu in 1860, but he does not consider that important. He feels that the day he became a Christian was the greatest day in his life. He says, 'It was in 1896 that I became a Christian. W. Remfry Hunt was the missionary in Chuhsien at that time. The greatest thing I ever did was to have enough sense to let Jesus Christ come into my life.'

We could stop Wang Yun Ting's story here by just saying he has been a follower of Christ from that day forth. His life, however, has meant so much to the people of his village and to missionaries that we must share it.

Wang Yun Ting was truly, in his youth, a prodigal son. From the age of twelve to the time when he became a Christian at the age of thirty-six he was, as he says, 'a bad man.' He cheated in business dealings, lied in personal relationships, and lived a prodigal life of wasted youth. He believes that his greatest sin during those years was his indulgence in opium smoking. He did not break this habit until he became a Christian. He has not touched an opium pipe since his baptism.

Wang Yun Ting left Wuhu and arrived in Chuhsien (formerly known as Chuchow) in 1888. He came in contact with Mr. Hunt who gave him a Bible to read. He read the story of the Prodigal son and was so impressed that he became interested in becoming a Christian. It was through the influence of his wife, a Christian, that he finally was baptized in 1896.

Dr. Elliot Osgood employed Yun Ting as his cook. He was a good cook and worked for the doctor for several years. He loves to tell stories of how the people in Chuhsien loved and respected Dr. and Mrs. Osgood.

Before 1900, China had no mail service between Shanghai and Nanking. Wang Yun Ting was the connecting link between the missionaries in Nanking and Chuhsien. He was a trusted servant of our Mission.

Nineteen hundred twenty-three is another red letter year in Wang's life. It was at this time he became an elder in the Christian church. He has been an elder for twenty-four years. One of his favorite sayings is, 'For years I was a servant for the Osgoods. And just look, now they have made me a servant of the church.'

He has been a real servant of the church. It has literally come true that the least of all the Christians in Chuhsien has become the greatest. Yub Ting stands by the communion table each Sunday morning. He talks for a few minutes and the people listen with eager hearts to what he says because they know his actions and his words are the same. He backs up his words with Christian living.

Elder Wang will not talk about it, but it has been reported that when the communists entered the Chuhsien community in 1927, he, at great risk to his own life, protected the lives of the C.A. Burch family. He hid them and later escorted them to a place of safety.

During this recent war (the Japanese occupation), when most of the Christians in our area left for the west, Elder Wang stayed to shepherd the Christians left behind. I asked him why he did not go west also. He replied, with a twinkle in his eyes, 'Why, young man, I was too old to go west. So I decided to look around and see what I could do to make myself useful.'

He did make himself useful. He went to the homes of the Christians and prayed with them there. He saw that the Lord's Supper was not neglected. He did his best to encourage the church community during the long years of the war. At this time he was only seventy-seven years of age, and a little more energetic than he now is at the age of eighty-seven. As more Christians returned to Chuhsien, he invited them to his home for the church services. Finally, in 1938, when Pastor Peter Cheo returned to Chuhsien, elder Wang turned over the arduous church duties to him. Elder Wang, truly with God's help, kept the church alive in a period when many other institutions were crumbling all around him.

How does this old man, who has now been a Christian for fifty-one years, feel about the Japanese who so cruelly mistreated his people?

Elder Wang says, 'The Japanese are like any other people. Some are good, some are bad. During the war Chuhsien was occupied by many Japanese soldiers and civilians. If the person was bad in his heart, he treated us badly; if he was good in his heart, he was helpful to the Chinese. One Japanese helped me very much. When I was hungry he gave me food to eat. When I was without good water, he brought me water to drink. When my lamp did not have oil, he brought me oil. You see, he was a Christian!'

Elder Wang gave me a message to the Christians in America. 'Tell them,' he says, 'that we are friends. In our hearts we believe in the same God. In our lives we experience the same saving power of Christ's love. At our deaths we have the same faith in God's power to save us into eternal life. We are friends.'

Today is Sunday in Chuhsien. Elder Wang will stand in the presence of his Lord at the communion table. He will continue to do this every Sunday until his legs will no longer bear him up; until his speech is too weak to be heard; until his funeral service is read in the church which he has served for fifty-one years. The Prodigal Son has returned."

- Adsit, Glyn B., Minister and Missionary, Hofei, Anhwei, China, letter to Mother and all brothers, sisters, nephews and dogs, January 4, 1948.

"Dear Mom and all brothers, sisters, nephews, and dogs, this new year has come in like an Indian summer.

The weather is unbelievably warm, and the sunshine is brilliant. Today is Sunday, and we are waiting for church time to roll around. We do not try to go to Sunday school since we cannot understand very much of what is said. We are getting better in our language. We study about four hours per day.

Nothing much has happened since my last letter. We know a General Jang and his wife who are stationed here in Hofei. They are Christians and also speak some English. They like to come over and visit with the missionaries. She invited us to a Chinese opera last night. The men play women's parts and sing in high falsetto voices. The costumes were magnificent, and the acting was not bad. It lasted for four hours. We arrived an hour late and were spared too much cold feet. Our group were the only foreigners there, and the general's wife had reserved seats right in the front, where every person could see us. It added to her prestige to be seen with us. She did not invite us for this reason, however, since she is a very humble Christian.

Our Christmas programs were well attended at the church. We sang in the choir, and on one night, I played my harmonica. They liked it, and I had to encore for several numbers.

Have changed my mind about sending mail by slow letter. It will take too long.

Mr. Goulter and I are starting a class for farm boys tomorrow. Mr. Wang, our Chinese co-worker, will do most of the teaching. Our job is to furnish the ideas. (I got my fingernail torn off monkeying with my electric light generator and am having some difficulty typing. Forgive these mistakes.)

Spunky, our dog, continues to be the center of attraction. He is learning to bark and does so quite freely. He chews everything in sight, but is so cute that no one gets mad at him.

We will be able to move into our house within two or three weeks. The paint is arriving, and the carpenters are about through with their part of the repairs. Cement is hard to get, and I am having our servant collect rocks and old bricks and break them up and lay on our sidewalk. We are having lots of fun working around the yard.

Missionaries learn to conserve everything. We have a stove in the kitchen that burns wood and coal. The pipe runs up through the bathroom. In the bathroom, we have a tank made of tin, through which runs the stove pipe from the stove downstairs. This warms the room and also furnishes us with warm water. We will use this system in the dining room and bedroom also.

There is a rumor that the railroad will be rebuilt from Wuhu to Hofei next spring. This railroad was in operation about eight years ago, before the war. The bed is still in good condition, and all they have to do is re-lay the rails. If this does happen, it will make it much easier for us to get to Nanking and Shanghai to buy materials.

We get world news quite regularly. Our radio is working fine, and the Goulters take the Shanghai paper. It reaches us two weeks late, but the news is new to us.

I am wondering if some of my undeveloped pictures I sent to the States ever reached you? I sent two boxes by a young Lutheran pilot who was flying home last September. I also mailed one from Nanking, altogether three rolls of colored film. I also received the last box you sent me, a box of pictures. The boxes you are sending are probably addressed to Nanking, and it will take them a month longer to reach us. Many people have not heard of our change of address and keep sending things to Nanking. Many church people sent us boxes, but only two have arrived in Hofei.

The Communist leader, "One-eyed Liu," is on the rampage again. He was the one who caused trouble in this area some two months ago. He is somewhere south and west of Hofei. There is no danger for us since Hofei has thousands of soldiers with the city wall. The wall around Hofei is one of the thickest and highest in this province.

I suppose Jean has told you what we eat every day. If not, here is a brief summary. For breakfast: tangerine or banana or pear, butter and honey or preserves, bread baked by our cook, eggs, and coffee. For dinner: Chinese food from the hospital. For supper: some meat dish or cheese and crackers, bread, three vegetables, butter, preserves, and two cups cocoa. We also drink milk for dinner, and we take vitamins early in the morning. You can see we are eating plenty. We sleep about nine hours a night. My bicycle is working all right. If you see Velva Dreese, tell her that the coat she gave Jean can sure be used. Also, that suitcase has served us faithfully. We have not yet opened the buttons and soap, but these will be used in the days to come.

Must go to church. Hope you are doing the same. Love, your son, Glyn."

- Adsit, Glyn B., Minister and Missionary, The Christian Mission, Hofei, Anhwei, China, Letter to Folks, January 17, 1948.

"Dear folks, I have never seen such lovely winter weather anywhere in the world as we are having here in Hofei. It is sunshiny most every day, and the temperature is pleasantly warm. California has nothing on us. I suppose the American papers are full of the troubles in China? If so, let me give you the facts as we see them from this side.

First, the Communist trouble in Hupeh and Honan Provinces. These two provinces are the ones to our west and north. There is a band of communists roving around at will over these two provinces. The main army of the Kuomingdang is up north in Manchuria trying to fight the Commies there; therefore, they do not have sufficient force to wipe out the Commies in Hupeh and Honan. These Commies are real "Red" ones and do not love us Americans. Three missionaries were killed last week by a band of robbers, communists no doubt, who stopped a bus and ordered all passengers out. When they saw the three foreigners, they said, 'You are Americans, and all

Americans must die.' The man was not American but Finnish or Norwegian. They shot him anyway, and he crumpled at their feet. The two ladies did not show fear at this procedure, and they promptly shot them too. Two Chinese who tried to intervene were also shot and killed. God bless them and rest their souls. At least they died a noble death. The bodies were recovered and taken to Hankow, where they will be given a Christian burial. This incident excited the American ambassador and the heads of the missions in that area. They promptly sent word that all foreigners in areas that are threatened by Communists should evacuate without delay. They sent an airplane to Hankow to help evacuate some five hundred missionaries in that vicinity. Our Doctor Corpron has been to Nanking recently and talked with Ambassador Stuart, and he reports as follows: 'You folks in Hofei are in no immediate danger. I want merely to caution you to keep on your guard and be ready to leave if trouble seems imminent. Watch out for Communist-incited riots and uprisings. The United States is going to give China much aid in the near future; and when the Commies learn this, they will really have it in for you US missionaries. Do not try to stay in an area where they will be in charge.'

We are keeping our eyes and ears open. Do not worry! We are in no danger and have enough sense to run before we are shot. If an accident should befall us, what of it? At least we are trying to do what Christ wants all of us to do.

In Canton, far to our south, there has been trouble between Chinese students and the British. Some British firms have large land holdings, and the Chinese encroached upon their land and built houses without permission. They call them squatters in America. The British had the police tear down the houses send burn them. They first warned the people in advance to move, but they did not. Therefore, the students stormed the British Consulate and burned the building. No one was killed. But this happening does indicate the feeling that is in China. It is briefly this: 'We fought Japanese for years alone. US and Britain owe us something for that. We will not tolerate other countries meddling in our affairs.' (They felt Britain was meddling, even though the squatters were on soil that belonged to British.) 'If you don't do what we say, we will force you to do so.' As you can see, we have plenty to keep us interested. We go merrily, nervously, hopefully on our way.

Now for more pleasant news. Our house is nearing completion. It is a standard joke around here. The chatter runs something like this. "Is your house finished yet?" "Nope." "Well, you better hurry or you won't have it finished in time for the Communist General to live in." We do hope to get to sleep in that bed for a while before the Commies run us out, when and if. By the way, your box with the dried fruit and maternity suit for Jean arrived. Thanks a lot. Jean is wearing the suit and enjoys it. Colored pictures also arrived. Our compound did not have a sidewalk, so I decided to make one. We had no cement; therefore, we collected rocks from all over the yard and had the servant break them up with a small hammer and put them along the path. It has made a real good walk. It was rather funny to see him pecking away at the rocks hour after hour, reminded us of a jailbird in prison. It is taking the carpenters just about ten days to make four doors. They are so slow. The carpenter making our toilet box had never seen one before. We told him how to make the lid with the hole in it and supposed he would do it right. We had indicated the hole by a small round circle on the paper. When we saw him making it, we noticed that the hole was rather small. He had made it about the size of a small saucer. I explained what the hole was for, and he has finally made it large enough for use, we hope. Our kitchen cabinet is finished. It is white on outside and blue inside. The top is made of tin, and the sink is made of tin. We have a pipe that runs behind the cabinet and out through the wall. So we do not have to carry out refuse water.

Money exchange is now CN$115,000 to $1 US. When we arrived in Shanghai last August, it was CN$30,000 to $1US. We get about $17,000,000 a month in salary. Rockefeller has nothing on us. Oranges are scarce and worth 10 cents each. We have really enjoyed the ones we eat here in China. They are much sweeter than the American orange and just as juicy.

Our little pup is sick. I am giving him sulfa, but he won't eat. I am teaching in our rural farm school. We have about forty boys from ages thirteen to eighteen. They are all boys from villages around here. I am teaching music, English, and recreation. I can teach these without using Chinese. Some of the Chinese are teaching the deeper subjects of religion and agriculture. Write us soon. Love, Glyn and Jean."

- Niedermeyer, Mabel, Missionary Education, The United Christian Missionary Society. Indianapolis, Indiana, Letter to Mr. and Mrs., Glyn B. Adsit, January 20, 1948.

"Dear Mr. and Mrs. Adsit, I can well understand your feeling about and inability to take those pictures for our China picture-story book. Yes, the spring time of this year will be satisfactory. We are not beginning our study until the spring of 1949 with the children, and the book can be ready by that time if we get the pictures by June 1. Would it be possible for you to send them to us by that time? I am being married next month, but will stay in the office while Miss Brown makes her trip in your direction, but will leave when she returns. So this should be written in June or early July, my last job of this kind officially as a member of the department.

We are anxious about you folks these days. News reports are discouraging. Sincerely hope you and our work will be unmolested. Our prayers and thoughts are with you. Yours most sincerely, Mabel Niedermeyer."

• Adsit, Glyn B. and Jean, Ministers and Missionaries, The Christian Mission, Hofei, Anhwei, China, Letter to Family, February 1, 1948.

"Dear family, all ten of you, no upset around here as of this date. The main fighting is in the far north, only sporadic bursts of communist activity near us. If serious trouble comes, we will let you know.

Mother, forgive us for not sending you a birthday card, and accept this letter as evidence of a happy birthday and many more years of good health. We continue to be in good health. I have a slight cold, but am not down with it. Jean is beginning to get so large she waddles like a duck.

Enclosed, you will find that check that I sent once before. Please cash it for me, as we cannot cash it here in China. Use the money in sending things to us. We need toothpaste and powders. I need some face lotion to use after shaving. Jean needs hand cream.

Our house is ready for us to move into five rooms. We will move in tomorrow, and the workmen will continue to work on the other three rooms. Sometime this year, a Miss (Lyrel G.) Teagarten, one of our single missionary workers, is to come and move into our house. She will occupy the three rooms that are not completed as yet.

We have just completed the unpacking of all our things we brought out. Tell Duane that the bed the Yellow Cab Co. packed came through in excellent shape. Not one thing was broken or lost. We did have a few small things broken. One cookie jar broken, one cooper boiler bent and pierced with a nail hole, one can of soap powder spilled all over the contents of one box, two lamp chimneys broken, one old platter broken. All other things came through fine.

We have not studied all this past week since it has taken all our time to move. My cook and I carried all the things over from the place where we had them stored. It was only about half a block away, but they got heavy before we reached our third floor. We used a pole and two of our tin boxes "coolie fashion" (carrying items on their shoulders stretched between two poles). My shoulder muscles are still very tender.

Since we have been living in the doctor's house, we are very close to the happenings that take place in the hospital. I have watched several operations. A soldier was carried in from ten miles out. He was shot through the stomach in a battle with Communists. He was weak from loss of blood, and his feet were very cold. He was suffering from shock. The doctor x-rayed and found the bullet lodged just under the skin in his back. He ordered the coolie to prepare the operation room and then, one hour later, started the operation. I watched as he cut open the abdomen and started looking for the places where the bullet pierced the stomach. He had to remove all the blood and water that the soldier had drunk and had leaked through the holes of his stomach into the abdominal cavity. The operation lasted for two hours. The soldier lived for nine days, finally dying from pneumonia and shock. He died this morning early, 2:30 a.m. The night nurse came running over to get the doctor. She was slightly hysterical and very excited. She began yelling under the doctor's bedroom window, 'Doctor Corpron, hurry. The soldier is dying.' Dr. Corpron calmly told her to give him adrenaline and went back to bed. He told us this morning that he knew that the boy would die since his body was too weak to fight the complications of pneumonia and liver congestion.

We have just emerged from our second snowy cold spell. It got down to 10 above. It really hurts your heart to see these poor thinly clad farm people without heat in their homes. When it is bitterly cold, most of the women and children stay in bed all day. People are constantly stopping me on the street, asking for clothes. I must tell them I have none to give.

Our home is rather nice looking inside now that it is painted. The walls are a little darker than ivory, and the woodwork is ivory color. We made a mistake in painting the mop boards and the thresholds the light ivory color.

They get dirty too easily. We will paint them darker this summer, when we have the floors painted. I am already beginning to use the carpenter tools I brought out. I made Jean a linen chest to put in the bathroom. I simply used one of our packing boxes, putting three shelves in it. She is going to hang a curtain around it to hide the roughness. Our cistern is slowly beginning to fill up with rain water. We are fortunate to have a cistern because the well water is very hard. The *Encyclopedia Britannica* arrived in good condition, and we will be using it before long. Thanks again. It was a wonderful gift.

Eggs are 35 cents a dozen here in Hofei, so we eat plenty of them. Most expensive items are milk and meats.

I want to tell you that I got Jean's sewing machine back together again and in good running order. I had wondered if I could do this, but it was very simple.

I am writing a short history of the Hofei mission workers. Will send that for you to read when it is finished. I sent that little story, "The Prodigal Son Returns," to our missionary magazine, the *World Call*. They published it in the January edition. You might borrow it from Joneses and read it if you wish. Tell the Joneses I am really glad to hear of Elnora's good luck; only wish it was a bigger well, and then we could all go and live with her when we get old. Jean is taking this opportunity to read a lot of books. She laughs about someone writing her to be careful while she is in "her delicate condition." She says she was never so big in her life and doesn't feel at all delicate. Write us soon. Love, your kids, Glyn and Jean."

- Adsit, Glyn B. and Jean, Ministers and Missionaries, Hofei, China, to Mr. Edwin Marx, February 4, 1948.

"Dear Mr. Marx: Thank you for sending our December salary to the amount of CN$18,000,000. We received this about one week ago.

Will you please send us CN$20,000,000; placing it in the Hofei bank as you did the other money? Will you also please advise us how much money is left in the US account after this twenty million is sent?

We are hearing it rumored that you are going home this April. If this is true, I wish to take this opportunity to wish you god speed and the best of sailing. Thanks for all the help you have been in explaining about finances and other things.

We have moved into our house and like it very much. The workmen are going ahead with the other three rooms while we are here. We are only living in five rooms now. Cordially yours, Glyn b. and Jean Adsit."

- Adsit, Glyn and Jean, Ministers and Missionaries, Hofei, Anhwei, China, Letter to Mother and all the family, February 6, 1948.

"Dear Mother and all the family, today is Sunday. What a beautiful sunshiny day it was. We walked around the city wall. On our trip, we saw a woman about thirty-five years old lying by the side of the road. Upon questioning, we found that she had lain herself down there, wanting to die. We never did get it straight just why she wanted to die. We think it was because her home and relatives were burned to death by bandits. We could not help her because it would have meant that we would be responsible to support her all the rest of her life. What a cruel system it is that prevents one from doing what is in his heart. You will never know how the heart can ache until you experience some of these things.

Speaking of heartaches, my little pup died. We are not sure what of, but I know the final thing that killed him was a heart attack. I buried him in our backyard. I won't get another one for a while.

These are days of testing and trying for us. I am, for the first time, beginning to feel homesick. When you feel like Jean and I do now, you wonder if you will ever come back to China once you get home, but time will tell. The oldsters here say they all felt like that their first years out here.

We have electric lights in our house now. We finally got the motor installed and running. It sure cheers up the old house. Will you please send us some light bulbs? We need several, say about ten. We want two 75 watt, four 60 watt, and four 40 watt bulbs. Be sure to pack plenty of soft stuff around them.

I have learned that the Chinese are like all other people. It is very easy now to tell the ones we know from the others. While in America, I thought they all looked somewhat alike, but this is funny now. Mother, are you keeping all of my letters? If not, please do, for many things I tell you are recorded in no other place. (Thank heavens she kept them all and returned them to Glyn when they returned.)

We are trying to train our servants. What a job this is. It has already made us nervous wrecks. You have to treat them like they do not know a thing, and most of them don't know Western methods at all. It will take Jean three years before she can turn the cook loose to prepare a full meal by himself.

No sign of Communists in Hofei. The hospital gets patients that have been beaten and robbed by them, and some are shot. Of course, the ones that are killed we never hear about at all. Traveling in any form is a little dangerous just now. The buses turn over on the slippery roads and kill some passengers almost every week.

Did I ever tell you how the farmers make a living in the winter? Some of them turn to bandits and rob their neighbors. That makes them an income all the year around. What a country!

Tomorrow begins the Chinese New Year season. If you think the Christmas preparations in America are something, you should see what these people do to get ready for their New Year. They celebrate for about one week. They cook for three days before the New Year Day to be sure and have enough food on hand. You cannot go on the street and buy things for about all that week. They have no iceboxes; therefore, they have to cook up their food for the week. They serve sweets, and this is the one period of the year when everyone gets his fill of meat. (Most Chinese do not eat meat each day.) Every Chinese tries his darndest to get home for the New Year. The family washes all the clothes or makes new ones to wear for the New Year. They clean up their yards and houses. I think this is the only time in the year they really do this. They must all take a bath before the New Year if at all possible. We cannot get any workers to come and paint or do carpentry work.

Did I ask you to send toothpaste and hand cream for Jean? We find that we did not bring enough of these. Also a box of pepper for the table; any edible things we can use, but don't break your pocketbook sending us things. We are not going to starve. Jean had her monthly examination day before yesterday. Dr. Corpron says she is perfectly normal and has not gained too much weight. I am anxiously awaiting the big event now. I really am curious to see what it will be, a boy or girl. We have decided that we honestly don't care whether it is a boy or girl, but if the first one is a boy, we want the second one to be a girl, or vice versa.

We are preparing today for the Chinese New Year. I mentioned several things before, but one of the main things they do is to go call on all their friends to wish them a happy new year. We have bought peanuts, sesame candy cakes, tea, peanut candy, watermelon seeds (which they just love to crack between their teeth and eat the heart inside). They will begin arriving tomorrow morning after breakfast. They come in and say, 'Gunsi, gunsi,' which means, 'Congratulations old fellow on having lived to see this wonderful New Year's Day.' We smile broadly and then serve them refreshments. They then go to the next house and repeat the performance. This lasts for two days. They shoot firecrackers just like we do at Fourth of July time. I suppose you know that firecrackers were invented in China.

Our home is very comfortable. Our oil stove burns too much oil, and that stuff is very expensive, but we manage to keep enough to stay warm. As usual, Jean is making the place look very cheerful. She has bright flowered paper window curtains in our dining room. She is making a set of drapes for the bedroom. We have put all the baby clothes and other necessities in one chest of drawers. It looks like the little stranger will be well clothed at least. Write us when you find time. Tell Duane and Hurshel's families to write, or we herewith disown them. Your China Kids, Glyn and Jean Adsit. P.S. Your last letter did not have sufficient postage on it. You put 15 cents and it takes 25 cents for airmail unless you use the envelope type."

- Adsit, Jean, Minister and Missionary, Hofei, China, Letter to Mom (Reecie Adsit), February 17, 1948.

"Dearest Mom, I must get a letter to you. We've been so busy moving into our four rooms (the other half isn't completed) and unpacking along with curtain making, etc. that we've been too neglectful of late on the letter writing.

Our spring rains are here. Hardly a day goes by without a shower. We planted some cherry trees and berries last week, plus a few flowers. After the rains, we'll make a garden. They tell us there will not likely be any more killing frosts.

Mom, Glyn, and I want our friends and relatives to know about our baby as soon as we can let them know. We wondered if we sent you and my two older sisters names if you'd mail out announcements. We'll send you three people airmails on the great day, and then, when you receive the information, you can pass it on. If you'll just let Oletha and all of the immediate relatives on Glyn's side know, my sisters will do my family and a few of our friends.

Glyn isn't feeling too well again. He has three or four days when he is himself and then feels punk. However, this time, he has the flu. He's in bed today, and I am being a nurse. I am joking him, telling him the only reason I am being nice to him now is that when I have the baby, he must be my nurse.

Things are still quiet here in Hofei. New Year's is just over, and I am glad. We had 250 some odd guests in one day. One of the older missionaries had over a thousand. They expect tea and Chinese candy and peanuts and watermelon seeds. They only stay a minute and say, 'Happy new year.' They spend the week before preparing for the celebration, and then they celebrate. Everyone has meat to eat, a bath, and a new outer garment if possible. We used this celebration to have open house too and get it all over at once. Write us when you can, and don't work too hard. I love you. Jean."

- Adsit, Glyn and Jean, Ministers and Missionaries, Hofei, China, Letter to Homefolks, February 26, 1948.

"Dear homefolks, Mother, your letter with the newspaper clippings arrived. For once, a newspaper got the details straight, but that was only half the story. It would take reams of paper to write everything about the political situation here in China. We continue to be safe, healthy, and happy. It seems that the national government is getting the worst of it in Manchuria but is winning most of the skirmishes south of the yellow river. We see bands of soldiers leaving Hofei to go and fight almost every month. So here we are in our little protected, walled city, pecking away at this great task of trying to win China for Christ. And the encouraging thing is that we are succeeding. I tell you, the doors are wide open for every type of Christian activity. The only thing that holds us back is that the war disrupted our training of leaders, and now we are tragically shorthanded. I have already mentioned the church at San Ho. This town is ninety li from here (thirty miles). The church there has about five hundred members and no pastor. It has a hundred inquirers ready for baptism this spring and no pastor. They are planning on building a new church to seat eight hundred to a thousand, and no pastor. God works in mysterious ways His wonders to perform.

Our days are becoming increasingly crowded. The many small things we do add up to a heavy schedule. I am trying to plan and plant a garden. Our cook is preparing the plots, and I am planting the seeds. I brought out several different kinds from America. We are using cow manure borrowed from Mr. Goulter's cow lot. You should see me crumbling up the manure and gingerly putting it around the lettuce, tomatoes, and pea seeds. But the darn stuff will grow, so just call me Farmer Adsit. I have also planted a dozen blackberry vines and six cherry trees. The trees will probably not produce this year, but we can look forward to next year. I suppose I told you my doggy died. You should see our beautiful narcissus plants. They are blooming in two plots in our south dining room window. They are a beautiful, petite plant with yellow, fragrant blossoms. They grew amazingly fast. Our yard will have several types of flowers this spring, summer, and fall. We have about a dozen rose bushes scattered around the yard. I transplanted several holly trees. They are really beautiful but sticky.

We get splendid radio reception from all over the world. From 5:00 p.m. to 10:00 p.m. is the best time for programs. We get Australia and the Philippines just as clear as if they were in the next room. Also Japan comes in good. The weather is warm here, around 60 (degrees). We have not had our stove on all this week. It is pattering rain on our roof today and filling up our cistern. We have about four feet of water in the cistern now. We have been in our home now for over three weeks, and it is beginning to seem like home. The painter is still working on three rooms, and we are looking forward to the time when the whole place will be prepared and the noise of hammer and saw will cease. A single missionary lady, Lyrel Teagarden, is coming to live with us around April 1. she is an old timer and will be a help to us. You should see my study! I made three bookcases and filled them up with books brought from America. We spent most of today straightening up the study and trying to find a place for all the doodads we brought out with us.

Jean is in perfect health. She now weighs 168 (lbs), a little too heavy, Dr. Corpron says. She must cut down on some of her eating. It really gripes her not to be able to eat all she wants to. Less than two months until the baby comes, and are we getting excited. Jean has washed most of the baby things and ironed them. We borrowed an old buggy-bed from Dr. Corpron and painted it up with white paint. It will serve as bed and buggy for the first few months. We seem to have plenty of clothes for the first few months, but after the baby starts walking, we will need more things. Our (*amah*) girl servant is going to have a baby about six weeks after Jean. They say they don't want to keep it. If it is a boy, they will give it to His mother; if a girl, to someone else. We are going to try to talk them out of it. She has hookworm and must undergo treatment to get rid of the worm.

The muddy lanes in Hofei are a sight to behold. It gets so sticky and deep that you think you are in a pigpen. It is on nights like this one that I feel wretchedly sorry for the poor in China. There are three families living just outside our front gate in straw huts. The huts are made from corn straw and grass. They sleep on straw placed on the ground. They have no windows for ventilation. Their clothes are lice infected, and they are very poor.

My teaching duties start again tomorrow. Our young farm boys return for the classes. I will teach English and music. We hope to choose several prospective leaders from this group of forty boys. I am teaching a Bible class on Friday nights to men who are interested in English and Christianity. Also, two young men are coming down from San Ho to have me tutor them in English. They are trying to prepare to enter Nanking Theological Seminary next year. They want to be rural evangelists. I am very glad to help them if I can.

Jean is learning how to bake in our little oven. She has turned out three good cakes. You think you have inflation in America. China is really having inflation. Prices have risen some 400 percent since we landed in Shanghai. Exchange is now 150,000 to 1. It does not hurt us since we get paid the same each month in US dollars. We get around $25,000,000 each month. Don't forget to send us some light bulbs. We really need them. Sizes again are 110-120 volt, 60, 40, and 75 watt size.

There is a little village some seven miles from here called Er Shr Pu. In English, that means twenty li village. The Hofei mission council has given me that village to look after and to try to start a church there. I am to go out each week, taking others with me and distribute seeds and medicines to create interest. We have contact with one family already who are interested in becoming Christians. We will start a Bible class and, if it grows, will establish a church. This is my first real job, and I am going to try to do it well. You will be hearing more about this project as the months go by.

The carpenter is beginning to make screens for our house. It is none to early since we have already seen several flies. Our little electric motor is a dandy. It runs over four hours on one gallon of gasoline. That makes our light bill around $10 a month; but it is worth all of that to have bright light.

New Year's festivities have passed. Over two hundred people came to call on us, and we had to guess at about half of what they were saying. The kids are out flying kites these windy days. I counted fifty of them playing just outside our compound. Where else in the world could you stand in one spot and see fifty kids of ages between two and thirteen? China has gobs of kids. No more news. Write us regularly as you have been doing. Love, Glyn and Jean."

• Adsit, Glyn and Jean, Minister and Missionaries, Hofei, Anhwei, China, Letter to Dr. E.K. Higdon, March 1, 1948.

"Dear E.K., your letter of February 9 concerning language study for newly arrived missionaries to China seems urgent, so I will try to answer it today.

As I previously stated, we have not found too much use for the sound scriber after our arrival in China. The main reason is that we are not connected with a school that will supply us records, such as, Yale or the language school of Peking. Mr. Marx wrote the Peking school, and I think they answered in the negative concerning their sending us records. I have not been able to get Yale to answer satisfactorily about sending us records from their office. Their last letter to me suggested that since we would not be on hand to hear the lessons explained before we listened to the records, they would be of no use to us.

We have been a little disappointed in that we feel that the language study provisions of our mission on the field have not been adequate. I asked Marx and McCallum to let us go to Peking immediately upon our arrival in Shanghai, but they said the policy was that if a person had had a year in the United States, they should not go to Peking for another year. I now feel this was a mistake and that we should have gone for at least six months. I know that about 150 of our friends from other boards that studied with us at Cornell and Yale did go to Peking immediately upon their arrival in China or shortly thereafter.

I approached Mr. Marx about the language problem, and he tried to get us a teacher but did not succeed while we were in Nanking and Chuhsien. That meant that we were three months without language. Adding this to the three months we were in the States without study, and it adds up to six months without it, which is too long to be off language study, at least Chinese characters. Upon our appointment to and arrival at Hofei, we immediately began asking what we were to do about language study. Oswald Goulter and Miss Wilkinson helped us with our problem, and they found a teacher who consented to give us one half day instruction. We were not too well satisfied with him because he did not speak Mandarin and his English was not sufficient to help us in explanation of words we did not know. We finally found a Mr. Tan who is an excellent teacher. We like him and are progressing under his teaching. We did not have a textbook to follow; therefore, we borrowed the China Inland Mission's "Primer." This book gives us new vocabulary and characters. It will last us for six or nine months. After that is learned thoroughly, I don't know what we will do. I plan to write Marx or Walter Haskell and ask them to contact the CIM and ask them to send us some more materials.

If we had gone to Peking, I feel that they would have been more willing to cooperate with us by mail. As it is, one has to have had at least two years under their system before they feel it will do any good for them to advise through the mails.

We have not taken an examination to see if our language is good or bad. No one seemed to want to give us one, and, therefore, we didn't take any. I can tell you how we are progressing however. We can say anything we have the words to say. Our greatest lack is vocabulary, and this will build up as the years go by.

We received your New Year's letter with all the good news about marriages and family reunions. Won't be long now before you and Pete will be Grandpa and Grandma. Jean continues in good health, and we are getting excited to know whether it is a boy or girl or just an "it." Your friends, Glyn and Jean Adsit."

- Adsit, Glyn B., Minister and Missionary, Hofei, Anhwei, China, article entitled, "Hofei Christian Hospital—Mission of Mercy," submitted to George Walker Buckner, Jr., Editor, *World Call*, International Magazine of Disciples of Christ, March 1, 1948.

- Adsit, Glyn and Jean, Ministers and Missionaries, Hofei, Anhwei, China, Letter to Central Christian Church, Enid, Oklahoma, and Lincoln Terrace Christian Church, Oklahoma City, Oklahoma, March 4, 1948.

"Greetings from China. How happy we are that we can say that these past six months have been the most exciting six months of our lives. Yes, we have been in China for one half a year. Much has happened to make us dreary and sad, but more has happened to make us cheery and glad.

We never cease to thank God that we are Christians and Americans. Being a Christian in China makes all the difference in the world. Morals here are very low and are crumbling even lower as the cancerous civil war eats the strength of the people away. Those who are Christians in Hofei need your prayers that they might remain true to that which they know is right. They are as a light set on a hill. They are the salt of this earth. Being Americans has made us see what a fortunate country we have at home. Believe me. All this Eastern world is looking to America to somehow lead them out of their chaotic troubles. They do not want to turn to Russia and Communism, but they, in many cases, are forced to in order to survive. The poorest person in your church would be well off right here in Hofei.

Fifty feet from our front gate is a family of six living in a grass lean-to hut. They migrated from the north to Hofei and have been living here for over a year. Their floor is the earth. They have no chairs, no table, no light at night, and no place to wash bodies or clothing. The men of the family try to find enough work to earn food. I noticed one of the little children sitting in the sunshine the other day, picking lice out of his clothing. I am going to go over there one of these days with my DDT gun and give them a few good squirts if they will let me.

The time of our baby's arrival is drawing near. We are getting anxious and excited. We have tentatively settled on the names: Timothy Lee for a boy, and Sharon Ann for a girl. Jean says she has enough baby clothes for it up until the age of one year. So please don't send any baby clothes for one under one year. Some of you have asked about things to send to help us and the Chinese. We are not in desperate need of anything just now. Jean could use some baby powder and Mexanna heat powders. Also, she has mentioned canned baby foods. As for what the Chinese need, the need covers everything, and the list could be endless. My suggestions are that if you wish to send things, the following are acceptable: winter clothing for next winter, (such as) used sweaters, boys' and girls' gloves, and wool clothing of any kind that is still useable. Have these cleaned and packed in boxes of around twenty or thirty pounds. Put a few moth balls in for safety. Send these to us at Hofei. Mark as follows: 'Used Clothing, for Relief Distribution.' Summer clothing: Low quarter tennis shoes, light duck materials, blouses and shirts, swimming suits (we have a pool on hospital compound, and several of the hospital employees can go swimming if they have suits), dresses, pants. Baby clothes: we can distribute any amount of baby garments, especially little undershirts and sleeping gowns. Mark same as wool clothing. Pack in cardboard boxes, wrap and tie securely. Notify us by airmail of your shipment and contents.

The church in Hofei has a revival series of a week's duration. I was asked to preach on the subject 'the relevance of the Bible for today.' I called the sermon. 'The Bible has a Message for Today.' As my Chinese is not yet sufficient enough to allow me to preach, I used an interpreter.

As you no doubt know, China celebrates two New Year's Days. The one they like the best is their old, traditional one. It is much different than our observance of the day. To begin with, they make elaborate preparations. The wife prepares cookies and goodies to feed the neighbors when they come calling. Everyone calls on everyone else, so they must have a great amount of candies and cookies on hand. The whole celebration covers approximately two weeks. The shops all over town are closed for this length of time. We could not buy even a dozen eggs during the New Year's period. On New Year's Day, people begin early in the morning to call on their friends and neighbors. We are newcomers to Hofei, but we had around two hundred visitors within three days. We served refreshments and tea to all of these. Old-timers like the Goulters report that about six hundred callers came to their home. Their only purpose in coming is to wish you a happy new year and to renew old friendships. They stay about five minutes and then go on to the next home. The men who were working on our house repairs took off for the two weeks. We had to send a note requesting them to return to work after two weeks. It is a time of resting, eating, and gambling. Having the people come to our home served two purposes. It gave us an opportunity to show off our newly repaired house and to pass the New Year in good Chinese fashion.

We have been told that when our baby arrives, we are to send boiled, red-colored eggs to all our friends. They, in turn, send some present to the baby. That will mean that we must boil several dozen eggs.

The garden tools and seeds we brought are being used almost every day. I have several blisters and calluses on my hands to prove that I am a working man. Our compound is a large one and affords an opportunity for a large vegetable garden. I love to work in the garden and am planning and planting everything that I can. I have three hot boxes of tomatoes and lettuce growing in the kitchen. These will be transplanted in about three weeks. We are planting trees all over the yard.

Our church in Hofei is an active one. We have several inquirers that will be baptized this Easter. Several Chinese Christians are enthusiastic and are going out to the neighboring villages to preach and teach. My work consists mainly of teaching so far. I am working in our farmers school at the present time. In this school, we have forty young boys who have had no previous formal training. We are trying to train them to be better farmers, and our main purpose is to influence them to be Christians. My personal hope is to cultivate several of them for leadership among our rural churches. This is a long-time project, but a start must be made now. This seems to me to be the greatest need of our brotherhood out here. We have no preachers to fill our little parishes. We need thirty preachers at the present time.

On Sundays, we visit surrounding villages where we have either schools or churches or both. The mission has decided to give the responsibility of one village. It is Ershrpu. That means 'twenty-mile village.' We have a good contact in this place. A family (by the name of Hsu) is well educated and is eager to hear more about Jesus and His way of life. We hope to first start a small Sunday school and later to develop it into a church.

I know that all of you are interested in our political situation. Strange as it might seem, you probably know more about what is happening in China than we do. I do know that something must happen in the near future to change the present situation. There are no Communists near Hofei. We are hearing reports of bandit activity almost every day. But this has always existed in China. It seems that the Kuomingdang is growing a little weaker day by day. President Chiang Kai Shek seems to lack the power to force a cleaning up of his party. There is much corruption, and the people do not trust or respect their government. Inflation is out of hand. Money is now 150,000 to 1. It was 40,000 to 1 when we arrived in China. That means it has grown up approximately 400 percent.

We continue to be in the best of health. Our well water is good. We have a cistern that furnishes water for washings. The well water is too hard to use in washing clothes. Jean says training the cook is the hardest job she has ever had. She laughingly relates that he at last has learned to boil water with scorching it.

We wish we had a million missionaries. We could use them, but if we had a million missionaries, we would need a million churches to support them. That would mean more work for someone. That is just what we all must do. Work, work for the night is coming. Your friends in China, the Adsits."

"China: You Shall Never Yield," *Time Magazine*, Copyright Time, Inc. 1948, reprinted with permission in *Front Rank*, A magazine of Christian Living for Adults and Older Young People, Volume 58, No. 10, Christian Board of Publications, Saint Louis, Mo., March 6, 1948, pp. 6-7, 10-11.

- Adsit, Glyn and Jean, Ministers and Missionaries, Hofei, Anhwei, China, Letter to Mother, Pat, Duane, Hurshel, and Bessie and all the rest, March 22, 1948.

"Dear Mother, Pat and Duane, Hursh, and Bessie and all the rest, it was sure good to get your letters, Duane and Hurshel. Don't let that be the last one to come from your households. You will be satisfied with my one letter to all of you I hope. I know you would if you knew how much postage is from this end and how our time is crowded.

First off, about the additions to our family. We have an old mother cat who will have kittens before long. I'll be a pickled ninny if she doesn't have a dozen. Also, another missionary is coming to live with us the end of this month, a Miss Teagarden.

The past fifteen days have been rainy and cloudy. We only saw the sun once during those two weeks. I did not realize how much happiness the sun gives until we had to do without it for so long. We are afraid that some of our garden rotted in the ground because of too much moisture. It really rains here. Our windows are not too weather-proof, and the water comes in the cracks if the rain is on a slant and wind driven. We got up quite a few times during the nights to see if we were floating in our rooms. We had to mop up water and stuff cloth and paper in the windows.

You should see the cute room we have fixed for the coming event. Jean has baby pictures pasted on the walls. I made a small box case for the baby books and toys we have. It is usable at least. I also made a screen to put between our room and the baby's room. It is painted with blue poster paint. Boy, I never dreamed that I could do so many things with my hands. But being a missionary draws out almost any ability that one has. It sure is teaching me one thing: I listen and don't talk much. That always my great weakness, you know, talking too much. Well, I think I will be different from now on.

I spent an hour today chopping dandelions. They grow like mad out here in our yard and in our garden. I planted six more evergreen trees in the front yard. We wish you could see our yard. It is beginning to look like someone lived here at last. We have flowers planted along our walks, which are made of crushed rock and bricks.

Jean continues to be in perfect condition, so says Dr. Corpron. Yes, Mother, he is a good doctor. He knows what he is doing and is examining Jean each two weeks. She is rather heavy now, weight 164, but she is big in the stomach. She has cut down her eating somewhat. Pat, Jean read your advice and says she will do everything she can to keep on nursing that baby.

Mother, stick a box of pepper in your next box to us please. We are clear out. You might (also) put in some more toothpaste. Your boxes have not arrived yet, but we have been receiving no mail these past two weeks because of rain and unusable roads. The trucks just do not run when it rains. We expect to be hearing about the boxes in a week or so however.

Radio reception has been very good the past few days. We have no trouble getting America. We particularly like to hear the news programs.

Almost every woman of child bearing age is going to have a baby pretty soon, it looks like. The women have several children in China, about eight or nine, but many of these die before they grow up. Our Chinese teacher, Mr. Tan, has had four children—that is, his wife has—and only two are alive. She is expecting about the same time as Jean.

When it rains, it soaks the mud walls of which the house are made. A woman and her son, a baby, were killed

Sunday morning (when) the walls caved in and the heavy, wooden beams above fell down on the bed. It smothered and crushed them. They were members of our church and had the funeral from the church. They left a father and five other children.

What does kerosene cost in America? It costs $2 a gallon here. Our wood and coal stove is disabled and out for repairs, and we are using a kerosene burning stove in its place. We burn $1 worth of kerosene a day. I think the baby should arrive in about two or three weeks. Jean is tired of waiting already. It is too healthy and kicks the devil out of her, she says.

Yesterday was Palm Sunday. Our church was packed with adults and kids. The children, about two hundred in number, marched in waving willow branches and singing Hosanna to the Lord. Quite impressive! I suppose you were excited when Jean mentioned my recent small illness. I was not very sick, just a bug that almost everyone gets out here. I wondered why you had put $1 worth of stamps on that envelope.

The carpenters are just about finished with putting up our screens. They are real good ones and will keep mosquitoes out this summer. Our foreign houses will be the only ones with screens in all of Hofei, probably. This month will be our seventh month in China. Time sure is flying, and before you know it, we will be walking in your front doors with a child or three, saying, 'Hello, you bums.'

The scenery is beautiful from our west windows. In the far distance, about ten miles, is a lone mountain that gradually curves downward. The sun sets just to the right of it and makes the most beautiful scenes around 6:30 p.m. We can also see a mountain south of us. Our river is rising now, and Dr. Corpron is getting his boat in shape in case we have to use it to leave Hofei. He proceeds on the philosophy that one had better be safe than sorry.

I am having a little trouble with a tooth filling. I might have to pull the tooth unless I can get to Nanking or

Shanghai this summer. It is a jaw molar on the lower left side. We took our smallpox vaccinations this week. Mine is itching now, and I think this one might be a take. I have not had a take since I was about seven years old.

We have been playing deck tennis, and we are now going to prepare the tennis court. Several people in Hofei know how to play tennis, and as you know, that makes me happy, for that is the one sport in which I excelled. I am having lots of fun teaching my farm boys. They like to study English but have a hard time making the letters *l*, *r*, *v*, and *n*. I must speak very distinctly so that they will imitate just right.

Exchange [rate] has gone up again. We now get 200,000 for $1 US. What a life. Eggs here are 30 cents a dozen. Fish is cheap, and also vegetables are cheap. Expensive things are canned goods and oils of any kind. We pay $1 for a package of breakfast food that you could buy for 25 cents.

Jean has washed all the baby things and has them ready for use. She has about four dozen diapers and scads of everything else also. People are always sending the mission packages here in Hofei. Whenever there is a real cute baby dress or hat or something, they give Jean a chance at it before they distribute the things to the Chinese. Also, her sisters are giving her baby things too. Where we will need clothes is when the baby is around eighteen months.

We will have to wait until later in the spring to baptize our converts. The weather is a little chilly since Easter is coming so early.

This is the way we are planning on taking care of Jean when the baby comes. The Corprons have an extra room. When Jean delivers, she and baby will be taken to the Corprons' room. They do not want to leave her in the hospital because Chinese all around will make her uncomfortable. Our nurse, Grace Young, will attend to her, and I will sleep at our home and stay and eat over there during the days Jean is in bed. That way she will have the proper nursing and feeding. Mrs. Corpron is a trained dietician.

I still love to read. Between all of us missionaries, we have a great number of magazines sent out. We exchange them and get to read all we want to. A friend has sent us the *National Geographic, Reader's Digest,* and *Omnibook, Good Housekeeping,* and one or two others.

I still have many other letters to write, so you all forgive me now for signing off for this time. Love, Glyn and Jean."

- Adsit, Glyn and Jean, Ministers and Missionaries, Hofei, Anhwei, China, Letter to Family, March 29, 1948.

"Dear family, your letters are coming to us regularly. We enjoy them so much. Do not be tempted to slacken up on your writing to us, even if our letters to you are sporadic. Easter was a beautiful day in Hofei. We had sunshine all day long. The church was crowded for the morning service. The choir sang the alleluias wonderfully, and I could almost imagine ourselves at home, in one of our churches. We listened Sunday evening at 10:00 p.m. to the sunrise service in the Hollywood Bowl in California. The music reception was clear and very strong.

I have been busy at teaching in our school, as per usual. We took our first language test the other day. It was a three month's test. We did all right and are now studying the next three month's lessons. Jean continues in good health right down to the wire. This is her last month, and she is beginning to pooch out a little lower down in the stomach. She does not get out too much now. She cannot sit still for a long stretch and, for that reason, does not like to go to church. She cooked the evening meal for the foreigners' Sunday dinner last night and seemed to enjoy doing it. Our neighbor across the road had her eighth baby last week. It was a girl. I asked Mr. Wang what they had named it. He said they hadn't even thought about giving it a name yet. He said, "You have a lot of interest in your first baby, but you will lose that by the eighth one." I hastened to explain that we did not intend to have that many. He did not even take his wife to the hospital but delivered the baby himself. He is one of our better-educated men. [I] don't know why he is queer on that point.

It is getting warmer day by day. It rains frequently, and that makes all the ponds fill up. The water level is very high around Hofei. You only have to dig three feet to strike water now. It drops to about fifteen feet later on in the year.

Our garden is proving educational. Our peas are up and look like they will survive. The beans are almost all eaten up by a small white little pest. Our potatoes are not yet up, and the corn is about half and half. Our cheery trees are blooming, and our berry vines, eleven of them, are sprouting leaves. I suppose I mentioned that a family gave us a cat. She is to have her kittens in about three weeks. She eats Chinese food, rice and vegetables, and likes the little fish that resemble a sardine. She looks like she will have a dozen babies. I don't know what the poor thing will do. She only has eight tits.

I have shot several magpies [birds] that are pecking around our garden. I also shot one big, black crow. I tied them up in a tree by the garden, hoping that the other birds will take the hint. Better add another crow to that list. Jean just called me and said there are several crows in the backyard, fussing around that old, dead one you hung up. I went out and shot at him once. I thought I had missed him because he flew about a hundred feet before he fell.

About baby food. We think it is a good idea if you can send a can occasionally. Just put a few in a package at once. Send out more fruits and strained meats because we have plenty of vegetables. You have asked about pricing boxes. My suggestion is to price them as low as you can. Never put value over $5.00 if you can help it. If you send used things, be sure to label them as such. You might label each box of things as "Gift Package, for Missionary Relief."

Money value has gone up again. It is now 250,000 to 1 US dollar. That means I get about CN$40,000,000 a month salary. But we live up all of that each month. So, being a millionaire has no attractions for us.

We sure are enjoying that bed you gave us. Jean says it is the one place she can get and be comfortable. She always sleeps at night. I think it is the best mattress in Hofei.

You know that song, 'Oh, how I hate to get up in the morning'? Well, we have a bunch of soldiers who practice their bugling just outside our compound. They start blowing the bugles at 4:30 a.m. It wakes us up, and we get up and put cotton in our ears and try to go back to sleep. One morning, they started at 3:30 a.m. I thought that a little too early, so I got up, put on my shoes and an overcoat, and went out and asked them [what was] the big idea. They said, the moon was shining so brightly they thought it was already 5:00 o'clock, and besides, they had no timepiece. I begged them to wait until later and let the neighborhood get some sleep. They now blow at 4:30 a.m. Ho, hum.

You would die laughing to see the grown men and young men flying kites. They make kites of all shapes and sizes. The most popular shapes seem to be butterflies and airplanes. There is so little to do in Hofei that even flying kites is sport for men.

I am still digging up dandelions. I dig about fifty every morning. I hope to get them cleared out this year. I will plant morning glory vines tomorrow. I want to let them soak in water all night before planting. Hollyhocks grow everywhere very easily.

We both are in wonderful health, and our spirits are good. Jean still thinks she would rather live in US than in China, however. Write us one of these days. Glyn and Jean."

- Adsit, Glyn and Jean, Ministers and Missionaries, Hofei, Anhwei, China, Letter to Loved Ones, April 4, 1948.

"Dear loved ones, this Sunday is a beautiful, bright, and cheery one. Our grass and garden vegetables grew an inch, I am sure. We have a grass similar to the clover that the

Chinese like to eat. We have been having an awful time keeping them out of the compound. Today, I let some very poor people into the backyard to pick some of the grass. They were thankful because they have little to eat besides just plain rice. I took a picture of them picking the grass, might be able to send it home. One little lad in it is eight years old, but he is about the size of our four-year-olds.

This week has not produced much news of interest. Jean continues to swell. She has a little trouble sleeping sometimes. But her health and spirit is good, so I feel she is okay.

Communists are fighting some forty miles from us, but there is no danger of Hofei falling. Hofei is the state capitol and is well guarded.

I am learning how smart crows are since I am trying to shoot every one that comes within eating distance of our garden. Lettuce is up and can be eaten in about two weeks. Potatoes vines are showing hope they will produce potatoes.

We had a little trouble at church this morning. A couple wanted to be married in the church. They asked our church board, and they said no, not on Sunday since that day was when the church needed the building. But this morning, around 11:30 a.m., the wedding party came anyhow. We had an awful time finishing the service and then persuading them that they could not take over the building unlawfully like they were trying to do. I think we won the argument; at least they left. Might hear from this later on. Our policy is not to allow outsiders who are not even Christians use our property because if we give one person permission, everyone in town will want to use our auditorium.

Jean is almost certain that she will not want to come back to China for a second term. She just simply cannot seem to make the necessary adjustment to the people. She is not to be blamed for this since it happens to many missionaries. In case she cannot change her feeling, it would be foolish for me to ruin our lives insisting upon her coming back with me, whether or not. So, I have told her that if she cannot make a change, we will not come back. I will stay in America and preach or teach in one of our colleges. We intend to go back to college and take more study. I will study at least and Jean work or take care of our family. I would like to suggest for your thinking—and you need not reply at once; in fact, it would be better for you to think a long time before you answer my question—that in case we stay in the States, you sell your business, rent our home there in Topeka, and come to live with us. We need you, and you will be crowding sixty by that time and will need to retire from working all the time. I said we need you. If Jean works, you could take care of the children or even have a little beauty business in our home, health permitting. We feel that of all us kids, we would be the ones for you to expect to live with. Jean and I have talked this out and hope you will give it your serious consideration. I know how you have said that you never wanted to live with any of your children, etc. But now that you are older and smarter and we are older and wiser, perhaps you will consider our request. We don't have our eyes out for your insurance either. Ha ha. This would give you an opportunity to see some new country and to have time to write a little if you feel so inclined. We will probably go to Phillips University, so you will get to see our old alma mater.

Old Pussy had five kittens. She hid them under the floor in our attic, but I found them. She makes a good mother. How she likes to eat fish.

Jean decided to try cutting my hair short. She started with the clippers, and before she finished, I had no hair at all. It is about one inch long now. I look like an idiot, I guess.

The magazine came. Did you have anything else with it? We are celebrating Jean's birthday tonight. She will receive presents from all the foreign devils, and I made her a rolling pin. I whittled it out of a block of wood with wood chisels and a knife.

We are in good health and in no danger. Write us soon. Glyn and Jean."

- Higdon, E.K., Executive Secretary, Department of Oriental Missions, The United Christian Missionary Society, Indianapolis, Indiana, Letter to Mr. and Mrs. Glyn B. Adsit, April 5, 1948.

"Dear Jean and Glyn, your letter of March 1 got here in just a week. The copy of your communication of March 4 addressed to the Central Christian Church and the Lincoln Terrace Christian Church was delivered on March 15. It is good to have such fast airmail service.

What you write about the language situation interests and concerns me. I am sending a letter to Dr. Kok to find out whether or not the Institute at Yale or the school in Peiping can do better by you than they have been doing if we bring a little pressure to bear at this end. We are sending twenty students to Yale for the summer term in the institute, seventeen for French and three for Chinese, and that should entitle us to the best possible service on the field.

Harriet and Hubert report that their Sound scriber has been repaired and they are making good use of it.

Don't be too hard on the men who might have given you a language examination and sent you to Peiping. Remember that they are all carrying tremendous loads. Furthermore, the arrival of new missionaries often adds to that load. This I know from personal experience, experience both as a new missionary who gave the older men and women a lot of headaches, and experience as a seasoned missionary who sometimes had headaches because of the attitudes of the new ones. When I think of some of the things I said and did during my first term, I wonder why my colleagues, both Filipinos and Americans, let me remain on the field. I suppose every missionary has that experience and gradually realizes that he needs to learn humbly from those who are older than he both in years and in service. If he doesn't, he grows increasingly unhappy, unpopular, and dispensable.

I have sent some extracts from your letter of March 4 to *Christian World Facts*, the annual magazine published by the Foreign Missions Conference. Thank you for sending me the copy so promptly. I note that you again write about supplies. This is in response to inquiries which you cannot ignore. It was to deal with such situations as this and the requests that come to us here at headquarters for special material projects that the project committee was set up in China upon my suggestion, and a similar committee in the Philippines. If all missionaries would submit their lists to the project committee together with the names and addresses of organizations or individuals, the whole matter could be much more efficiently organized. Do you agree?

You are often in my mind these days. I am thinking and praying for both of you, but especially Jean, as the great birthday approaches. We shall all be on alert for the cable announcing "its" arrival and name, not only because we are eager for the news, but also because we shall forward it by telegram to your relatives. Yours, E.K."

- Adsit, Jean, Minister and Missionary, Hofei, China, to Mother (Reecie Adsit), April 10, 1948.

"Dearest Mom, I continue to feel fine, darn it. I'd like to have this baby and see what it's going to look like. We got the little sweater, cup, and booties set as well as the colored slides. They had no duty on them; in fact, had not even been examined. We also got the magazine. The article in it was very interesting and enlightening. I hadn't thought of what might happen if one put a child on its stomach while so small before. If you want to share all this letter with the kids, you can; otherwise, it's just to you.

In Glyn's last letter, he mentioned of my not being able to adjust to China and the people here. I've been in quite an emotional upheaval ever since I arrived here in China. I had kept this to myself, hoping to be able to adjust my feeling toward the people, for Glyn's sake, but like all things usually do, I couldn't curtain my feelings any longer. The whole problem was affecting Glyn and my life together. We had one of our heart-to-heart talks, as often we do when something troubles us, and I told him I had been most miserable since I'd been here in China. I hardly know how to explain my feeling. I was indeed sincere when I decided with Glyn to come to China. I hope you do not feel I've let him down, for he doesn't, thank God.

We will do what we can in our time here, and if within the term here, I change my feeling of complete unhappiness, we will come back, but I imagine we'll stay in America and do some kind of church or teaching work there. Glyn hasn't decided whether he would rather have a church or teach Bible in one of the colleges of our church. He has been doing quite a lot of teaching here and has been enjoying it a lot. These things being considered and talked about, we have made some other plans that include you. We want you to live with us if you will only forget and forgive all that's ever gone on before in some of the things that have been said. You see, Mom, we've grown up a little more perhaps since we've been here. Life has a different meaning to us now. Somehow, material things are even less important, and life and loved ones and happiness with them is, after all, the key to everything that's worthwhile in the world. So you will be doing us a service and pleasure by thinking over seriously the idea of sharing our home with us. Don't answer right away. Think about it, and answer when you feel like it.

Glyn's health is much better. Fact is, he's gaining weight now. I was blind, but probably his whole trouble was based on my words and actions. I was taking spite out on him because I was so miserable here in China. Now that we both see that point clear, he is happier and so am I. I've never known anyone more loving and gentle than Glyn has become. He has been more than a lover and a gentleman while I've been carrying the baby. We both have read everything we can on baby's care, for we hope to be good parents. Well, I'm sure you have had enough of all this; sometimes though, we have to pour our hearts out to someone who we know will understand.

I love you, Mom, and may God bless you and keep you. Love, Jean."

- Adsit, Glyn B., Minister and Missionary, Hofei, Anhwei, China, Letter to Home Folks, April 19, 1948.

"Dear home folks, well, no baby yet! Jean says it is bound to come any day now. She feels so heavy. Today, she said she thought it had dropped down a little. Doctor says that is a good sign that delivery is not far off. It is beginning to warm up in earnest these days. It takes me about one and a half hours to water my garden in the late afternoon. Some days, I do not get all the garden and flowers watered. We had a baptism at the church in Hofei yesterday. Fifty-one were baptized, thirty-five men and boys, and sixteen women and girls. It was very impressive and shows that the church continues to grow out here on the far-flung Christian battlefront. Before the year is out, we will baptize about fifty more. It is not easy to have a baptism service in Hofei. It was quite chilly for baptizing, and therefore, we had to order heated water. This was arranged the night before, and the coolies started carrying water to fill up the baptistery long before dawn on Sunday morning. They have to time it just right so that the water will not cool off too quickly. We got up at 6:00 a.m. and had breakfast and were at the church at 7:30 a.m. The service lasted until 9:45 a.m. The pastor had to ask each person individually if they believed in and accepted Christ as their personal Savior. Then Pastor Chyan and our Mr. Goulter baptized them. It was a rather long morning, lasting from 7:30 to 12:30 a.m., including baptism, Sunday school, and church.

In the afternoon, Dr. Corpron sent a note asking me to bring my camera and come take a picture of a woman who had a difficult delivery before her. Upon examination, he found that this woman's baby had broken out of the uterus when about three months old and had lived for seven months in her abdominal cavity. It was a ten months baby. He had to cut through her stomach and remove the baby. It had been dead for five days and was quite a sight to see. Dr. Corpron says that such cases are rare in medical history. I have been watching quite a few operations, and it does not bother me anymore, so I think we got some good pictures. He wants to write up the case and send it to the *American Medical Journal.*

I am spending most of this week taking pictures for a book that a woman in our society in Indianapolis is going to write. It is to be of a typical Chinese family and will try to portray their daily activities such as eating, playing, worshipping, etc. Jean continues in the best of health.

Our old Pussy cat sure pulled a good one on us. I have caught her carrying the babies to other places than where we want her to stay. I always put them back in their box and keep her locked up for a day or two, hoping that she will finally give in and let me be boss. I finally decided to trust her and left the door to the room open, and what did she do but take all five kittens and hide them where I could not find them. It was really a spectacular feat. She carried them over an eight-foot wall, across three small fields, and hid them in a straw stack and in an old building. I heard her fighting with another cat and followed her and discovered where she had hidden the babies. They are now up in my study, smelling the place up.

It keeps us busy running people out of our yard. They like to come in and look around and just mess around. We hate to let them start it because they pick things up and walk off with them. (This is a polite way to say steal things.) It used to be that people threw rocks at missionaries years ago. I reverse the tables and throw rocks at them if they won't get out after I have politely asked them to.

Your box with the little baby set and pictures arrived. Also the box with the hand cream, toothpaste, and light bulbs [came]. Three of the seven bulbs were broken. Jean likes the hand cream very much. You are labeling boxes okay. Just remember not to put too high values on them is all.

Communists have been fighting rather close to us lately, but government troops have been able to handle the situation so far. We are making frequent trips into the countryside, teaching and preaching. I am spending much time in teaching English. It is a splendid way to get a contact, but one must be careful not to let it take all his time.

As I have mentioned before, the summers here in Hofei are unbearably hot and humid. We are going to do our best to get out for a vacation if at all possible. Dr. Corpron advised that we leave with a small baby by the first of July and return September 1. We want to go to Kuling, a mountainous region south of us. It is pleasant there, and one sleeps under blankets at night. We will be forced to live like campers, but that will be no hardship for me since I have loved that type of life along. We do live in houses but have no conveniences at all. You have to cook on a Chinese stove and sleep on a cot.

You should see our new screens. A mosquito can hardly get in the house now. Flies are thick outside, but we have only one or two inside. We also had a clothes closet made for me. The baby took our one chest of drawers, and we needed more room.

We have heard all along about Chinese women having so many children. They do have about eight or ten, but only about one half of them survive childhood. That was one reason they had bound feet. It was suppose to make them walk in such a way as to broaden their pelvic bones, making it easier to bear children.

I am enclosing five negatives in this letter. Please have them enlarged to regular size and ship them back at your convenience. I will try to explain what the pictures are:

Number 5. A typical picture of a door during New Year's Festival. They put gay-colored paper on the door with characters that means happiness, etc.

Number 11. Picture of Lyrel Teagarden and an old Chinese Gentlemen, Mr. Wang. He is around seventy and does some preaching in our rural churches.

Number 16. Picture of the Shaw family at Christian Cemetery, on Easter day, standing before the tomb mound of his father and her husband, who was killed by Japanese for being a good Christian and for standing up to them. He was beaten to death.

Number 19. Picture of primitive communications. Taken on the road to Ershrpu, just outside Hofei. You will notice the man in the foreground pushing the wheel barrow and men on dykes carrying things on a pole. These with poles are farmers bringing their produce to Hofei for market.

Number 17. Picture of Mr. Hu and yours truly. Taken in the cemetery on Easter day. Mr. Hu is one of our promising young men who will eventually develop into a pastor.

Please send me two prints of number 16, three of number 17, three of number 11, and one each of the other two. You might keep the negatives, putting them in your strong box. I have several more negatives that I will send a few at a time. Write soon. Love, Glyn."

- Adsit, Glyn B., Minister and Missionary, Hofei, Anhwei, China, Articles sent to George Walker Buckner, Jr., Editor, *World Call*, International Magazine of the Disciples of Christ entitled, "China's Sorrow," "I Baptize Thee," and "Easter in Hofei," April 25, 1948.

- Adsit, Glyn B., Minister and Missionary, Hofei, China, Letter to Grandma, Uncle and Aunts, May 1, 1948.

"Dear Grandma, uncles, and aunts, what a day April 26 was. All of us foreigners were eating Sunday evening meal together. Jean felt like she had passed a little blood but did not say anything to anyone about it. At 9:30 p.m., she began flowing a little more. We then knew that something was soon to happen. Dr. Corpron advised us to stay at their house that night because of the difficulty of traveling the dark streets, and because of the curfew that prohibits walking on streets after 10:00 p.m. So we took our things and went over for the night. All this was on the night of the twenty-fifth. At about 11:00 p.m., Jean began to have recognizable regular pains. It did not bother her too much until about 4:00 a.m. She did not sleep any, however. Doctor examined her at 7:00 a.m. and said she had begun to dilate but was some time off from delivery. She was grunting pretty hard by that time, but she is not the yelling type. She only let out one pretty good scream at all. I sat by the bed with my watch, keeping time of the regularity of the pains. At 9:00 a.m., they were coming about six minutes apart. Doctor said not to get too anxious, that we would not take her over to the delivery room until the pains came every three minutes apart. So I settled down to wait for nature to take its course. Believe it or not, I never did get excited but once. It was pretty hard to watch Jean when the pain came. She gripped the bed and pulled for all she was worth. At 11:00 a.m., Doctor examined again and said he figured it would arrive around 1:30 p.m. So we ate dinner, and then I began the clocking process again. The pains began to come every three minutes, and the groans were more audible, so we put her on a stretcher and carried her to the operating room. This was at 1:30 p.m.

By the time Dr. Corpron and Dr. Gang were scrubbed up, the baby was ready to deliver. They painted Jean's stomach and womb with some red sterile medicine. Then they shaved her. Dr. decided to give her a whiff of ether every time she bore down. This helped take away the edge from the pain. She bore down about six times, and the baby's head appeared. Boy, I then began to realize that I was soon to be a father. The hair was black. Dr. pulled and stretched Jean as much as he could to help the delivery. He did not want it too fast because of the danger of tearing. Finally, he was able to get his hand under the baby's chin, and then told Jean to bear down real hard on the next pain.

She did, and out Timothy Lee came. We were all standing with bated breath to see whether it was a boy or a girl. As soon as Doctor [Corpron] saw it was a boy, he said, 'Well, you have a big boy.' They gave Jean a good whiff of ether as soon as the head was born, and she went out for about five minutes. The baby was very blue when born, and the cord was wrapped around his neck once. But as soon as his body was born, he began to cry. No whipping needed. He has a deep cry and pretty powerful. As the doctor worked on Jean, the nurse [Grace Young] began to clean up the baby. As soon as the baby began to cry, he began [to turn] deep pink instead of blue. He still gets very red when he cries. We put him on the scales, and he weighed 8 lbs. 3 oz. Pretty big boy. Doctor says Jean had plenty of room for a 10 lb. baby if need be. She did not tear at all. She now says she thinks she could have a dozen if they all came that easy.

As they were tying the cord, I asked the doctor why it was that Chinese babies died from tetanus when their cords were improperly tied. He said it was because of the things they put on the cord to dry it up. He mentioned ashes as one of the things they put on cords. Jean heard the conversation through her half-awakened ears and said to me, 'Why are they going to put ashes on his cord?' I told her, 'We were not going to put ashes on Timothy's cord' and for her not to worry. She also said the following: 'Don't forget to ask the doctor about circumcising the baby. Don't forget to write to Shanghai and register the baby. I really wanted a boy but was afraid to say so because I was afraid it would be a girl. Won't daddy be proud now that he has a grandson?' She doesn't remember saying those things, but as I told her about them, she laughed.

Timothy is on a three-hour feeding schedule. Jean is nursing him, and her breasts are full and overflowing. We have had to use a pump on her once to relieve the pressure. Timothy got too hot and broke out with the heat, but it is clearing up, and his new skin begins to look much better. We are staying at the Corprons' for the ten days and then will go home. Miss [Grace] Young, our foreign nurse, is taking care of Jean and Timothy. I also help by getting up during the night for one of the late feedings. Can't tell who the baby looks like. I think he favors Jean more than he does me. If he resembles anyone, it might be her brother, Ralph. Jean says he looks like me when he cries. He is five days old today and is already spoiled. He has learned that if he cries enough, someone will come and pick him up.

Well, we have another dog. It is a she, and we named her Lassie. I don't know what type she is, just a Chinese wunk, I guess. Our five kittens are almost ready to be weaned. We will give them away very soon now.

We are eating lettuce and radishes every day from the garden. Our corn is twelve inches high. Our peas and beans will soon be ready for eating. I am having a little trouble with the vine crops: cucumbers, pumpkins, squash, and watermelons. There is a little, orange-colored bug that eats the leaves. I sprayed them yesterday, but it rained last night and washed off all the poison. I will have to spray again as soon as it dries up.

I haven't done a thing this week but run back and forth between Corprons' and our house, getting things for the baby and Jean. Oh yes, his eyes are gray-blue, but they might change color. He has a lot of hair. His hands and feet are huge, and his fingers are long and slender. He had long fingernails when born and scratched his face. He already sucks his fingers when he gets hungry.

The box with light bulbs and toiletries came yesterday. It got by customs free. They are going to catch you sending things without marking them down one of these days. But as long as you can get away with it, okay. My potatoes are just about ready for eating. Boy are those new potatoes and peas going to taste good.

We have killed about four snakes in our yard. One of them was a four-footer and poisonous. You see, we live in the country, and snakes are quite abundant. Write us soon.

Old Father Adsit, Glyn. P.S. Please send me one of each and keep negatives in your box. Attached baby announcement which reads: 'Now I intended to surprise, the parents I selected; But someone went and put 'em wise—I found I was expected! But say! I fooled 'em anyway, in spite of all their guesses—They didn't know for sure 'til now if I'd wear pants or dresses! P.S. In case you're interested—I wear pants; My name is Timothy Lee; I arrived April 26, 1948 at 2:00 p.m.; I weigh 8 lbs. 3 oz., and my parents are Glyn and Jean Adsit. I have black hair. Jean and I are doing fine. Jean was in labor from 11:00 p.m. April 25 to 2:00 p.m. April 26th, and the doctor did a good job.'"

Adsit, Jean and Glyn and newborn son, Timothy Lee, Minister and Missionary, Hofei, China, Letter to Grandma, uncles, aunts, and cousins, May 1, 1948.

"Dearest Grandma, uncles, aunts, and cousins, well, here I am. I am a good-looking 8lb 3 oz. boy, and maybe you think my mother and daddy aren't proud of me. Oh boy! What a setup! I can really get all of everything I want. My daddy comes and talks to me when I am awake, and if I get mad because I can't get my fingers, he helps me get my hands free from my long sleeves. You know, I've got nice, black hair like daddy's and blue eyes and big feet and hands like Uncle Dewy. I will probably be so big I can whip cousin Mike in a fistfight when I get to America. Daddy has already promised to teach me to swim and fish and all those kind of things we boys like to do.

I don't think I want to be president of the United States though. I think I'll be something that will cause me less worry. My mother is doing fine. Although she started having pains Sunday night at 11:00 o'clock, and didn't have me until Monday at 2:00 p.m., she didn't have a hard labor and no tearing. She'll stay in bed here at the doctor's house for ten days. The foreign nurse takes care of her, and the doctor is right here to check on our progress every day. After ten days, we'll go home if all is well, and Daddy will help Mother with me. He already helps get Mother ready at bedtime and gives me my last feeding before night and sleeptime for them. Of course, I sleep all the time. Just eat, sleep, wiggle, and stretch, and, of course, wet my pants. That is all I do right now, but just wait. The fact is, I don't cry; only when my pants are dirty and about ten minutes before time to feed me. I do this so I'll be sure to be fed on time. I am like my Daddy; we men like our food to be good and on time. My mother feeds me. She has good milk and lots of it, but I don't let any go to waste. No siree! The twenty-ninth, I got your telegram and was mighty surprised to hear from you all, and so quick too! Daddy has taken pictures of me. Of course, he'll take some more and send them to you all. The Chinese send red eggs when they have a new baby. Daddy bought three hundred some odd, and the cook colored these red, and Daddy took a picture of me and my big basket of red eggs. The thirtieth of April, Daddy got the second package of light bulbs, and none were broken. Mom is going to save the little razor for me to shave with when I start growing a beard. I better close now and take a nap or mother will be cross with me for not sleeping. Love, Timmy Lee. [Jean actually wrote the letter of course.] P.S. Dear Mom, A week from tomorrow is Mother's Day. Congratulations on having such a fine family and especially such a good Timothy Lee. May you live to be a hundred, and hope your health is good. Love from your sons, Glyn and Timothy."

- Adsit, Glyn B., Minister and Missionary, Hofei, Anhwei, China, Letter and Pictures to Mabel Niedermeyer, Missionary Education, The United Christian Missionary Society. Indianapolis, Indiana, May 7, 1948.

"Dear Mrs. Mabel Niedermeyer, you will please excuse me for not knowing your married name. The reason for this letter is to start sending you the negatives for the pictures that I have taken in relation to the children's book you are to write.

When you first contacted Lyrel and Winona about taking these pictures, they immediately began thinking about the project. Lyrel made out a tentative list of things to be photographed. She then had to go to Nantungchow and could not finish the taking of the pictures. When she arrived in Nanking, she asked me if I would tackle the job. I told her then that I was not an experienced photographer but would do the best I could. The idea of the type of pictures is Lyrel's. I selected the family to act as the main characters.

I decided to use two cameras in taking the pictures. My idea was that if one failed to produce a good print, perhaps the other would do better. This helped some but added to the expense a little.

Lyrel's idea was as follows. The family had gone West during the war and had returned to Hofei. She wanted to show them viewing their ruined home, nothing left but dirt walls crumbled. Then they gradually worked themselves into the life of Hofei again.

Story of pictures: [The reader will note that the author is in possession of each original picture as Glyn took it and that I have included only a few of them in the photo section of this book; however, all the captions have been included here as they appeared in the original letter, which continues below.]

[Glyn continues.] You will notice that small negatives have a number on them.

Picture no. 35: This is the Jang family. They are standing in front of a typical Chinese building. The roof corners slope heavenward. (These first few pictures are of the members of the Jang family.)

3: This is Jang-Shu-Ling, the fifteen-year-old son of the Jang family. He is a very happy boy, as his smile will show. He is happy because it is spring and the flowers are in bloom.

4: Shu-Ling standing tin front of the Communications building in Hofei.

31: Grandfather Jang, who is nearing seventy and who is proud of his white, flowing beard. Grandfather preaches in the hospital clinic each morning.

25: Mei Li, which means 'beautiful package.' She wants to show you her two beautiful teeth and the bow in her hair. She is the baby in the Jang family.

33: Jang family with city wall in background.

24: Mother; and Jye Jye, the older sister; and Mei Ling, the baby sister, standing in front of rose bush.

10: Auntie, sitting in chair working on a pair of shoes. Notice the bound feet, which are fast passing out of existence in China. In rural China, people make almost all their shoes. They are made from cloth resembling a poor grade of canvas.

116: Large negative of Jang-Shu-Ling, standing in doorway of Chinese home. The badge on his chest indicates that he is a student in our farm boys' school. You will notice how the Chinese houses are formed by several courtyards. This picture shows three of them.

End of introduction of members of family.

Picture no. 7: Jang family looking at ruins of home after returning from West China. The Chinese houses are built of mud and straw. They have wood beams, and some of them have tile roofs. The Jangs are very sad looking because they know that all their belongings are lost and they will find life very bitter for a few years.

20: Mother receiving two cans of milk from the hospital dispensary. The milk was very much needed because the baby was undernourished during the war. The hospital gives out hundreds of cans of milk each month.

32: Mother preparing meal in their Chinese kitchen. The stove burns straw and wood. It takes two people to successfully run a Chinese stove, one person to crouch behind it, feeding in the fuel, and the other to cook the food in the deep iron *gou*. They do not have facilities for baking; therefore, all their foods are boiled or fried. All their food is served piping hot. They do not drink water at meal time.

5: Jang family, who are Christians, standing as they say the blessing before eating. Grandfather is saying the blessing. They are very thankful that they have such good food. Many of their neighbors are not so fortunate as they are.

9: Jang family eating evening meal. They all eat with chopsticks. Jye-Jye; and Di-di, older sister; and younger brother are too small to sit in chairs and have to eat while on their knees. It is perfectly polite to pick up your bowl and hold it just under your chin. The food is in bowls that are placed in the middle of the table. There are no individual plates. Each person just helps himself from the common bowl as he needs food. An average meal consists of a dish of green vegetables, a dish of fat pork, a dish of some kind of bean sprout, usually a dish of fish, and then some soup to top off the meal. They, of course, eat three or four bowls of rice with each meal. After eating, they retire to the parlor and drink tea.

Small negative, no number, of family standing in front of their new home that is under construction. Up until now, the Jang's have been living in a rented house. Now they are having a new one built. Notice the smiles, in contrast to the gloomy faces at the time when they were looking at ruins of their old home.

17: Father working on his accounts. He is using the age-old system of reckoning with the abacus. He does this very quickly, almost as fast as we add with our adding machines. He is trying to figure out if he has enough money to finish the building of their new house.

8: Jangs—Mother, Father, and Di-di—saying goodbye to Shu-Ling as he goes to school. They are standing in front of their newly completed house.

18: This is Shu-Ling's message to boys and girls in America: "Americans and Chinese are good friends." This is written on blackboard in his school.

11: Mother, who is teaching in nursery school sponsored by the church. The children are playing a rhythm game. Di-di is standing in front of mother, and Jye-Jye is the one in the checkered dress.

12: Children of nursery in playground. Mrs. Jang is leading them in a game.

14: Shu-Ling lives in a country village. He loves to drive the old pig to market. He does this by tying a rope to its hind leg and switching it with a small stick. The pig always squeals real loud.

26: Father and Shu-Ling at well. Father is drawing water by using a grass rope and wooden bucket. A girl is washing clothes at the well.

27: Shu-Ling likes to go with his father to the well. His father always lets him carry the water bucket as they go home. Father carries the water in two large buckets attached to a pole, which is carried on the shoulder.

28: Mr. Jang is manager of the farm center and has to work. Shu-Ling helps Father by watering vegetable plants in hot weather.

30: Shu-Ling and his classmates. He is learning how to be a better farmer in one of the classes taught at the farm center. This is a church project.

29: Shu-Ling playing volleyball with his school chums.

23: Mother taking Mei-Li to the hospital (Christian) clinic to be weighed. Jye-Jye thinks this is great fun as she watches the nurses weigh the baby.

Large negative showing Shu-Ling playing horseshoes with Wu-Soo-Hun, his classmate.

Large negative showing mother and children at nursery school.

Negative showing mother and baby at well-baby clinic. Mei-Li is being weighed. She is laughing and having a wonderful time. If she is underweight, the clinic will give her some milk.

Negative showing mother receiving milk for baby.

Negative showing Shu-Ling working with classmates in farm center.

Negative of boys sitting on small stools. Teacher with hand upraised. This is Shu-Ling's class in the farm center school. He is sitting in the second row in the center.

20: Shu-Ling goes to his uncle's farm and watches his cousin Wan-Ren prepare the rice paddy for planting. This is a water buffalo. Water is let stand on the land for a few days to soften it up. Then the buffalo pulls a plow through the mud to turn over the soil. Little rice plants will be set out in the plot a little later.

I have asked about names for the Chinese children. Some suggestions are: for boys, Tsung-Ren and Gwo-Gwang. For girls, Feng-Yin, and Shu-Yin. These are in addition to the ones used to accompany the pictures.

There are still a few more pictures that I want to take, which I will send you just as soon as the weather is a little more conductive to picture taking. We have had a constant ten days of rainy, cloudy weather. But I hope these negatives reach you by June 1, which was the deadline you set. If these pictures are not suitable, please tell me and I will try to take some more for you.

As payment for the film used, I will wait until I have finished taking the pictures and then send you the amount of film used. Since most of these pictures are very typical and some of them quite clear, I will appreciate it very much if you will have a negative made for me and send it to Hofei. My idea is that perhaps you can have a negative made of each one I am sending you and maybe even make them into a small set of slides. Please let me know if this is possible. The picture of the boy and water buffalo is one I took some time ago. It seemed appropriate; therefore, I put it in. Will you please return that negative when you are through with it?

- Adsit, Glyn, Minister and Missionary, Hofei, China, Letter to Robins, May 10, 1948.

"Dear Robins, I am offering no apologies for delaying this letter for two weeks. I have been so busy. Well, as you have all no doubt heard, it is a boy. We have named him Timothy Lee. Timothy arrived April 26 at 2:00 p.m. He was a good-sized baby, weighing 8 lbs. 3 oz. Jean had no trouble with the birth and is up now and nursing the hungry, crying infant. Boy, this becoming a father sure is tiresome. I have already lost lots of sleep. Also, I have become an expert at watching Jean change Timmy's diapers.

We China Robins received the two Robins within ten days of each other. This one is rather old, and most of the news was already known, but we still think it a good idea to keep two going.

I have been having lots of fun and have gained some experience in taking pictures for a book, or rather, a booklet, Mrs. Mabel Niedermeyer (married name unknown) is writing on China. I spent ten whole days taking pictures. I have found that our Argus C-3 takes good pictures.

As I have mentioned before, the pressing need in our rural church program is more trained leaders. We have started a school for farm boys of ages ranging from fourteen to eighteen. We teach them twelve courses, a little of everything under the sun. We have found that if we send our prospects to Nanking Theological Seminary for training, they do not want to return to the country areas to work. They get big city ideas and are not willing to rough it anymore. Therefore, we are keeping most of them in our schools or are sending them to special Bible courses, etc.

We are enjoying fresh lettuce and radishes from our garden. (We) also ate a mess of spinach and peas from the garden. Corprons and Goulters have strawberries. There are three refrigerators in Hofei station; therefore, we have plenty of ice-cream. Ho hum, the life of a missionary!

We are still tussling with the army buglers. They start blowing at 5:30 a.m. If they could only blow in tune, it would be possible to endure it.

When it rains in Hofei, it really rains. We spend most of the time wiping up water that comes in through the windows. We have had about eight inches of rain this week. I suppose you Africans have that much in one day? Hofei had a wonderful Easter with over fifty being baptized. We had to wait for three weeks for the baptism because the weather was too cold. Our China National Convention is slated for this week. The group from Hofei, some twenty people, have chartered a truck to go to Nanking. As it is raining today, it looks like their trip will be delayed. We are not planning on going because of the small baby. I could go but decided to stay since we do not know when the bandits or communists will come.

I forgot to tell you what it costs one to have a baby, especially a boy, in China. The Chinese custom is to send red-colored eggs to one's friends. As you know, everyone is supposed to be the missionary's friend. But we had to pick out a few dozen special friends and send them eggs. Each family receives eight eggs. I bought several hundred eggs and spent the better part of one day delivering them. They reciprocate by sending a present to the baby. When the child is one month old, the proud parents are supposed to give a feast, inviting all those who sent gifts. We ask some restaurant to cater for this meal. They prepare the food at their place and bring it down and serve it at our home. This will set us back several million Chinese dollars. One US dollar is worth 606,000 Chinese dollars now.

Several funny things have happened to our packages coming to China. One package had a package of gum in it. Someone opened it and took out one stick, leaving us four sticks. Jean received a package with, supposedly, three pair of nylons in it; but upon arrival, only one pair were left. Goulter's freight was held up in customs for over a week because they had some salt in a box. They went out on the street and bought the same amount of salt and gave it to customs, and they let them keep their American salt.

The Communists in our area seem to be migrating northward. We have not heard of any large bands too near for weeks. Verla had an interesting experience I hope she tells. There is a jail just back of our compound. We frequently see the jailer leading bandits outside the city wall to shoot them. "An eye for any eye" still rules, but if you could only know what the bandits do to the country people, you would not feel too badly when one of them is caught. I visited a fifteen-year-old girl in the hospital who had been raped and then burned. Dr. Corpron gets about two bandit cases a week in the hospital. They torture their victims, trying to make them tell where their valuables are.

Let me share with you one of the valuable lessons I am learning on our mission field here in China. Most of us, I at least, have come to the mission field expecting to do a great work. I have wondered just what that 'great' piece of work was to be. I think I have learned that no work is great of itself. A 'great' work is made up of many, many little works. I have been trying to analyze Mr. Oswald Goulter and what has made him so popular here among the Chinese. It is not because of any one 'great' work he has done. It is, I feel, because he is big enough to do the little works day by day. Therefore, my sermon to myself is, 'Don't go around looking for a great piece of work to give yourself to, Adsit, old boy, but plug away day by day at the necessary tasks.' Finally, my brethren and sisteren, 'He, who would be the greatest among you, shall be the servant of all' (a biblical quote). With constant thought, and we are praying for all of you. Adsits."

- Adsit, Jean, Minister and Missionary, Hofei, China, Letter to First Christian Church, Amarillo, Texas, Reprinted in their church newsletter, May 16, 1948.

"Letter from the Adsits (Dr. Snodgrass, Pastor at the church writes, 'Such an interesting letter was received last week from Jean and Glyn Adsit that we are publishing it. They were former members of this church and have been in the mission field in Hofei, China since last August.)

"We were certainly thrilled when a week and a half ago, we received packages from First Church. I suppose the best feeling of all was to know you all still claim us as yours—for we always feel like it's coming home when we're in First Church, Amarillo—so much of our lives were lived there—even though we were only there a short time after we married. The contents of the packages were all okay—except the half gallon of Karo had all leaked out in that box. We salvaged everything else by washing it, except one package of paper napkins. Candy is a luxury, and the custom officials had taken that out. (I hope they liked it.)

The mission work moves on in full swing here in Hofei. Last Sunday, there were fifty some odd baptized in a beautiful service that started early Sunday morning and went on into Sunday school and church. Glyn has been the busy one of late. He teaches in the rural school (for future leaders of the church here in China) about twelve hours a week. He has a special class of six fellows who are trying to qualify so they can enter Nanking Theological Seminary next fall. He is teaching them English. He also has an English Bible class every Friday evening, to say nothing of his two hours every morning of Chinese language study.

We have found, however, that to keep busy (without endangering our health) is good medicine to keep one's mind from wondering what we might do if the Communists took over our city. The older missionaries feel there will be a new drive on Hofei in the late spring, when the harvest is ready; however, no one can say. We just go on working, doing what we can each day and thanking God for it.

Our baby hasn't arrived yet but should any time. Its arrival is almost as uncertain as the political situation, but for one thing, we know it will arrive. [The reader should note that this letter was obviously written and mailed some time before April 26, 1948 since Timothy Lee Adsit was born on that date.]

Congratulations on the presidency of the convention. How busy you must be now with that responsibility plus the church and all that goes with it.

The mission here in China is already planning furlough schedules. We will study some more when we come home. We have been granted a two-year leave to let Glyn get his BD. We are not sure of what college we would like to attend as yet. We had talked of TCU (Texas Christian University, Fort Worth, Texas). What do you think? Of course, we will have our family then, and a suitable place to live will have to be a consideration wherever we go. Who knows? We might end up in Phillips University again.

I've rambled on. Will you see that a hearty thanks and whatever portion of this letter you want to read gets to the people responsible for all those lovely gifts? You and all the church are always in our prayers as you move forward for Christ. Sincerely yours, Jean Adsit."

- Adsit, Glyn B., Minister and Missionary, Hofei, Anhwei, China, Letter to Home Folks, May 26, 1948.

"Dear home folks, our son is one month old today. What a boy he is. He weighs 9 lbs. 3 oz. now. He gains about six to seven ounces a week. Timothy is just beginning to sleep longer at night. He slept from 10:30 p.m. to 4:30 a.m. This is a long stretch for him since he has been on a three-hour feeding schedule. Jean gives gobs of milk. We call her our old Jersey cow. She looks pretty with her new permanent, a 'Toni.' She is letting out most of her clothes. She gained a little around the hips and bust. Timothy has blue-gray eyes and light brown hair. He is losing his hair now. We are anxious to see what color it will be when it comes back in.

It begins to look like we might go to Kuling, a mountain summer resort, for July and August. It is two days and nights from here by train. I hate to take the trip with Jean and baby, but heat during those two months is almost unbearable. They say we can wear our winter clothes and sleep under blankets even in august. But when you consider that the mountains reach above the clouds, you can see it could be chilly. President Chiang Kai Shek vacations up there also.

Are you eating things from the garden? We have had strawberries, lettuce, potatoes, peas, green beans, radishes, mustard greens, spinach, chards, corn, tomatoes, beets, cabbage, cucumbers, pumpkin, squash, watermelon, and cantaloupes coming on soon. The soil here is Hofei is very rich.

I bought a hat on the street today, one like they wear in Africa, and paid $1.50 in our money. I also purchased enough cloth to make two short-sleeved shirts, 85 cents a yard. Jean loves to sew, and this helps me.

I saw them making silk today. It is a very slow process, and all the worms have to die in order to produce the cocoon. We'll write again soon. Love, Glyn. P.S. Your letter of May 16 arrived today."

- Adsit, Glyn B., "Hofei Hospital—Mission of Mercy," *World Call,* June, 1948, pp. 16-18. (Reprinted by permission, White, Cyrus N., President and Publisher, Christian Board of Publications, 1221 Locust Street, Suite 1200, St. Louis, MO 63103).

"It is not an easy task to serve as superintendent, surgeon, diagnostician and 'general handyman' of any hospital. But that is not the question. If the Disciples of Christ Christian Mission at Hofei, China, is to operate a hospital with only one missionary doctor, that doctor must try to carry on all phases of the work. Dr. Douglas S. Corpron is not trying to do four men's jobs; he is doing them.

Superintendent. As Superintendent, Dr. Corpron must buy and dispense all the necessary medicines and materials used in medical work, a most difficult task in China today where inflation has made the prices of medicine and food almost prohibitive. He must call staff meetings. He must try to keep up on new medicines as they are discovered and explain their uses to his Chinese co-workers. And he must regulate the cost of hospital care to the patient's ability to pay.

What would you do if a man came into the hospital and said, 'This hole in my leg is a bullet wound. Bandits burned and ransacked my village last night. I am one of few survivors. See my hands? Look closely at the ends of my fingers. See how burned and bloody they are? Those bandits thought I was a rich farmer and tried to force me to tell where I had money hidden away. They drove bamboo splinters under my finger nails and set them on fire. I am just a poor farmer. I have no money left. Doctor, can you help me?'

So many people came to the mission hospital wanting free help. Where to draw the line and still keep the hospital in operation is a hard decision to make; yet it is one that confronts the superintendent in Hofei Christian Hospital often.

Sometimes the superintendent is called upon to settle disputes as well as to administer medical assistance. One time a young Chinese officer was carried into the hospital by four of his friends. He had been shot in a skirmish with communists several miles from Hofei. He was very weak from loss of blood and exposure to cold weather. His friends, one officer in particular, demanded that the hospital take the wounded soldier in immediately, threatening the hospital workers if any delay was encountered. There was just one thing the workers could do, call the foreign missionary doctor. He was the only one who had enough 'face' to stand up to the army officer. Dr. Corpron suggested that he should go to a military hospital because the Hofei Christian Hospital was open to civilians only. The officer, however, had heard of Dr. Corpron's hospital and wanted to be treated in it. Finally, it was agreed that he could enter if he accepted the role of a civilian; paid the regular fees; and, most important of all, if he would get a trustworthy person to take the responsibility for his admission. He was treated, the bullet was found and was removed, and the problem was fairly solved. Being a superintendent could be a full-time job.

Surgeon. But Dr. Corpron must find time to act as surgeon too. It is easy to understand the nature of a missionary doctor's job a little better if one realizes that the patients usually wait until their physical condition is all but hopeless before they come for treatment. It is not unusual for Dr. Corpron to do five or six major operations in one afternoon.

Dr. Corpron has become a specialist in delivering difficult baby cases. Most Chinese women do not come to the hospital for delivery but are treated at home by a midwife under the most unsanitary conditions. But many times, when complications arise from improper treatment and ignorance, the mother is brought into the hospital, where the doctor must use all the skill at his command to save both mother and child. Dr. Corpron could easily devote all his time to the surgery, but there are other tasks.

Clinic. The morning clinic presents a picture that reminds one of some of the scenes that are recorded in the Bible. The cripple coming into the waiting room on crutches, a sick man carried in on a bed by four of his friends, a blind man coming in hope that the 'foreign doctor' can perform the miracle necessary to make him see again, people with open sores, tuberculosis patients, all of these and more are seen in the clinic at Hofei. Dr. Corpron must diagnose each case carefully. He must decide what treatment to give. But even after diagnosis, his job is not done, for many of these Chinese do not want to enter the hospital for treatment. He has to reason with them. 'This is your last court of appeal. If you go home, you will surely die.' It is not pleasant to see a man go home to die, especially when you feel that you might save his life if he would but give you a chance.

Handyman. What does a handyman do around a hospital? Dr. Corpron, as handyman, sees to it that the electric plant is in good running order. He goes to Nanking or Shanghai occasionally to buy food and medicine. He helps conduct a short chapel service in his home each morning. Dr. Corpron says, jokingly, that in his spare time, he serves on the mission building committee, attends church services, writes letters, and finds time in between for reading and recreation.

His tasks are made lighter by the help of his wife and the hospital nurse, Grace Young. Mrs. Corpron is not content to be just the mission doctor's wife. In addition to planning the meals for the Corpron household, seeing to it that the diet is proper and sufficient, she writes to her three children, two of them in Shanghai and one in America attending school. Her greatest joy, however, is obtained from working with Chinese babies and their mothers.

Baby clinic. Each morning Mrs. Corpron is busy in the baby clinic, checking the weights of babies and deciding whether or not they should be allotted some of the milk powder given the Hofei Hospital by UNRRA. Almost every baby needs additional milk, but she must exercise great care in its distribution, for some mothers take it and sell it on the streets. Milk is too precious to be wasted in this way.

There are many pathetic little babies that are far underweight. An old Chinese grandmother was on a trip from Pengpu to Hofei. Along the road she saw an abandoned baby girl only three or four days old. Hoping that her daughter would nurse it, the old woman picked it up and took it home. Her daughter refused to take the baby, however, so the woman was left to care for the wee babe. She had no way to feed her but managed to keep her alive by feeding her the water drained off rice gruel. But the baby did not thrive on this food. In desperation, the woman began asking around to learn if anyone would help her. She heard of the Hofei Hospital's program of saving babies and hurriedly brought the six-week-old baby to let Mrs. Corpron look at her. When the baby's weight was checked, she weighed but five pounds! The baby was given some milk in a bottle, but she did not know how to feed herself. Now the nurses at the hospital are trying to teach the child how to take milk from a bottle.

Well baby clinic. Three afternoons a week, the Chinese mothers bring their babies to the 'Rotary Friendship Well Baby Clinic.' This clinic is supported in part by the rotary club of Yakima, Washington. Here, they learn how to bathe their babies. Since the average Chinese home is not sufficiently warm to bathe a small baby, the mothers are grateful for an opportunity to come to a warm room for this task. Mrs. Corpron says that it is not uncommon to see a baby who is four months old who has never had a bath. Scabies is a common disease among such babies.

Several native nurses help in this clinic. They give medicine to those who need it and try to teach principles of cleanliness to the mothers. In addition, baby clothes sent by the people of America are distributed to those who have need.

Responsibilities of nurse. Miss Grace Young is the only foreign nurse on the hospital staff. She has spent many hours in helping to get the hospital back in shape. (The Japanese lived in the hospital during the recent war, and when they retreated from Hofei, the place was left in a dirty mess.) When Miss Young arrived in Hofei six months ago, she immediately started to work at dividing the relief materials given by UNRRA. There were tons and tons of material, enough to set up and run a hundred-bed hospital for months. She supervised the storage of all materials in addition to her regular responsibilities of keeping the drug room well stocked and supervising the laundry. In addition, she must assist in the surgery.

Grace is a stickler for cleanliness. She chases after the coolies and nurses to see that they keep the hospital decently clean. Dr. Corpron refers to her as his 'old Dutch cleanser.'

Being a missionary nurse demands much of a person. Miss Young is called upon many times to do work apart from regular nursing. She teaches English to a group of young hospital trainees, music to the Chinese workers, and leads the music for the hospital staff devotional periods.

When Jesus performed a miracle of healing, he turned to his followers and said, 'Greater things than this ye shall do.' As I watch our Christian hospital workers go about on their mission of mercy, I think I know what Jesus meant."

- Adsit, Glyn, Minister and Missionary, Nanking, China, to Mother and Home Folks, June 9, 1948.

"Dearest Mother and home folks, greetings from Nanking! I am here to meet the two Corpron girls who have been in Shanghai American School. They are Ruth and Mary, ages seventeen and sixteen. It is raining very hard this morning, and it is delaying our bus trip home to Hofei. I think it has rained two inches in the past thirty minutes. We do not know how long we will be delayed. You see, our roads are dirt and rock. It takes at least two days for them to dry.

Vacation time will soon be upon us. We will go to Kuling. We are scheduled to leave Nanking by airplane June 24. We arrive one hour and forty-five minutes later, a very short trip via air. If we had to go by boat or train, it would take two days. Since Timmy is so small, we have decided to risk the air trip. We have rented a house for all of July and August. We will share it with one of our young missionary families from Wuhu, the Joe Smiths, who have two children ages six and two. We will leave out servants in Hofei to look after the house and compound. I want them to can some garden vegetables. I have been canning without canning machine and cans. Jean doesn't trust the pressure cooker, and I run it also.

Timothy is gaining right along. He now weighs 9 lbs. 14 oz, almost a 10 lb. Catfish. He has been a little fretful with his smallpox vaccination and his circumcision. Boy, it was hard to take him to the doctor for that operation. Jean is making a wonderful mother. Timmy is getting where he smiles whenever he hears our voices now. Jean's milk is plentiful. We have started the cod liver oil and orange juice. We also have several boxes of pabulum, which we will start him on at three and a half to four months. He is changing his looks and personality from week to week. I believe he is beginning to favor me a little now.

Jean's Roswell, New Mexico, church sent a box for Jean and Timmy, and it was loaded with lovely presents. Before

I forget it, let me suggest that you send no more boxes until the later part of July. We will be home by September 1. It is taking boxes six weeks to reach us now. The box for the baby contained, among other things, a silver spoon and fork, a potty, a plate into which hot water can be poured to keep food warm, rubber pants, a brush and comb set, a silver bracelet, and a sweater and bootie set.

We have some pictures taken and developed of Timmy and will send you some as soon as I get home.

Our health is fine, no sickness for a long time now. I am a little tired since we have to get up several times every night to take care of Timmy, but that is part of it, I know.

Our rural work is going ahead. We have baptized two from Ershrpu, the little village in which we are trying to start a church. The prospects are very hopeful for this place. We also baptized eight of my students last Sunday. It is wonderful to see the church growing day by day!

I will be sending you a check right soon to help pay for the boxes and pictures and postage you have been sending to us. We got a raise just recently, and it will enable us to do a few things like this.

It is my deepest prayer and desire that we can work out our lives here in China. I know you will be praying that Jean will be able to make the adjustment. Workers are so desperately needed here in China.

Tell Hurshel and Duane to write! Love, Glyn."

- Adsit, Glyn B., Minister and Missionary, *Lot 15-B, Kuling, Kiangsi, China*, Letter to Mother and Family, June 30, 1948.

"Dearest Mother and family, Kuling is a most beautiful spot. Our house is situated on the side of a mountain. We look across the valley and see the beautiful mountainside with its tall fir and pine trees. It is nice and cool here all the time. We sleep under a blanket and quilt each night. It has rained constantly for four days. We are having some trouble in drying baby diapers. We left Hofei by bus, going through bandit territory, but were not molested. Timmy was a little shaken up by the trip. He has settled down now. We ate in a Chinese restaurant. We usually order eggs and pork scrambled together, rice, and a soup. We picked up a diarrhea bug somewhere; however, we both are over that now. We stayed in Nanking for six days, waiting for our plane to leave. It rained us out one day, but we got away on Friday the twenty-fifth. The trip by plane was wonderful. It was not bumpy, and Timmy slept all the way. It only took us one hour and forty-five minutes to make the trip from Nanking to Kiukiang. The pilots were Chinese. If we had gone by boat, it would have taken at least forty hours. We were met at the airport by The China Travel Service man who made all necessary arrangements to get us and our baggage up the mountain to Kuling. We traveled by Jeep to about one fifth the way up the mountain, and there, we were unloaded and told to register with the Kuling land office. Much to our surprise, we met the Joe Smiths at this place. They had left Wuhu by boat, and we made perfect connections. Smiths are the family we are living with us here. We hired chairs and carriers to carry us over the mountain. Jean, with Timmy, required six chair carriers. I got by with four. I did walk about one-third of the way up, however. It is not very pleasant to ride in a chair. I felt ashamed to be carried on the shoulders of other men. The scenery reminded me of the Ozark Mountains. The mountainsides are slashed by many small, dashing streams of clear, cold water. We felt the air getting cooler as we climbed higher.

This is a good place to sleep and rest. I intend to study a little, play tennis, hike, and read. Timmy sleeps and eats a little better now. He weighs about 11 lbs. 4 oz. He still nurses Jean. Her health is fine, and it looks like she will be able to breast feed him for the necessary length of time. Prices are very high in Kuling. It is a summer resort, and prices go up when the foreigners arrive. There is not one car road leading into this place. Everything must be carried over the mountain, up the steep steps by coolies using carrying poles. We can buy almost anything if we have enough money. President Chiang Kai Shek's summer home is right next to our place. He has not come up as yet.

Timmy can recognize us now. He is nine weeks old. He is beginning to goo and laugh. We are feeding him one bottle of milk a day, orange juice, and cod liver oil.

Chinese money is getting progressively worse. It is now 1,500,000 to $1 US. It was 40 to $1 US when we arrived last August.

Americans in Kuling are planning a Fourth of July celebration. We will have a treasure hunt for the children in the morning, baseball game in the afternoon, and games for adults and children.

Address our mail to us at: 15-B, Kuling, Kiangsi, (China). Love, your son, Glyn."

- Adsit, Glyn B., Minister and Missionary, Lot 15-B, Kuling, Kiangsi, China, Letter to Home Folks, July 17, 1948.

"Dear home folks, Mother, at long last here are three negatives of little Timmy. The one of him in the basket is at six weeks of age, others are at first week and, I think, one month. His hair is growing some now, and it will be light like Hurshel's. He favors Hurshel some around eyebrows and eyes. He looks like you when he frowns.

I am helping run a swimming pool here at Kuling and am enjoying the cold-water swims. I am enclosing some small pictures with the following explanations: 1) Glyn in Sudan chair returning from San Ho on a country trip; we got caught there in a snowstorm and had to stay nine days and, finally, had to ride chairs back to Hofei; 2) Chinese girl with baby brother. Hat is a very decorative one worn by boys in country villages. Silver ornaments around the hat show parents' love for the boy. The hat is a bright red. His dress is blue with red flowers; 3) Girl minding her little brother. Girls must watch brothers, and they carry them about by tying them on their backs; 4) Water oxen plowing ground in fall; 5) Water buffalo pulling a harrow through a rice paddy. I tried to get the boy to look at me, but he said, 'I do not dare.' He meant he was afraid of me; 6) A grave casket placed out in the rice field, or near it. Water level is too high to permit digging graves. They sprinkle lime on the body and place it in a coffin made from thick boards and then set it close to their house for about a hundred days. Then they move it to the field; 7) Country woman grinding wheat to make flour. The hammers are heavy, about sixteen pounds. They pound in perfect rhythm, and you have to be healthy to keep this up all day long; 8) A schoolboy holding a stick with a string of firecrackers on the end. They are popping away to welcome our visit to the school; 9) A woman carrying grass to town. Town people will buy this grass to burn in kitchen stoves. It weighs about eighty pounds; 10) An old eighty-seven-year-old woman flaying wheat. She beats the grains out and then sweeps them up and winnows them; 11) Glyn in tomato patch with Lassie the pup; 12) Glyn in corn. Building in back is a jail. We see them march prisoners out to shoot them every now and then; 13) Lassie throwing a kiss to Shang; 14) Our house from front yard. Lawn is beautiful, and trees give wonderful shade; 15) Glyn with three hundred eggs in basket. These were hard boiled, painted red, and sent to our friends when Timmy was born; 16) Mrs. Corpron holding Timmy, Tuxedo their dog, and the basket of eggs.

Will send more pictures right along. Can send negatives of any of these you want.

Timmy and Jean are fine. We are having a little trouble getting him to take any orange juice or tomato juice. He likes his cod liver oil, however. We have not weighed him for about a month, but we know he is gaining right along. He sleeps good at night now. This gives us a rest that we have been needing.

The Communist situation is not too good. They are getting closer to our Hofei, but not close enough for us to leave. If the war keeps going like it is, we might return to America next year. No one can tell what will happen.

Kuling is truly a beautiful place, such a contrast to some other parts of China. We are beginning to feel the pinch of being parents. We cannot go just when we please anymore. This is hard to get used to. But we know it goes with having Timmy. What is Lawyane's draft status?

Will close for this time. I am feeling fine and hope to get all my correspondence caught up and hope to write another article or two for our *World Call*. You can borrow the Joneses's and read what I write. I wrote an article that they printed in their May or June or July issue. I am not sure which. I haven't seen it in print yet. Love, from your son, Glyn."

- Adsit, Jean, Minister and Missionary, Lot 15-B, Kuling, Kiangsi, China, Letter to Mother (R.L. Adsit), July 21, 1948.

"Dearest Mom, we have thought of Hurshel and Bess a great deal and the children's tonsil operations. By now, they are up and eating everything again.

The mountains are really beautiful. Last evening, we hiked to a place called Nan Chang Pass (or the northern pass). We took a picnic supper. The whole disciples mission group (went). One of our ladies has an ulcer, and she couldn't walk the two miles there and back, so she offered to watch Timmy. He slept all the time we were gone. The moon was supposed to be exceptionally beautiful on this particular evening, but heavy clouds kept us from seeing it shining on the lake below. However, there was a marvelous sunset, and the clouds made it even lovelier. Glyn remarked, 'I wish mom could see this. It would cause her to start writing all the beautiful things she sees in that sunset.'

The baby is growing so quickly that when I hold him, he seems to have gained a little more every day. He coos and makes cute little noises. His daddy, however, is going to spoil him rotten. If I've done all I can to make him comfortable and then he cries, I just let him cry, but the daddy walks in and picks him up. Oh well. They are only little once, so if he wants to love him to pieces, I'll let him.

We think of all of you and miss you and love you lots. Write when you can, and remember, Mom, take it easy. Love, Jean."

- Adsit, Glyn B. "China's Sorrow," *World Call*, July-August, 1948, p. 27. (Re-printed by permission, White, Cyrus N., President and Publisher, Christian Board of Publications, 1221 Locust Street, Suite 1200, St. Louis, MO 63103).

"For centuries, the Yellow River has been called China's sorrow. It is rightly named. During the early part of the war, the Chinese forces tore down the dykes which controlled the river and it was allowed to flood thousands of square miles of farm land. This helped the war effort, but it brought untold distress to the many farmers who were forced to leave their water covered homes. China's sorrow had become their own sorrow.

Jang-Da-Fan and his family migrated to Hofei, coming more than six hundred miles from the north. His was one of the families forced to leave the flooded area. In past years members of his family had been good farmers and had accumulated a few worldly belongings. They were forced to move without any warning and saved only what clothes they were wearing and what they could carry on their backs. It was not easy for the mother to walk all this distance because she had bound feet. She also had to look after two older children and a baby. The Jangs begged their way as far as Hofei, and here they stopped because Mrs. Jang was soon to have another child.

We see the Jangs every day. They live in two small grass huts not far from our front gate. Their 'house' is pitiful, almost beyond description. There are no windows; the ground serves as their floor. They sleep on a pile of straw.

Their diet consists almost wholly of rice. Once is a great while they eat meat. Several crows and magpies have been bothering our garden. I shot some of them with my rifle and the Jangs came running to ask if they could have the birds to eat. I gladly gave them the birds, and now frequently shoot some in order that they will have a little more protein in their diet.

The Chinese have learned to eat almost any green thing that grows. Our yard has grass resembling clover. The Jangs come frequently to pick some of the grass leaves for food. What a mixed up world! In America, we feed our cows grass; in Hofei, people gladly eat our grass.

It is not an exaggeration when I say that the Jang children have very few clothes. One of the children has no summer clothes at all. Fortunately, Hofei's climate is warm enough to allow him to go naked.

These people keep body and soul together by working at odd jobs wherever they can find them. At present they are making mud bricks and selling them for about two cents each. Their family can live on fifty cents a day. They demand only the barest necessities of life. Dr. and Mrs. Corpron, our missionaries in Hofei, have hired the father to do the garden work. Mr. and Mrs. O.J. Goulter have hired the mother to do some sewing. The policy is to allow them to do some useful work and receive pay for it. In this way the Jangs will not be pauperized and will still be able to make a living.

China's real sorrow is that people like the Jangs have such little hope of improving their miserable manner of living. We are doing what we can to bring them the joy of Christian hope. We pray that friends in the churches at home in the United States will feel China's sorrow and will help her in her hour of need."

- Adsit, Glyn B., "Easter in Hofei, China," *World Call*, July-August, 1948, p. 41. (Re-printed by permission, White, Cyrus N., President and Publisher, Christian Board of

Publications, 1221 Locust Street, Suite 1200, St. Louis, MO 63103).

"Easter in Hofei, China. Easter Day in Hofei was very beautiful. Daybreak came, bringing with it the realization that it was a morning just like this on which Jesus arose from his rock-hewn tomb. We knew that all over the world believers in Christ's resurrection were singing, 'Hallelujah! Jesus Christ Is Risen Today.' Hofei Christians were remembering what Christ's resurrection had meant to them, and what it was still meaning. They were thinking, because he lives, we too are alive. We are free from ancient superstitions and fears that had us buried in a tomb of despair. We have risen from our decadent Chinese religions and are now members of the world religion, Christianity.

Hofei Christian Church was packed and overflowing for the morning worship service. Strangers and Christians came early to be sure to get a seat. Pastor Chyan was at his best and preached a good message. The choir was robed with splendor, and they really shone with their white, waist length robes. They sang all the familiar Easter songs, and surprised the congregation by singing two specials.

All the Christians were wondering how many people would be added to the church during this Easter period. Pastor Chyan announced that we were to have over fifty for baptism, but that the service could not be held until later since the weather was still too cold.

Over 200 Christians gathered for the fellowship hour which was held in Mr. and Mrs. O.J. Goulter's front yard. The Chinese preferred meeting in the afternoon to meeting at the early morning hour. They felt that they would be more wide awake and would enjoy themselves more. The meeting was called for the express purpose of having a good time with Christian friends. We played several games and ate light refreshments. As night began to fall, we all drifted toward out homes, feeling in our hearts that

Jesus had not only risen years ago, but that he is still living in Hofei."

- Adsit, Glyn B., Minister and Missionary, Lot 15-B, Kuling, Kiangsi, China, Letter to Mom and Folks, August 13, 1948.

"Dear Mom and folks, yes, the dog Lassie is ours. We continue to enjoy our mountain vacation. Timmy has escaped the heat. We weighed him today. Weight: 14 lbs. 4 oz. He is three and a half months old today. He is gaining weight every day, and I feel it as I carry him over these mountain trails. We will leave Kuling for Hofei around September 6. We hear Commies are still to north of Hofei and we can return with safety. Many missionaries have been captured by Communists, but almost all are turned loose without harm. They do instruct missionaries not to return and not to support the government forces. President Chiang Shek and Madame arrived last Monday. I saw them come in by chair. He looks very tired and old.

Jean and I are getting a good rest in this cool climate. We want you to send a print of each picture of Timothy to Jean's sisters and to our three churches. The addresses are: 1) Mr. and Mrs. Phil Wilson, P.O. Box 660, Lakin, Kansas; 2) Mr. and Mrs. Joe Etheridge, 4244 West 10th, Amarillo, Texas; 3) Mr. and Mrs. Marrion Nilsson, First Christian Church, Roswell, New Mexico; 4) Mr. and Mrs. Norman Stacey, Lincoln Terrace Christian Church, 21st and Kelly, Oklahoma City, Oklahoma; 5) Rev. and Mrs. Ray Snodgrass, Central Christian Church, Broadway and Adams, Enid, Oklahoma. You should receive a picture from Jean's sister before long. Do not send negatives back to us, but keep them for our return. I am writing articles for our Church magazine *World Call*. I have had three printed so far. I enjoy writing very much and might try a book someday.

Our missionaries here have just finished holding a conference. We are making plans for our fall campaign.

We start an intensive evangelistic campaign immediately upon our return. We will travel from place to place and be gone from Hofei for two weeks. Jean will stay in Hofei and keep house. We got a 10 percent raise this week and also a children's allowance. We can now leave $50 a month in the United States to help buy things we need, to pay insurance, and to save for Timmy's education.

Everyone is saying the Communists will eventually win all of China because the present government is unable to purge itself of corruption and take care of the poor. We should pretty well know for sure within a year whether we can stay in China or not. We will keep plugging away at the evil here until forced to leave. Love, Glyn."

- Adsit, Glyn B., Minister and Missionary, Lot 15-B, Kuling, Kiangsi, China, Letter to Home Folks, August 23, 1948. (Documents never-before-published pictures of President Chiang Kai Shek and Madame Chiang Kai Shek.)

"Dear home folks, it has been raining here for five days. We are having a hard time drying baby clothes. It is rather disgusting to sit on this mountaintop in the clouds and look down on the plain below, where the sun is shining and everything is clear.

We are all in good health. Timmy weighs 15 lbs. He is beginning to gurgle and coo with a loud voice now at fourth months. Finally, his hair is coming in. It is light brown, almost a 'toe head.'

The Chinese government has just started a new currency reform. Our US $1.00 is worth 4 Chinese dollars. This helps us because bills are fewer and smaller. We also use silver dollars and 10, 20, and 50-cent bills. The enclosed map will show where Hofei is in respect to the strong Communist forces. They are closer to us now than when this map appeared in *Time Magazine*. Also, small bands of Chinese Commies roam around the countryside almost at will.

I had a couple more short articles appear in *World Call* in the July-August issue. You can borrow Joneses' copy. How is Elvira's oil well coming? The picture is of our missionary group during a week of conference.

We will probably be in Hofei before we write you again. Write us at Hofei; no more to Kuling.

Is Duane continuing his law course? I thought he was junior instead of a senior.

Let me suggest again that if you do not hear from us, there is no cause for worry. If something happens, you will get word right away. In this respect, no news is good news. I am feeling fine but have gained no weight. I do have a sun tan. The swimming pool I have been helping manage has made a profit, and we are making some much-needed repairs.

A week ago last Sunday, President Chiang Kai Shek and Madame attended church. I took about eight colored pictures of them, and you will get the slides one of these days. They were very kind in letting the foreigners take their pictures. They can go nowhere without a heavy bodyguard, even to church. Write us soon, to Hofei. Love, your son, Glyn."

- Adsit, Glyn B., "I Baptize Thee," *World Call*, September, 1948, p. 47. (Re-printed by permission, White, Cyrus N., President and Publisher, Christian Board of Publications, 1221 Locust Street, Suite 1200, St. Louis, MO 63103.)

"Fifty-three Chinese believers were baptized in the Hofei Christian Church on April 18, 1948. Of this number, thirty-five were men and boys and eighteen women and girls.

It is not an easy thing to be baptized in Hofei. There are no adequate dressing rooms, no baptismal robes, no hot and cold running water. Most of the Chinese have only one change of clothing, which means that something is going to get wet. Even though it is hard to baptize people, this service in Hofei last April went along with apparently no trouble.

When it was decided that more than fifty people were asking for baptism, the church board began to make arrangements. The following committees were appointed: decoration, filling baptistery, robing, baptizing, instruction.

The committee on instruction was charged with the duty of explaining to the candidates just what it meant to be baptized. Pastor Chyan, the minister in Hofei, had been working on this for months, and the inquirers were well prepared to take the long looked for step.

Finding enough robes for fifty-three people really presented a problem. It was finally decided that the church would borrow gowns from the Christian hospital. They were white and served the purpose quite adequately.

The platform was covered with green, wavy bamboo branches with large peonies scattered amongst them. The result was very beautiful and lent a rustic atmosphere.

At three o'clock in the morning, coolies began carrying water by bucket. They first carried enough cold water to fill the baptistery three-fourths full. Then they carried warm water to make the water more comfortable for immersion. The baptismal service began at 7:30 a.m.

'Do you believe that Jesus is the Christ, the Son of the Living God, and do you accept him as your personal Savior?' was asked of each person. They each answered, 'I do.' Then, as the congregation sang, the candidates marched to the rooms in back of the church. As they walked by where I was standing, I looked to see who they were. They were children coming from Christian homes, old women with tiny, bound feet who could hardly read a character in the Bible but who, at their late age, wanted peace in their hearts. A husband and wife who lived across the road from our house were among them. Some of them I did not know, but at that moment, I felt strange kinship with all.

Oswald J. Goulter, the missionary, was asked to act as the arms of the pastor in baptizing those who were ready for immersion. Pastor Chyan gave the person's name, and then Mr. Goulter said in Chinese, 'Upon your confession of faith in Christ as your personal Savior, and in obedience to his command, I baptize you in the name of the Father, the Son, and the Holy Spirit.'

It took two full hours to complete the service, but we all felt that they were most wonderfully spent. We could see that out here on the growing edge of God's kingdom, people were interested in hearing about this strange man who called God his father and who loved men so much that he died for them.

Over a hundred friendly non-Christian Chinese witnessed the baptismal service. Many were asking, 'What is this they do?' It was easy to answer, 'Behold, they are being born anew.'"

• Adsit, Glyn and Jean, Ministers and Missionaries, Hofei, Anhwei, China, Letter to Mom and Folks, September 12, 1948.

"Dear Mom and folks, home again! How nice it is to be home and eating our own food again. It was wonderful to live on the mountain for the summer months. But it is better to be back here among friends and to tackle our work again. We came down the mountain in Sudan Chairs (Jean and Timmie that is). I walked down two days early to secure passage on the boat. I stayed in Kiukiang in the Catholic hospital. They treated me real nice, and their French cooking was superb. They are French Catholics. The boat we road to Nanking on was the *Sze Ming*, a rice carrying boat that takes passengers. We had a good cabin for just the three of us. It was private and nice. Little strangers like cockroaches and spiders invaded us once or twice, but that is mild for China. We did not study while in Kuling, so our minds are rested and I am ready to tackle it again.

We bought several things this summer. Our biggest buy was three rugs. One is brown. The other two are smaller ones. We also bought some Chinese idols. We stayed in Nanking for two days before coming on to Hofei. We bought our winter's store of groceries. This set us back about $200 but can be taken out of the next ten months' salary. Timmy is fine. He is so fat that he is just one roll after another. We haven't weighed him yet, but we think he will come close to 15.5 lbs. Your box was here awaiting us. The gifts were very nice. Timmy's eyes just popped when he saw the exerciser. Jean particularly appreciated the rubber pants. Tim did not have any of those.

Our fall schedule is heavy. I begin to make trips this week. We will visit all of our stations, ending up at San Ho, some thirty-five miles away. One place near Lyang Yuan has some Commies, but we hear they will let us come, so don't be worried about this. Hofei is the provincial capital and has many well-educated people working in office jobs. I am thinking of trying to start an English preaching service just to attract them. I can do it through an interpreter. Making a trip into the country each week, studying three hours per day, teaching in our rural school, and writing articles occasionally promises that I will be busy this year. I hope to have some time for Jean and Timothy.

I have lost a few more pounds because of hiking so much in Kuling Mountains. I intend to get these back right away. I have already started eating ice cream in abundance as the first step. Our icebox is working fine so far. We have our second crop of potatoes coming up. Our tomatoes are also coming in again. You might send a couple boxes of Pabulum and a can or two of baby foods in next box. Jean says green vegetables will be best in baby foods: asparagus, beans, spinach, etc.

The Chinese government is making a valiant effort to establish a sound economic system. Our (US) dollar is now worth four Chinese dollars. This makes it easier for us to figure. Instead of millions, it is now tens. You cannot appreciate what that means to us until you stop to think that last month, our salary amounted to over a billion dollars and we had to keep books with astronomical figures. Several people have been sent to the firing squad for violating the new economical laws. Maybe they mean business this time.

There is fighting ten miles from Hofei today, but they say they are not coming this way. Let's hope not or our homecoming will turn into a fast home leaving. One thing can be said about the life of a missionary: it is never dull.

Our floors were painted while we were in Kuling. It makes our place look 100 percent better. They are dark brown. Write us when you have time. Love, Glyn and Jean."

- Adsit, Glyn B., Minister and Missionary, Hofei, Anhwei, China, Letter to James McCallum, September 22, 1948.

"Dear Mac, this letter is in regard to specials (money gifts from Christians back in America) that Jean and I have received during the past few months.

My June financial account, received from Walter, shows that we have two specials amounting to $55. I would like to ask that we be allowed to use this in helping to repair the rural center buildings. We are using these buildings now, and they are in bad need of repair.

Our July account shows that we received two more specials amounting to $85.45. We have permission from the Hofei Station Council to use this money in helping run our farm center school. Will you please consider this request and advise as to action taken?

Last March, we received a personal gift of $50 from a Mr. George Bell in Great Bend, Kansas. He wrote asking if I had received the check for $150.00. I answered that only $50.00 had come. He again wrote explaining that $50.00 was for personal use and $100.00 for our work in country places. E.K. Higdon advises that they received credit for the $100.00 toward their Crusade goal. He also advises, 'I cannot present to our Board of Trustees a request for the appropriation of this $100 gift until I have from James H. McCallum a statement to the effect 1) that the project which you propose for its expenditure has been approved by the administrative committee, or 2) that you desire to use the $100 to apply on the repairs of a building or the equipment of an institution and that that project is in the Crusade financial objectives prepared and approved in China. Please get this information to me so that I may present the matter to the board of trustees when it next meets in November.'

The Hofei Station council has approved the use of this $100. It is suggested that it be used as follows: 1) to send two or three students to Wuhu Bible School, these are not far enough advanced to go to Chuhsien; 2) to help repair farm center buildings and buy needed equipment for our farm center school; 3) to buy materials for use in school, such as, pencils, tablets, books. Will you please consider this as soon as possible in order that E.K. can be notified in time to present it to the November meeting? Also regarding the above $140.45. Will it be possible for you to consider this before the next regular meeting of the council? Our school is underway, and we are in dire need of repairs. I hope this can be done, as I feel this school is badly needed and is a great step forward in our training of future leaders for our churches. Cordially yours, (Glyn Adsit).

- Adsit, Glyn., Minister and Missionary, Hofei, Anhwei, China, Letter to Mr. Walter Haskell, Treasurer, UCMS in China, Nanking, China, September 22, 1948.

"Dear Walter, in reply to your letter about all of us putting our salary in the bank and handling it ourselves, Jean and I are in favor of your suggestion. Will you please put our money, including our September salary, in the bank in the following manner: 1) We have no account in Nanking and wish to ask you to open one for us at the Shanghai Commercial Nanking Branch. Just put in the minimum amount needed to open an account. Please send us the necessary papers to fill out, and the checkbooks; 2) Place the rest of our money in our Shanghai account.

If you cannot open an account for us in Nanking without our being present, just let it go until I come to Nanking. At any rate, we are going to need GY 1,000, one thousand dollars, right away. Will you please place that amount in the Shanghai (account) right away in order that I can write checks on it by next Monday, September 27? We are buying oil and kerosene and are borrowing money to buy it and want to pay it back right away.

Tell Mythel that we got her note regarding pans and buckets and thanks for her trouble. Timmy is growing fine. Weighs 15 lbs. 14 oz. now. Jean is recovering from a sore throat. I have just returned from a country trip and find I have a nasty cold. Verla and I are planning on going to San Ho very soon. Hope you are not too busy to root for the Dodgers. Sincerely yours, (Glyn Adsit)."

- Adsit, Glyn B., Treasurer, Hofei Station, Anhwei, China, Letter to Mr. Wang, September 24, 1948.

"Dear Mr. Wang, will you please advise me when I should make my monthly financial report to your office? Also, will you tell me what method you will use to send me our budget money for October? Will it come via bank, or will you send it by some person?

I have paid the following tuition, which I understand your office will refund to me:

Wang-Chi-Tyan69.00

Wu-Sing-Tan36.30 of Chuhsien, he has a daughter in San Ruh middle school.

Jyang-Jau-Hong18.70

124.00 GY

Sincerely yours, Glyn B. Adsit, Treasurer, Hofei Station."

- Adsit, Glyn B., Minister and Missionary, Hofei, Anhwei, China, Letter to Joy Snow, September 24, 1948.

"Dear friend, your letter of September 4 arrived, and I hasten to answer.

One of the first things to remember about Christmas is that China is not a Christian nation yet. This means that only a fragment of China's society will be celebrating the birth of our Lord. But what a blessing it is that He is not forgotten in China. There will be no national holiday. The stores will not be loaded with gift suggestions. There will not be bright strings of lights that rival even the Milky Way. And most sad if all to one away from home, there will be no tender, fresh, green Christmas tree in the windows. You see, the birth of Jesus means little to one who has never heard of him.

Those who do know that Jesus is born will celebrate his birth in many ways. The Christian homes will have a prayer service of thanksgiving to God for his precious gift. The Christmas story will be read to little, black-headed, eager-eyed boys and girls. Their hearts will be moved just as ours were in our more tender years. Perhaps small gifts will be exchanged. If so, it will happen on a small scale. This, please keep in mind, will happen in the home. If you happened to walk onto the street of Hofei on Christmas Day, you would not know that it was a special day. The life of the town goes on, and your heart is hurt in the realization that so many do not know and do not care.

The newspapers will probably carry the story of the birth of Christ. President Chinag Kai Shek will see to that.

The Christian churches in China will make elaborate plans for the Christmas Day. You would think you were in America when you heard the carols being sung by the young people's choir. Hofei Church gives a Christmas pageant each year. It depicts the birth of Jesus and the story of the shepherds. One amusing thing stands out: the shepherds have many servants. This is typically Chinese because their way of showing a man of importance is to show how many servants he has. I said that shepherds had many servants. I should have said, the three wise men. The choir will sing the traditional Christmas tunes and a few Chinese ones. Gifts of tangerines, candy, and popcorn will be given to the children of the church.

Several groups in the church will go caroling on Christmas morning. Last year, we were awakened at 4:00 a.m. by the caroling of the young nurses and interns from the hospital. We thought this rather early, but got up and gave them some refreshments just the same.

The hospital group put on a Christmas program that is rather on the light side. They have the children recite and sing. They use Christmas as an opportunity to get together and play. It is a good thing because much of their life is dull and uninteresting.

Christmas in the missionary's home is a wonderful time. Even if there are no children to urge us on, we celebrate just the same. Hofei has several holly trees. We cut off a branch and make a lovely holly tree. We string it with lights, and it is just as if we were home in the USA. All of us missionaries exchange gifts and wrap them and pile them around the tree. Christmas morning finds us together, opening our presents and spending a wonderful day in eating duck, chicken, or goose. And we always (open) the gift packages that come from home.

I hope this can be of some use to you in your program. It is rather hard to give you any original material on Christmas in China. We foreigners have brought Christmas to China, and therefore, it is patterned after our type of celebration.

Give our love to all our friends. We are well, busy, and happy. Timmy is five months old and full of energy. He now weighs 16 lbs. and begins to look a little like his pop. Sincerely yours, Glyn."

- Adsit, Glyn B., Minister and Missionary, Hofei, Anhwei, China, Letter to Administrative Council, United Christian Missionary Society, Nanking, China, September 24, 1948.

"Dear friends, we are trying to rehabilitate our farm center so that it can be used as a center to train young men for the leadership of the church. This property has had no repairs for about ten years now.

Last year, Mr. Goulter, Mr. Wang, and I set up the school and ran it for about six months. We did this without any authorized budget and on 'a shoe-string' so to speak. The school proved a success, and we believe we should continue it again. In fact, it is now under way. We are cooperating with San Ruh Middle School. They are sending their boy students to the farm center to live, and we, in turn, are allowed to send twenty of our students to the school. Last year, we taught our boys reading, writing, science, etc. We felt that it was a duplication of effort for us to teach these subjects when the school was already teaching them. They felt the same way, and, therefore, we are trying out this new plan.

Now the reason for this letter is to ask that we be allowed $400 to help put the building in shape. This would be used to buy:

30,000 tiles for roof	$150
white wash	$60
cement	$12
bricks	$15
nails, wood, and paper	$20
labor	$100
doors and windows-labor included	$43
Gold Yuan	

This does not include glass for the windows. We are not planning on fixing the glass this year but would like to do it next year if money is available.

As the school is now under way and the repairs are urgently needed, will you please consider this request as soon as possible, before your next scheduled meeting if possible. Sincerely yours, Glyn B. Adsit (Treasurer)."

Adsit, Glyn B., Minister and Missionary and Treasurer, Hofei Station, Hofei, Anhwei, China, Letter to Administrative Council, United Christian Missionary Society, Nanking, China, September 24, 1948.

"Dear friends, a letter from Mr. Sen, of Liang Yuan came today requesting money to move his belongings from Liang Yuan to Shr Tan Chao. He is also requesting that we allow him money to buy necessary furniture for his house in Shr Tan Chao.

We feel that his requests are legitimate and relay them on to you. You will notice that in our budget suggestions, we included such items as this under the heading 'Travel.' That is one reason it is as large as it is. He states that the moving and furniture will amount to 251 GY. He has some furniture in Liang Yuan but is leaving it there for Mr. Jyang Jau Hong to use when he moves there.

My suggestion is that there are two ways we can handle this request. You can consider it outside of our budget suggestion as a special request, or you can include it in our budget as was our original intention. Will you please advise which way you prefer? Sincerely yours, Glyn B. Adsit, Treasurer."

- McCallum, J.H., United Christian Missionary Society, China Mission, Nanking, China, Letter to Glyn Adsit, September 29, 1948.

"Glyn Adsit, here are several matters accumulated that I want to write to you about. Your budget received and we are studying it along with the others that have come in. We note that there are no receipts whatever. Is it possible to show any in any of your enterprises or from the farm, etc?

Moving. We have been talking over this problem. It is proper to ask us for the furniture for Swen. Such things as beds, table, chairs, water kong, if they have a kong that is not necessary. As to moving we think that moving within a station should be part of the station budget, but from station to station that the mission may provide, though even there, we hope that when some church invites a new man they may pay part or all of the travel. Therefore, if you can take care of the moving from your travel budget, do so, even though we have to formally pass the new budget.

Special. I have circulated the AC (Administrative Council) members and they approve the use of the 55.00 and 85.45 specials total U.S. 140.45 Adsit specials for the use you suggest and the Hofei station approves. If Walter has these on his books you can have them any time.

The U.S 100 and the special you wrote about seem to be related. On the basis of the need of the repairs, we are approving the use of the 400 G.Y. Since there is in the Crusade an item for the Rural Center I think we can ask for it on that basis, and in the mean time, carry it on the suspense account. If that does not go through, we can still try to put it on regular repairs. You know any income from rents belongs to repairs. There should be something coming in from some of the people living on the Rural Center grounds.

That covers your letters. I better send a copy of this to Grace so that if money is involved, you will both have the information. How is Timmy and the wife? Best regards, sincerely, J.H.M. P.S. I suppose Walter will send money through Grace. However, this is his business and yours, not mine."

- Adsit, Jean, Minister and Missionary, Hofei, China, Letter to Mom, September 29, 1948.

"Dearest Mom, what I ever did without a baby to love, I do not know. Glyn and I just stand and look at Timmy and wonder how we were ever fortunate enough to have God bless us with such a perfect formed and beautiful child. I suppose all parents feel just like we do over their child, and later children, for we want Timmy to have a brother or sister one day. I want you to keep up with Tim's growing and his cute things, so this letter will be full of him. Now he eats cereal, egg, banana, and, of course, orange juice and cod liver oil, and he nurses. Oranges are 35 cents American money apiece here in Hofei, so Tim either has an ascorbic acid pill or canned orange juice.

He sleeps through from 7:00 p.m. or 7:30 p.m. to 5:30 a.m. or 6:00 a.m. This pleases his father and mother, of course, because they were afraid there for awhile that they wouldn't get any more sleep. He laughs out loud and coos lots. He is already mischievous. He will stop in the middle of his nursing, and I'll think he's almost asleep, but he'll look up at me and laugh and his eyes just dance. I can imagine that Glyn used to be just like that. If you've baby pictures of Glyn, will you compare them with Timmie? I want him to be just like his dad so much.

The box with the little toys, the exerciser for the bed, etc., arrived and were we happy over it. Tim loves the red bears on it. The only rubber pants he had were too small, so, needless to say, I was glad for them. Tomorrow, I am going to go and have one of the ladies teach me to knit. I am going to knit two pair of leggings for Tim. When he starts crawling, he'll need something warm, and the things I've ordered from the States won't be here by cold weather I am afraid. Last Monday, Tim was five months old. We weighed him, and he weighed 15 lbs. 14 oz. By now, it's probably 16 lbs. He tries to sit up alone already. He can roll over now by himself. I have to watch him when I leave him now. I also think we're going to have a tooth before long the way he chews his lower lip and slobbers.

My, you should see him look at his hands. He seems so pleased with himself. He turns the hands over, and sometimes he fusses at them as if he were mad at them because they wouldn't do what he wanted them to. He holds a rattle pretty well. One of the missionaries gave him one, and he has fun with it.

Glyn and I read all the baby books we have to see what schedule he's supposed to be on and what he should be doing next, but we have decided that Tim is writing a book all his own. [Little did they know what a prophetic statement that was.] He doesn't do anything just like the book says, except, of course, cry. This is quite a volume on our boy, but he's our main topic of conversation at this time, and I thought you'd enjoy it all. Love, Jean."

- Adsit, Glyn B., Minister and Missionary, Hofei, China, Letter and article sent entitled, "Precious Package," to George Walker Buckner, Jr., Editor, *World Call*, International Magazine of Disciples of Christ, September 29, 1948.

- Adsit, Glyn B., Minister and Missionary, Hofei, Anhwei, China, Letter to Mac (James McCallum) and on the back of the first letter, Letter to Walter (Haskell), October 11, 1948.

"Dear Mac, enclosed, you will find some suggestions for the new missionaries coming out to China. Some of the Hofeites have not given me their lists yet, and I don't think I should hold these any longer.

In relation to the children's supplement, Timothy has been receiving the $12.50 per month, but has not received any 20 percent supplement or increase. What has happened to the suggestion about children's allowance that were made in Kuling? Has the society taken any action?

One reason we wanted the $20 left at home was to pay bills that arise in the USA. How can we pay these if you have it sent out here? Is it possible to have this $20 per missionary left at home if we wish it? If not, when it is sent out here is there some way we can get Walter to keep it in the US$ (gold) account until we want it used? I am thinking of writing Payne, asking him to withhold $40 per month for us and deposit it in our deposit account. Would this mess up your plans in relation to the $20-per-month business?

We have not been able to find any merchants to take checks and give us money for them. The Hofei Bank will take checks, and we have to wait from a week to twelve days to get the money. They are, at present, asking 2 percent.

In relation to the money the banks are charging to send money to Hofei: who is to pay this percentage? In lieu of the fact that we are on a cost-of-living basis does it seem proper for us to pay this 2 percent, or should the mission handle it?

As an example, I have just had 1,500 GY sent to Hofei via Hofei Bank. It will cost me GY 30. That ain't hay.

I have been getting up at 2:00 a.m. to listen to the World Series. I thought Boston would sure take more than one out of four games. I am still plugging for Cleveland. Sincerely yours, Glyn. P.S. What action have you all taken in relation to getting Ju-Shau-Tan's mother moved from the rural center? You wrote us a letter asking that we hurry Mr. Chyan out of the church property. We cannot move him until Mrs. Ju is moved from the Rural Center. It seems to me that no preacher should be allowed to use property in two stations. Can you strongly suggest that he quickly come to Hofei and move her, lock, stock and barrel? GBA."

[On back of same letter.]

"Dear Walter, I notice by your statement to me for September that you deposited the entire salary of $133.74 in my Shanghai bank account. Just at present we do need this money in our account, but later, we would like to ask you to *not* deposit our salary as it comes but to please wait until we notify you to do same. Is it possible for you to do this?

The Nanking Bank sent me forms to fill out. How much money will we have to deposit there to open the account? Will you please ask them and deposit the necessary amount for us?

Having our $20 per missionary sent out to China presents a problem for the Adsit family. We want to use this money in the USA. Just recently, we had to buy around $100 worth of baby clothes and doodads. We are also buying baby foods and need money in States to pay for these. What should I notify Mr. Payne in order to get this money left there? Do you want the letter to go through your office?

The statements for August-September have arrived. That means you are about caught up. Congratulations, I know you must be breathing a little easier now. Our railroad is functioning. Why don't you run up for a visit

Thanksgiving? Will you please ask Hwang when he is coming to Hofei to help me set up a good system of bookkeeping? Please remind him that he was going to bring along necessary books also. Sincerely yours, Glyn."

- McCallum, J.H., Letter to Glyn B. Adsit, October 14, 1948.

"Dear Glyn, the matter of Timothy's allowance is between you and the Society. I only passed on the information which we seemed to have through correspondence. Smith's did not know either, so it is from the Reynolds. Better look over your remittance amounts carefully, for it will not be listed under Timmy's name but will be in the total amount. They generally figure those items automatically and are not often mistaken. Anyway, it is not part of our accounting.

We have a deposit account with the society, but more often take out of it rather than put in it. If we send in bills to be paid at home, they take it out of salary even when the amount is more than our salary (like insurance). If it does not come out this month, it will the next. Fact is, they are generally a month late in taking it out. What they give a statement for this month actually often comes out the next. If you use sight drafts, you need to distinguish if it is from salary account or from personal deposits account. They often make mistakes here.

Walter will tell you about money. I think we are prepared to lay your money down in Hofei without cost to you. I do not know if it is practical to keep track of all the checks you issue on money after it has been deposited to your account. It would seem simpler to try to keep two weeks ahead of the game rather than two weeks behind.

We have done our best to get Chu to move his family out. We do not approve of his occupying places in Hofei and Chuhsien and then renting out his own property. We are in a jam here, and Pan does not seem inclined to move until we get Chien out. According to our last information,

Chu should be in Hofei now and we hope things will start moving. Sincerely, J.H. McCallum.

- Adsit, Glyn B., Minister and Missionary, Hofei, Anhwei, China, Letter to James McCallum and Luther Shao, October 23, 1948.

"Dear Mac and Luther, What a headache the making out of this budget is! Mr. Hwang has made several suggestions that have led us to change the form of our budget somewhat. The enclosed is the result.

Salary may be broken down as follows:

Wang-Ji-Tyan	120	per month	Hofei
Jang-Liang-Yu	60	""	Hofei
Hung-Chang-Gwei	60	""	Hofei
Shr-Bau-Ling	60	""	Hofei
Swen-Shu-Ren	60	""	Shr Tan Chao
Jen-Shr-Yung	20	""	Liang Yuan
Teacher (not chosen)	15	""	Shr-li-tou
Teacher (not chosen)	15	""	Jang-da-yindz
Li-Timothy Medical Worker	60	""	Swen-den-ji
Jya-Da-Long	*60*	""	Swen-den-ji and Liang Yuan

530

The last item on the proposed budget is in relation to the rural center. We are dividing the men into the salary class and wages class.

Salary for four men as follows:

Shu-Jya-Hwa	60	""	Government pays 48, we pay 12
Sun-Franklin	20	""	San Ruh school and mission pay 40 of his salary and our depart-ment pays 20
Hu-Jyan	40	""	
Fang-	*40*	""	
gy-	160 or	per year	
	1,980		

Mr. Shu, is the government man who runs the rural center farm. The other three men help run our farm center train-ing school.

Wages for seven men as follows:

5 workmen at gy 20. per month	1,200
1 workman at gy 23. per month	275
1 cook for students at gy 16 per month	*192*
gy 1,668 for the year	

I believe the rest of the items are self explanatory. Sincerely yours, Glyn B. Adsit."

• Adsit, Glyn B., Minister and Missionary, Hofei, Anhwei, China, Letter to James McCallum and Luther Shao, October 23, 1948.

"Dear friends, to be quite blunt so you will know what this letter is about, I am finding it a little hard to satisfy Mr. Wang-Ji-Tyan with the budget. He seems to feel that his salary is way too low and is trying every way he can to supplement it.

We are suggesting that his salary be GY 120 per month. This means that he will get an added 12 as his personal social allowance for each month. This is all right so far. He is also asking that he be given an oil allowance (kerosene). His reason is that there is a constant flow of guests at his home and it necessitates his burning an extra lamp or two each night. He asked for 10 more per month. What I want to know is what policy our mission is going to take in relation to this request? Mr. Hwang says Mr. Wu-Sing-Dan does not receive an oil allowance. If we give Wang one, will not this complicate matters somewhat? If you do decide to give him this oil allowance, I feel that 10 is too much. It would be more reasonable to give him 4 or 5 per month.

Another sore spot is the social allowance we give him for keeping visitors who stay at his house. As you know, there are visitors who are constantly coming to Hofei for one purpose or another. They usually stay at Mr. Wang's home because he demands it. He says it costs about gy 1 per day, per visitor who stays there. Is that reasonable? Also, I would like your office to tell him, and me, just what can be considered a legitimate visitor. He has a tendency to turn in a bill for everybody who stays there whether they have come to Hofei on church business or not. Also, will you advise me whether it would be possible to expect our church workers, such as Pastor Li and Mr. Hwang, to pay their board when they stay at his home? We know they are provided with travelling money, and it seems unfair to the stations to expect us to pay their board when they are provided money for that purpose. This allowance amounts to 20 per month.

If you add up all the money Mr. Wang actually gets, it is:

120 salary
12 personal allowance
10 proposed oil allowance

20   visitor allowance

5   stamp and telegram money, etc.

gy   167per month

In our last budget meeting, there was some feeling as to the wide margin between Wang's salary and the rest of our workers. We tried to explain that he was better trained, had longer service and had more mouths to feed, and had more responsibilities. Just what is the criteria for paying salaries now? We have heard that it is length of service and mouths to feed. Is this right?

Which one of these three do you give more weight? Also, shall we pay a single woman as much as we do a man with a family of three children? This question came up in relation with Miss Shr-Bau-Ling and some of our married men. We had proposed that we pay her 50 per month and pay the men with families 60 per month. She felt that it was too much a loss of face. She has had more experience and is better trained. But I feel that, regardless of training and length of service, we should put heavy weight on the number of mouths to feed. I do not see how a man with a wife and three children can live on gy 60 per month. Can you give me a little help on this matter? Sincerely yours, Glyn B. Adsit."

- Adsit, Jean, Minister and Missionary, Hofei, Anhwei, China, Letter to Clinton P. Campbell, October 26, 1948.

"Dear Mr. Campbell: This will acknowledge the receipt of your most welcome letter announcing my assignment as service link to the church in Stratford. I have known these good people for many years. In fact, I was baptized in this church. I know Mrs. W.O. Bryant very well. Before my mother died, she and Mrs. Bryant were the best of friends.

I can assure you that I will do my best to keep the Stratford church interested in our mission work. I know, all too well, that they need encouragement in giving to our unified programs. Both Glyn and I are very happy about this assignment.

Will you tell Mrs. Higdon we are very sorry for her and that broken arm? Also tell E.K. that we *just baptized another twenty-six people in Hofei.* Nine of these boys were from our rural center training class. Sincerely yours, Jean Adsit."

- Adsit, Glyn B., Minister and Missionary, Hofei, Anhwei, China, Open Letter to Dear Friends no address or name given, but sent to all Living Link churches, documenting an incident where Glyn and others got shot at, October 26, 1948.

"Dear friends, the last trip to ErShrpu was an exciting one. I almost got shot! Miss Verla Elliot, Miss Shr, and Mr. Fang and I were on the road as usual. We were riding our bikes and thoroughly enjoying the trip. All of a sudden, we heard the ping of a bullet as it whizzed by us and lodged in the dirt embankment behind us. This was the one time in my life that I have been consciously aware of fear. I was terribly afraid. I was also mad because I could not see who had done the shooting. Miss Elliot said, 'Glyn, we better stop. Maybe they yelled at us and we didn't hear them.' I agreed, and we got off our bikes. We had no more than gotten off when, zing, another shot whizzed over our heads. Our first impulse was to jump into the ditch and stay there, but we decided to keep going toward our little village. We had talked of going back to Hofei but decided that would not be wise since the person doing the shooting was behind us. We jumped on our bicycles and practically flew to Ershrpu.

At Ershrpu, we had our Sunday school services. It was very hard to concentrate on the service because, by this time, my stomach had decided to get nervous and tie itself into a knot. I had to appear brave for the sake of the other three. I was responsible for their safe return to Hofei. The suggestions I mentioned were three: 1) Try to get a truck to stop and pick us, and our bikes, up and carry us to Hofei. 2) Change our foreign clothing for Chinese dress, walk home and have our bikes carried home later.

And 3) Wait until dark and ride or walk home. We talked it through and decided to return via bike a little later that day. It was with fear and trembling that we got on our bikes and started the return trip home. We made it in safety, and we were very thankful to God.

A person never realizes just what the promise of a future and eternal life can mean until his life is almost taken from him. That lesson has been strongly driven home to me by this experience. It is a wonderful thing to realize that even though one might lose his body by being shot, his spirit will live on.

We do not know who shot at us. We do not understand their motive. We are guessing that it was somebody trying to frighten us for some reason. It might be anti-Christian, anti-foreign, anti-American, or maybe a Communist who did it. Let me say that if his purpose was to frighten us, he succeeded!

Our Christian program is in full swing here in Hofei. The Hofei church baptized twenty-six people last Sunday. Nine of these were boys from my rural center training class. We are very proud that they have the courage to step out of their decadent beliefs and accept our Lord's way of life.

We are still plugging away at studying the Chinese language. That is our main job for this year. I have been appointed treasurer for our rural work. This is a hard job and takes a great deal of time. We are kept more than busy and are happy that we have more than we can do.

Hofei is celebrating its fiftieth year of the Christian church. That means that our church here is still very young compared to the church in America.

This week, we are having our home and family life meetings. The young are discussing how to develop a Christian home. They are being encouraged to marry Christians and to take a more active part in church life. Our young people are active in the choir and a young people's society.

The Goulters are moving to Chuchow this month. Lyrel Teagarden is moving to NanTungChow. We had been using some of their furniture, and their moving means we are having to have new furniture made. It has been difficult to find wood dry enough to make the needed chairs, table, desk, settee, etc. We have just had a bed and playpen made for Timothy Lee. The bed is completely enclosed with wire and is mosquito proof. Mr. Goulter has just been operated on for a hernia (rupture). He is recovering nicely. He got this rupture on our last trip to Liang Yuan. We had to ride donkeys for about twenty-five miles. The constant jiggling caused his rupture to burst out. I am not ruptured, but I am sure sore in a certain spot.

Our hospital nurse, Miss Grace Young, fell from her bicycle and broke her left ankle. She is past sixty and is a little slow in recuperating.

I saw a woman who came to the hospital to have a tumor removed from her stomach. It was huge thing. They weighed her before and after the operation, and it was found that the tumor growth weighed a hundred and twenty pounds. The woman only weighed sixty pounds when that monstrous thing was removed from her body. The shock of having it removed killed her, but she would have died anyway had it not been removed.

Buying our winter's supply of groceries has been a chore this time. We made a list and gave it to the Corprons who purchased the groceries in Shanghai. They turned them over to a shipping company who guaranteed their delivery in Hofei. The boat, which was carrying the goods, was held up by robbers, and our things were taken off. The robbers notified us that we would have to pay about 30 percent of value if we wanted the groceries sent to us. We finally got the things, but only after much bargaining and loss of time.

The military situation is slowly worsening. City after city is falling to the Communists in north China. Everyone here is expecting the Commies to arrive in Hofei this fall or next spring. We intend to sit tight until we have to leave.

The economic condition is also bad. We had hoped that the currency reform would work. It seems to have failed because the people are not cooperating with the government. It is almost impossible to buy anything on the streets. The government has put a ceiling price on goods, and the farmers and merchants will not sell their goods. If a farmer carries rice or straw into Hofei, he is stopped on the streets by the soldiers and half of his rice and straw is taken by the soldier. It is plain robbery, but the farmer cannot do anything because the soldier has the gun. We do not blame him for not bringing his produce into town. The common man is almost hoping that the Communists will come. They reason that any change would be a good one. The present government has too many corrupt men in power who are thinking only of their own welfare.

Our garden is producing wonderfully for this fall. We are now eating tomatoes right off the vine, sweet corn so tender one hardly has to chew it. Our second crop of potatoes is coming on.

I have saved the best for the last. Our boy is growing every day in every way. He is six months old today. He jabbers all day long and wakes us up every morning with his own version of Chinese opera. We are very much afraid that he is being spoiled, but I suppose we could hope for little else when we realize that he is the only foreign baby in our mission station. Timmy loves his bath and kicks water all over the room. He has a special toy, a stuffed deer that we call Babie. And most important of all, he is beginning to look a little like his father.

We will be waiting for you to write. It helps a lot to hear from you. The days go faster, the nights are shorter, and our hours are brighter because you care. Love from your China friends (Glyn and Jean)."

- Adsit, Glyn B., Minister and Missionary, Hofei, China, Letter to Mother and Home Folks, Also enclosed article entitled, "Hope For the Soul of China," to be sent to George Walker Buckner, Jr., Editor, *World Call*,

International Magazine of Disciples of Christ, October 27, 1948.

"Dear Mother and home folks, as you can read by the letter I sent to our churches, I was really excited when that guy took a pot shot at us. I think it probably was a soldier just trying to scare us and have himself some fun. But as Jean says, 'You must remember that you are not only a husband but a father now.' So, I will not take any unnecessary risks. The military situation is steadily getting worse for the national government. They keep losing one city after another. We know that there is fighting within a hundred miles of us. We do not feel, however, that now is the time to leave. Dr. Corpron and I are talking of trying to stay and see if we can work under the Commies. The women and children would, of course, go to Nanking or Shanghai or America. Jean says she prefers me going with her or her staying with me. She does not want to separate our family. But as I say, it is too early to make that decision.

We need about six generators for our Aladdin Conversion 1944 Gasoline Lantern. Perhaps these can be bought at a store that handles Aladdin products. If not, will you please contact the Aladdin Co., which can be reached at The Mantle Lamp Company of America, Inc., Chicago, Illinois? We also need one dozen mantles for this same lantern. We are enclosing a travelers' cheque for $10. We are making it out to your shop. No one will know but what I signed it in your presence.

Today is the coldest day of this fall season. I have on two sweaters and a coat and two pair of socks, and my feet are still cold. We are not turning on the stove until we have to. Fuel is our most expensive item. Gasoline is $1 per gallon, and we use a gallon every day. Kerosene is 66 cents per gallon, and we use three quarts per day. Fuel oil for the big stove will run 75 cents per day. Wood and coal for the kitchen stove will run $1 per day. That means about $3.30 per day for fuel of one type or another. You can see why we try to save fuel.

Tell Duane not to try to do too many things. He will probably end up doing none of them well. Has he given up the railroad completely?

Timmy has no teeth yet. He has developed a real cute trick (we think). He shakes his head no when he does not want to drink his milk from the cup. He can almost wave good-bye but doesn't do it every time. His hair is still very fine and sparse. It is getting darker as it gets thicker.

About that shooting. We have decided not to go to Ershrpu for the rest of this fall and winter. By that time, maybe the situation will have corrected itself. The Chinese will continue to go, but the missionaries will not go.

I am enclosing some Chinese currency. The green bill is worth about a quarter of a cent. The blue is worth 2 cents. The red bill is worth 1 cent. You all can divide it up to suit yourselves. The picture is of Dr. Sun Yat Sen, China's first president. The 10-cent bill is more recently issued, the picture is of President Chiang-Kai-Shek. It is worth 2.5 cents. Love, Glyn. P.S. Hello, folks. Just another little article for *World Call*. Don't know whether they will print it or not. We are fine, and Timmy is growing every day. He eats egg, bananas, and cereal now. Please mail the film to us. Just send it via airmail alone, not in a package, and register it. Love, Glyn."

- Adsit, Glyn B., "The Bible Has a Message for Today," sermon preached in Hofei, China, October 10, 1948, pp.1-3.

"The Bible Has A Message For Today

Introduction: The Chinese people do not need to be told that there is trouble in this world. You can see war, confusion, poverty, corruption, and selfishness on every hand. So many Chinese are becoming despondent. They are losing hope. They are saying, there is no hope. Our Central Government is going to fold up and go to Formosa, or some other place of safety. It is a very dark picture that we look at; and the question I will now ask is, 'Is there any hope?' Does Christianity have any solution to offer us who need help so badly?

What China and all the rest of the world needs to hear is that there is a solution to our problems. We need not give up in despair and commit suicide. There is hope for the troubled world, and for all of us.

Even though it is true that we see our world changing everyday; we can find great comfort in realizing that God does not change. He is the same yesterday, today, and forevermore. If God loves us, and our Bible tells us that He does, He will love us whether the Kuomingdang is in power, or whether the Gungchangdang is in power. It really does not matter who our rulers are. We have a Father who loves us and who cares doe us. He will not forget that we are his children. Although our life on this earth is bitter, he is preparing a better home for us in Heaven. We sing a song, 'nobody knows the trouble I see, nobody knows but Jesus, nobody knows the trouble I see, glory halleluiah.' This song tells us that Jesus knows our troubles. Do not forget when you pray that Jesus knows and cares.

As long as brother fights brother, as long as men are selfish, as long as men are sinful, we Christians need to point to god's wonderful World and say, "The answer to your doubts and fears lie within this book. When everything else in changing and you are about to give up hope, remember God still lives and he will not forget us.

The Bible has a message for today. God is still speaking to his children. What is the message? The first message that the Bible has for us is that God is our Father and He created us.

God Creates

Some people believe that we human beings are no more than animals. They say there is no God, no Heaven. Believing that there is no God, they think they can live just like they want to. But the Bible says there is a God. We as Christians must share our conviction that the world and all that is in it belongs to God. In the beginning God created all life; vegetable, animal, and human. The flowers grow up in their beauty to glorify God. The animals were created to serve man. But man, here is God's finest creation. It is said that man is created in God's image. This means that we have a soul. We are more than mere body. We are a Spirit. This part of us will never die.

Because we belong to God, we are not free to act as we wish. We are responsible creatures. If we were animals we would not be responsible. But we are human beings made in God's image; and we are responsible to Him. Most of us have a little money that we consider our very own. But we must be very careful how we use our money; because the money is also God's money. On the final judgment day, we will have to report how we have used our money.

Some people say it is nobody's business what I do; I can do what I want to. But it is God's business how you act. You are responsible to God for your every action. (Stop) A father came home drunk and was staggering around the house. The mother noticed their small son imitating his father. He was playing like he too was drunk. This father was setting a bad example and will be partially responsible if his son turns out to be a drunkard.

We are responsible for our neighbors. Have you ever heard this story? (Read Luke 10:25 about the Good Samaritan.) I want to ask you a question. If you do not love your neighbors in Hofei enough to be friendly and helpful to them, do you think that you deserve eternal life? I am afraid the answer is no!

God created us and we will not be at peace in our hearts until we fulfill the purpose for which we were created. That purpose is to become as Christ like as possible. God is still creating new personalities. Our Bible tells us that: A man called Nicodemeus came to Jesus and asked him, 'How can a man be born again?' Jesus answered something like this. Your physical body cannot be born again. You cannot enter again into your mother's womb, and be born.

You must have a new Spirit born in you. You must let my Spirit come into your life. I am love. If you have a spirit of love you will be born again. This, my friends, is what Christianity is trying to do. We are seeking to give men a spirit of love. We want them to be reborn. When the Spirit of God comes into your life you will be born again. In the beginning, God created man, and today, he is creating new men out of old ones. China needs to hear this message: *You can be born again.* If you are not happy with your present way of living; if you are a sinner and want forgiveness; listen to Jesus say, 'You can be born again.'

The second message that the Bible has for today is that God has a plan for the world and for you.

God's plan for the physical world is that it will produce the needed food for man to eat. He expects man to develop the natural resources of the world. There is enough food in the world for all to eat; if man will only learn to share. Nature cooperates with God and produces many wonderful harvests. But man has not yet learned that he must cooperate with God.

God wants all the people in the world to live peacefully together. But we are all quarreling and fighting. What a great country China will be when her wars are over and her sons come home to work at a more peaceful business. How happy we all will be when every home in Hofei has running water and electrical lights. How easy it will be to travel when the railroad is rebuilt to Hofei. These developments are coming. But, I am wondering if China is as deeply interested in Spiritual things as she is in material things. Our spiritual resources must be developed.

God is interested in the development of our spiritual life. His plan is that man shall love his fellow man and live peacefully with them. He has given us some moral laws to help us learn how to be peaceful. He says a peaceful man is more important than a fighting man. Look around the world and see who the greatest men are. The greatest men today are Ghandi of India who has just been murdered,

Kagawa of Japan, and Sweitzer of Africa, a missionary who is a doctor in that lonely place.-Our Bible says: (read Matthew 5:3-12)

God gave ten commandments as His plan for the world. These commandments, 'You shall not kill, you shall not steal, you shall not lie, you shall not worship false idols, you shall not be covetous, etc.' Men disobeyed these and by so doing destroyed themselves.-You cannot break God's laws you only break yourself on them. For example: If you climb up on the Hofei city wall and jump off and fall down fifty or seventy five feet, you do not break God's law of gravity, you only illustrate it by breaking your body to bits. God's plan is that men shall obey His moral law of living peacefully together. If we fail to do this we destroy ourselves.

Look at the atomic bomb. One bomb was so powerful that it destroyed a whole city in Japan during the last war. The people of that town; Hiroshima, have learned that God is not only a God of love, but also a God of law.

God created us and is our Father. He gave us a plan to help us develop into good peaceful men. His moral laws insist that we love our fellow men and live peacefully with them. We have failed to believe God and are suffering the consequences today. But God loved us enough to give His Son for us. He has not given up hope.

God Gives His Son as part of His plan.

John 3:16, 'For God so loved the world that he gave His only begotten Son, that whosoever believeth in Him should not perish, but have everlasting life.'-The third message that our Bible has for us today is that God loved us enough to give us a part of Himself. The world will never know what it cost God the Father to give His only Son to the world. It was a gift of great sacrifice. God knew then, and we know now, that unless our giving costs us something, it will not accomplish very much.-Jesus came as a part of god's plan. Before He came all that the world had was a book, the Bible. After He came, they had a person to look at and to follow.

Jesus told us that the ten commandments were good and should be obeyed. But, He said, there are two commandments of greater importance: 'You shall love the Lord your god with all your heart, and with all your soul, and with all your mind; and your neighbor as yourself.' Love God and love your fellowman. This is Jesus's answer to your problem of life. Find out about God, and find out what He wants you to do.

We Christians must tell our friends that Jesus can change a man's life as Confucius, Budda, or Mohammed never can. Why can Jesus change a man's life? Because He is the Son of God and God has given Him the power to change lives. This was His special task. He came into the world to live for only a few years, but because what He taught was truth, His teachings live on and are changing lives every day.–How can He change your life? This is no mystery. I have seen men who were sinners change into good, useful citizens. What happened to them? They heard about Jesus, they read his teachings and believed them. They lived like He told them too. They changed from useless to useful men.

Jesus idea is that if a man wants to serve God; he must serve his fellowman. 'You shall love your neighbor as yourself,' Jesus says. There is no other way to serve God. The Chinese have a saying, '*Mei you ban fa*.' If you see a person in serious trouble you say there is no way to help. But as Christians we must never stop trying to find a way to serve our fellowman. As long as men will love their fellowman, there is hope for China.

Conclusion: The Bible has a message for today. It tells us that God loves us and wants each one of us to strive for a Christ like character. It tells us that God created us and that we can be reborn. It gives us a plan for living. It shows that God gave His Son to save us from our sins. Is there one here today who is seeking for peace in his heart?

Is there one here who is interested in learning more about this Jesus who came down from Heaven to save us from our sins? Listen then to Jesus, 'Come unto me all who labor and are heavy laden, and I will give you rest. Take my yoke upon you, and learn from me; for I am gentle and lowly in heart, and you will find rest for your souls. For my yoke is easy and my burden is light.' Matthew 11:28.

Let us pray."

(Many answered the alter call and were baptized later as a direct result of this sermon inspired by God and delivered by Glyn through an interpreter.)

- Adsit, Glyn B., Minister and Missionary, Hofei, Anhwei, China, Letter to James McCallum and Luther Shao, November 6, 1948.

"Dear Luther and Mac: We are facing a minor financial crisis. The salaries for October and for November are nowhere close to adequate. The salaries for October should be at least doubled, and the November ones tripled or quadrupled. This means that if a man's basic salary was 50 for September that he should get 100 for October and 150 for November. Every day we delay makes it imperative that we pay more. I am speaking here of the basic salary that you had been paying. This is not taking into account the raise that we were going to give them.

I am sending a wire today asking for money and for instructions as to how much salary to pay. Will you please answer this letter giving me details so I can pass information on to the workers? As treasurer, you can see how they are on my neck and expect me to take care of them.

We had a little surplus money and I paid the workers one month in advance. But the money has depreciated so badly that even that will not enable them to buy enough rice to feed their families.

Our rural center workers were getting gy 15 per month. This was okay in September, when they could live on 6 dollars as far as their food was concerned. In October, it cost them gy 9 to live. This month, they cannot possibly get by on less than 20 for food alone. The workers' basic pay should be gy 60 for November.

The military situation is still calm around here. People are worried because prices are going up and they cannot buy goods.

Oswald is still in bed. He had a setback from his operation. Seems neuralgia set in his chest, and it was extremely painful when he tried to breathe. He ran a fever of 101, but it is down to normal this morning. He will probably be in bed for the next two weeks. Grace Young is up on crutches and with her leg in a cast. She is busy taking inventory at the hospital.

Sincerely yours, Glyn B. Adsit."

- Cabot, John M., American Consul General, Letter to All American Nationals Residing in the Provinces of Kiangsu and Anhwei, Circa November 1948 (No date given but found attached to a letter from Glyn to Hofei Friends dated November 15, 1948 mentioned below this message).

"To All American nationals residing in the provinces of Kiangsu and Anhwei, military developments in North China make it appear possible that hostilities might spread farther south with the result that normal transportation facilities from Shanghai might be disrupted. Also, with the approach of winter and the increasingly acute shortage of food supplies and fuel, those remaining in Shanghai and its environs might be subjected to undue hardships.

Accordingly, it is suggested that unless you have compelling reason to remain, you consider the desirability of evacuation while normal transportation facilities remain available. John M. Cabot, American Consul General."

- Adsit, Glyn B., Minister and Missionary, Puko, China, Letter to Hofei Friends, November 15, 1948.

"Dear Hofei friends, we arrived safe in Puko at 4:30 p.m. (with two steamer trunks and a leather suitcase).

We did not have any trouble along the way, except it was rather tiresome. Timmy behaved beautifully.

Mac has written a long, three-page letter sending it by Wang tomorrow morning. I think he answers most of our questions very well. One thing we want to emphasize is about the money situation. They are having a very hard time getting money. The bank will not take drafts, and that is serious since that is our only source of income.

Reynolds and Smiths are in Shanghai now waiting for passage for US. Hubert and Joe will return from Shanghai and try to stay for a while longer. There seems to be several thousand soldiers between Hofei and Puko. We noticed several thousand around Twein Chou, and they say here that there will be a battle there right away. This will mean that the bus road will be cut off if that battle materializes. All the government people have gone, and about one half of the missionaries, men as well as women. I will have to decide tonight what I am going to do. I will either go on to US with Jean and Timmy or will see her off and return to Hofei and try to work under Pinks.

Rice is 400 a Dan in Nanking. The exchange is still four to one instead of twenty to one. The banks are not recognizing the other higher rate. George and Marge are going to try to stick it out a little longer. Marge is here at McCollum's now. Eva and Mac will try to stay even if Pinks take over. Ethyl will probably go home and leave Walter here. Everyone here hopes that Winona will come on out and go home. They are worried about her and hope that a vote or something will be taken there and that she can be forced to come out. I told them that being a Hofeite, I would not vote that way since everyone there had to make up their own mind.

It is very hard for me to make up my mind as to what I should do. I want to come back to Hofei, but I also want my wife to be happy. She insists that if I stay, she and Timmy will stay also. I cannot hardly ask her and the baby to stay under the present situation, and that probably means that I will return to America and hope to return some future date. That will mean that I am the only man going, but my shoulders are broad and can take the criticism if any is cast our way about that. Suchow is supposed to be surrounded by Commies, and it should be a matter of days until the city itself will fall.

They suggest that you ask families to move into our house and try to keep it from disappearing that way.

Mrs. Reynolds and kids are trying to get to Philippines to work there, but passage that way is very difficult [and she has] not [been] successful yet.

They are sending our families to Shanghai and taking whatever passage they can get from there on. The American Embassy is helping them find passage.

Now as to my opinions: it looks to me like the money issue will be the main deciding factor. If we cannot get money, we cannot carry on our work. Also, another factor is whether you want to work under Pinks or not. I feel that it is only a question of time until the change comes. If you pack to come out, bring only essential things. No one is going by air, but boats are restricting poundage on baggage. They say around 400 lbs. per family will be allowed. We will do a little repacking and try to take most of what we brought with us.

If I go, and it looks at this moment like I will, please remember that each one of you has created a special place in our hearts during this last year. Verla had that place through the past seven years. Irene was a good friend in the States, and Oswald naturally won our love. Grace, stubborn as she is, makes us proud of her because of her bulldog tenacity, Winona for her optimism, Doug and Grace for being mom and pop during this difficult, hard first year. Jean is sure that Doug is the best doctor in the world. Timmy sends a great big GOO and DA, which means you GOOPS hurry up and get out of DAT place. I am sure he will not mind my translating for him because his Hofei ‘*Hwa*’ is a little hard to understand. There is so much more I want to say, but I am so tired tonight that I cannot think any more. Love, Glyn."

- McCallum, James, Office of the Secretary-Treasurer, United Christian Missionary Society, China Mission, Nanking, KU, China, State of the Mission Letter to Mr. Virgil Sly, November 18, 1948.

"Mr. Virgil Sly-State of the Mission Letter: As long as we can, I will try to get word to you as to what is happening. We might be clear off on what we expect, but we are in a position to judge the will of the people, and it looks to us like this part of the country and all of China will be taken over by the Communists. Means of communications are apt to be broken early. I know that you will have inquiries about our missionaries, so first, I will go down the list, and hereafter, whenever there is a change, I will try to let you know. I might repeat what I have said before, but would rather do that than make omissions.

Joseph Smith and family. We put Winefred, Freddie, and Douglas on board a converted destroyer in Nanking November 14 bound for Shanghai. They were supposed to have reservations at the Navy Y there and were assured of evacuation accommodations soon. They will have to let you know from there on. We have not heard from them. Joseph left here the thirteenth for Wuhu and intended to go by train to join the family in Shanghai, but his intentions were to return to Wuhu and continue his residence there.

Reynolds. Hubert, Harriet, Virginia, Jane, and Douglas all boarded the same destroyer on the fourteenth for Shanghai. It was Hubert's intention to return to Wuhu after a few days and continue on at the Wuhu academy as long as that is possible. The Reynolds are interested in going to the Philippines if possible and are making efforts while in Shanghai to go that way. However, Hubert would not go with them to the Philippines now, but in case he had to evacuate China latter would make efforts to join them there.

Adsits. Adsits came to Nanking by bus on November 15 and, through luck, managed to buy some unused tickets on the night train, and we saw them off at 10:00 p.m. November 16 for Shanghai with all their baggage piled into the train compartment. They all expect to return home (to US) by the first available evacuation ship. I understand there are three navy transports available or soon will be. They will have to send you final word from Shanghai.

Starn-Teagarden. We have had letters from Lyrel and Pauline, November 9, 11, 13. All is peaceful there, and they think they should stay there. However, Lyrel's household effects got moved only as far as Chuhsien and they contained important food stuffs. Most of Pauline's things including food stuffs we had accumulated are still in Nanking. With the jam in transportation unless we can include some things for them in the next evacuation ship to Shanghai, I do not see how we can manage to get more things to them. They are very accessible to Shanghai though, and there does not seem to be the *panic* there that we have here. (No more thin paper in this mission except letter head paper.)

Hofei. Corprons, Goulters, Young, Wilkinson, Elliott. The people in Hofei seem to be unaware as to what this is all about and we have been sending word to them by every means possible. They are well stocked with food and supplies to last the winter if it is necessary and they are apt to be cut off from us any day now, although we might be in the same unit of the country administratively, again, if Nanking falls or a new kind of government is formed…

Goulters. Oswald is still bedfast from his operation and will not be able to be moved for another week. Irene is sticking with Mr. Goulter. He does not want to leave but wants to get to Chuhsien as soon as possible. Oswald had one serious relapse but is doing nicely now. In eventualities, he wants to stick in China, any part of China he can. Their household goods were moved to Chuhsien, and the house there formerly occupied by the Burches has been repaired and put in good shape for their occupation. Mrs. Goulter sent most of her winter things there and their provisions also.

Corprons. They wish to stick with the girls, Doris and Jean, or stay together as a family unit. We have had no information that the Shanghai American school is closing, but we are assuming that that question is being seriously discussed now. Events are moving too fast for them. They cannot easily leave Mr. Goulter now, and their leaving they think would mean the breakup of the hospital there. They are not favorable toward working in a Communist regime even though medical work is one of the accepted avenues of service.

Young. Grace has always said, 'When the doctor goes, I go.' She still wears a cast and is using crutches and the bus line, which is the only avenue open now, if it is still open, is a very rugged trip.

Wilkinson. Wenona will not think of leaving as far as we can get reports. We have urged her to evacuate because of her health. The doctor thinks it very unwise to stay through even if they all stay.

Elliot. Verla is reported to want to stick with Wenona or Hofei.

Chuhsien. Cherryhomes. Today, they are both in this same room at another typewriter. Marge came here because there is a hospital and doctors handy. George comes and goes but intends to stay in Chuhsien and has a group of young men organized into a little cooperative group that hopes to scatter into the country and carry on Christian work. They are not highly trained but are willing and able to eat bitterness and can maintain themselves in the country pretty well. They have built up a stockpile of supplies to carry over several months. Those could be easily lost in looting overnight, but they have scattered them widely and they are the most enthusiastic little cell in the mission that I know of. Marge and George are unhappy in being separated and some of our group is urging them to go to the Philippines. In case the hospital here folds up, that might change their situation so that they would consider this. But George is determined to make a try of it here [in Chuhsien] first. On leaving for Chuhsien this morning, he wishes us to send Marge to the Philippines when that seems best.

Nanking. Bates. The university is struggling to make its decision. They have decided to try to carry on as long as possible and not to try to move. But the case will not easily stay decided. They will not have the means to continue long if they are cut off from outside support. They do not have the means of helping any of their staff to evacuate (Chinese staff), and for political reasons, you might understand there is real danger to some Chinese in staying here. Searle thinks it would be criminal for some of us not to stay and see what we can do in such a situation as faces us. Lilliath has no idea of leaving Nanking now.

Smythe. Lewis and Mardie are all for staying. Mardie has reservations for Shanghai on Friday the nineteenth. She has in mind that it might be necessary to arrange for their two daughters, Peggy and Joan, to evacuate, though this is not determined. She is concerned that she be not cut off from return to Nanking.

Gish. Edna is uncertain what to do. It is so near her furlough time that she does not want to be caught here. She is very sympathetic with the Chinese who wish to move on to another part of China, and if she does not evacuate in a few days, she might consider moving with missionaries of other missions who contemplate going to Hunan and on south. We talked with her yesterday.

Haskells. Mrs. Haskell is also uncertain. Walter insists that she goes this time, because of her health condition, and she is in the packing stage so we will have to wait and see. We in the office have been too busy to think of what we would do.

McCallums. No thought of leaving up to today. This is our job as long as it lasts. We are too young to think of retiring and too old to start over again somewhere else. If there is anything to do here, we want to try it.

We are in sympathy with the moving of mothers with children out of this area. We do not approve of families being separated unless all members themselves decide that way and insist upon it. We do not try to order anyone to go or to stay. We do give group advice and counsel.

Conditions have eased in Nanking the past few days. A week ago, we could scarcely get any money. Even now the banks, government and private, refuse to take a draft or check. We are trying to find out what the condition is in Shanghai. But we have been able to get a hold of some American currency that we can change at from twenty-two to one to thirty to one, which is favorable according to present prices. Prices have come down some due to the fact that there is little money and, therefore, few buyers. In general, we have secured enough to pay up to the end of January and to lay by food supplies for about that long. We are able to buy again in Nanking, where the food shortage is most severe.

We have four dangers or problems. 1) Food and supplies. There is not enough this winter to sustain the population of China. Dividing the land and cutting off the heads of landlords will not increase the supply right now, so a new government might have as hard a time as the old one to give the people what they need. This is almost a quotation from our conference with Leighton Stuart. 2) Money. If we can get a supply of nationalist money, which is not easy, it might be worthless. We might be cut off so that we cannot draw on any resources from you for some period. 3) Disorder. Danger from mobs, riots, retreating and defeated soldiers, or a victorious army. 4) Problems of a hostile government, which we are trying to solve now. We are trying to formulate what we can hope to do and we are trying to form a united Christian Front in Nanking, but I am afraid we have not done enough on that to say we really have any front. If we can have months or weeks rather than days, we will make progress.

None of our Chinese have left. It is natural for people to return to the place they call home in a time like this, and some families have been sent home. There is a wavering among our Chinese leaders, and I shall have to report separately about them. I am sure that Victor Siao, who was last year at TCU will be one of our mainstays. Luther Shao has been in the hospital with an infection but will be out this morning.

The present government could still win in this struggle *if* they would make the reforms necessary and *if they had the will to struggle.* But it looks like it would take more help than now seems to be in prospect. We hope for a breathing spell to better prepare to meet whatever is in store for us. Next and reported last evacuation ship to leave Nanking probably the twenty-first for Shanghai. Very sincerely, James McCallum."

- Pickens, Reverend H.B., Editor, The Butner Bulletin, Vol. 9, No. 35, *USS General H.W. Butner*, December 11, 1948.

"*Last Word On China.* Nanking, Dec. 9 (AP)—The official Chinese Central News Agency reported today that Col. Chiang Wei-kuo had arrived in Pengpu. The adopted son of Chiang Kai-Shek previously was reported with the armies trapped southwest of Suchow. He is Chief of Staff of the armored corps.

Paris, Dec. 9 (AP)—Dr. T.F. Tsiang, head of the Chinese Delegation to the U.N. said today Chinese diplomats have no intention of accommodating themselves to any Communist regime in China.

Peiping. Dec. 9 (AP)—An explosion of a boiler in the Peiping-Hankow Railroad Adsitration building shook Peiping's banking district today. Two workers were killed and four injured" (p.1).

- Adsit, Jean, Minister and Missionary, Story Outline Jean Wrote About The Trip Leaving China, Aboard *USS General W.H. Butler*, December 11, 1948.

The Harrowing Trip Out of China

Jean often told the harrowing story of the time when she, Glyn, and Tim were forced to leave Hofei, China. The significant events that occurred were outlined by Jean on note cards as she returned home on the *USS General W.H. Butner* while they were still fresh in her mind. Jean writes,

"We received our first telegram in 1948 telling us that the situation was getting worse and that we might want to think about returning to the United States. Other personnel, Grace Young and Doctor Oswald Goulter, also encouraged us to return home since we had a young baby. Then a second telegram arrived from the secretary of state's office encouraging all Americans to leave China. We had an offer from one of General Chiang Kai Shek's generals to use a troop transport truck to carry us and our belongings. The general, a Christian in our local church, said that when the troop transport truck pulled up to the mission, we would have eight hours or less to leave. The truck arrived. We could hear guns off in the distance. Our mission met, and it was decided that families with children should go south to Nanking. The decision was made to go. We packed for a series of destinations. We left an eight-room house and put all of our belongings in two large steamer trunks and a leather suitcase. One trunk had baby stuff in it, and the other had our clothes and some personal belongings, slides and pictures of China, a camera, etc. Some missionaries left by bus, some by boat, and some by truck.

On the way out of Hofei, at the halfway point, there was an incident at Puko. We got caught in a skirmish but were not injured. We traveled through Chiang Kai Shek's Nationalist army troops coming toward the north and the Communists as we were going south toward Nanking.

We arrived in Nanking just before dark and just before the gates of the walled city closed. To be caught outside the gates after dark might have meant that robbers would attack us or something worse.

After arriving in Nanking, we stayed there for awhile, and as the military situation was getting worse by the hour as the Communists came south, the American Ambassador, J. Leighton Stuart, advised that we leave China. Our final decision to leave was made for these reasons: the effects of inflation and sinking funds; the difficulty we were having in overcoming the language barriers; we feared for the safety of our small child, Tim; we needed food for the baby; and the rest of the missionaries appeared to be coming out in three months anyway, except for those placed under house arrest.

We left Nanking for Shanghai on the last train available. While in Shanghai, we exchanged diapers and personal belongings for a bit of China culture to bring home, such as baby shoes, cotton and silk robes, dolls, vases, chopsticks, napkin holders, framed pictures, a set of brass bell chimes, a pagoda planter, some Chinese money and Chinese stamps from both free China and Communist China, etc. These were carried in a leather suitcase. We were fortunate to board the last ship leaving Shanghai, a large U.S. troop carrier ship named the *USS Butner*. The ship started north along the east coast of China, picking up Americans and others as we went. We became like refugees returning home. The ship got off course on occasion, and the ship's accommodations were very crowded. We reached Tiensin near Peking (now Beijing), and from there, we went to Japan, where we visited the missionaries working there. We set course for San Francisco, California, arriving there the week before Christmas 1948.

We learned while in China that people's clothing and customs differ but their hopes and dreams for the future are shared and similar to ours. We also learned that the Christians in China hold to their faith that God is in heaven and all will be right with the world. (Adsit, Jean, Minister, Missionary, and Mother, Story Outline About the Harrowing Trip Leaving China, Aboard *USS General W.H. Butner*, December 11, 1948.)

"Son of Topekan Heads Home From Warlands of China With Wife, Baby," Unsigned news article, paper, specific date, and page number not identified, Topeka, Kansas, December 1948.

"Son of Topekan Heads Home From Warlands of China With Wife, Baby. According to a cable received Monday by Mrs. Reecie Adsit, 634 College, her son Glyn, along with his wife and baby are bound for San Francisco and subsequently Topeka.

Adsit has been serving with the Christian Mission of Hofei, China. Hofei is the capital of Anhwei Province located north of the Yangtze River.

A former telegrapher at Newton and one-time pastor at Great Bend, Adsit recently received a 'gift for the Chinese on behalf of Kansas.'

Residents of Harvey County contributed stores of flour to the Chinese Relief Drive, and in some way that same flour was delivered to Adsit's mission. It was used to feed 120 undernourished children in the area.

In a letter of thanks to the contributors of Harvey County, Adsit said:

'One year ago those children had pinched faces, sores on their bodies and many were sickly. Today, partly because of your help, they are happier and healthier. They are learning there are friends in America who care about people no matter where they live.

'However, all in the Hofei area is not as pleasant as it might sound.

'It is our first term of service and we are afraid it might be our last,' the native Topekan wrote ominously. 'The Communists are coming closer every day and we are expecting to evacuate any hour.'

Mrs. Adsit was unable to say whether the Red advance had anything to do with her son's coming home."

- Author unknown, "Missionary Personnel in China," *World Call*, January, 1948, p. 14 (Re-printed by permission, White, Cyrus N., President and Publisher, Christian Board of Publications, 1221 Locust Street, Suite 1200, St. Louis, MO 63103).

"Missionary Personnel in China. Missionaries of the Disciples of Christ Mission in China were affected by national conditions in the closing months of 1948 even as they have been in the several periods of adjustment in that great country before this time. The United Christian Missionary Society has kept in close touch with the missionaries and reports on word as to their plans based on decisions reached in conference together, with other Missions, and with the best advice available from authorities. Some of the information as to individuals and families follows:

On Monday, November 22, Mr. and Mrs. Glyn Adsit and young son, and Mrs. Joe Smith and two boys left Shanghai aboard the transport ship, General Buckner, for San Francisco.

Mrs. Hubert Reynolds and three small children have arrived in Manila in the Philippines.

Mr. Reynolds and Joe Smith have chosen to remain in China, feeling they could help to carry on the program which the Mission is working out, even though it is not the policy of the Mission to approve the separation of families.

Mrs. George Cherryhomes has moved from Chuhsien to Nanking where medical care is available. She hopes to proceed to the Philippine Islands to be with her parents, Mr. and Mrs. Paul Kennedy, if transportation can be arranged.

Three serious problems made this evacuation necessary. First, there is a serious shortage of food, fuel and other necessities. Second, there is a serious financial crisis. Third, there is a strong probability that hostilities will bring this area under control of the Communists from the north very shortly.

Even in Nanking, the capital of the country, missionaries have for some time been unable to but such things as bread and rice and flour. The cost of living has doubled in a single day. Restrictions have so limited the withdrawal of money from the bank that the daily amount did not even begin to meet the needs for any one of our stations.

All missionaries now in Nanking intend to remain there for the present. It is not known how Communist control would affect the program of Christian missions. Reports indicate that some missionaries have carried on a Christian program in Communist areas, but this has never been tried on as large a scale as would be required in Nanking with the several Missions now at work there and the large institutions already established. The National Christian Council of China believes it should be tried.

Other United Society missionaries in China, and planning to remain for the present, are Miss Lyrel Teagarden and Miss Pauline Starn in Nantung; Dr. and Mrs. Douglas Corpron, Miss Grace Young, Miss Wenona Wilkinson, Mr. and Mrs. O.J. Goulter, Miss Verla Elliot in Hofei; George Cherryhomes in Chuhsien; Mr. and Mrs. James McCallum, Dr. and Mrs. Lewis S.C. Smythe, Dr. and Mrs. M. Searle Bates, Mr. and Mrs. Walter Haskell and Miss Edna Gish, Nanking..."

- Adsit, Glyn B., "Hope for the Soul of China," *World Call*, January, 1949, pp. 27, 29 (Re-printed by permission, White, Cyrus N., President and Publisher, Christian Board of Publications, 1221 Locust Street, Suite 1200, St. Louis, MO 63103).

"The Chinese people, who are caught in the crushing juggernaut of war, are desperately in need of spiritual help. The present time seems to be one of the worst China has faced in centuries; but there are those who are doing their best when times are at the worst, and there is hope for the Soul of China.

As Lyrel Teagarden, a missionary in China, was traveling to Hofei from Nanking by bus, she learned that Communists and bandits were very close to the route the bus was to follow. There was great excitement and many people on the bus were afraid. One Chinese gentleman said to Lyrel, 'You are a Christian, aren't you?' Lyrel said, 'Yes, I am.' The man then said, 'Please, pray that we may all get through safely.' This Chinese man was probably not a Christian. He knew, however, that Christians prayed; and that praying in such a situation might help. The message of Christian prayer is reaching the minds of the Chinese people, and is giving them hope.

Many signs reveal that both the upper and lower classes of Chinese society are finding hope in Christianity. My radio had gone bad and I took it to a professor in Nanking University who knew how to repair it. He told me this story: 'I attended high school in a church supported institution. Many of the boys there became Christians so that they might have free tuition and special favors. I did not want to be that dishonest so I did not become a Christian. Many years have passed and now I am a professor. I still am not a Christian, but I now want to be one because I have seen how the Christians endured the war without losing their honor. My country is in need of good men and I believe that if I follow the teachings of Jesus, I will be a good man.' There is hope for this man and there is hope for the Soul of China.

Not only does one hear men and women stating their intention of becoming Christians; there are also other indications that Christianity is on the march in China. Early one Sunday morning I was having my shoes shined in one of the sidewalk chairs in Nanking. As I watched the people walking by, I noticed a man leaving a drug store. He had a Bible under his arm. We did not say a word to each other but I was thinking: 'There goes a man who is trying to follow Jesus. He is doing his best while times are at their worst.' Seeing the Bible under his arm gave me new hope.

Last Spring, In Hofei, we were teaching a Bible class in English. Several government men and soldiers attended this class. One of these men was a member of the Chinese legislature. He became interested in the Christian message and we baptized him along with several of his Bible class friends. He is a man of influence and it is wonderful to know that he is on the side of those striving for good. His conversion makes us feel that there is hope for the Soul of China.

Our one greatest need in our church program in China is leadership. We have many small country churches without pastors. In order to meet this need we have opened a leadership training school. We invite young men to come into Hofei from the villages where we have a school or church, to attend this school. Our purpose is to train leaders, both laymen and preachers. We have about forty boys in our classes each semester. We pick out the best ones and encourage them to take more schooling. Our hope is that within the next ten years we can train about forty men for the rural ministry.

Many of these boys are not Christian when they arrive to begin their training. We tell them, quite frankly, we expect all of them to become Christians before the year is over. We spend the year trying to win them to Christ and his work. Last semester we baptized ten of these boys. As we remembered that these boys will someday be heads of families, it adds to our feeling that there is hope for the Soul of China.

Er-Shr-Pu is a small village seven miles from Hofei, Until recently there were no Christians living in Er-Shr-Pu. One family, named Hsu, became interested in our program and invited us to come to their home. One cold winter day we went to visit the Hsus' and found a pleasant family, eager to have us start a Sunday school in their village schoolhouse. They offered us the use of the building free and said the students all wanted to attend. This was a wonderful opportunity and we began making visits to Er-Shr-Pu. Today there are two Christians there. One is a student, and one is Mr. Hsu's son. This young man has dedicated his life to full-time Christian service. Two of the three school teachers have enrolled as inquirers. The villagers have become interested and they are opening their homes to us. Within a few years, we expect to have a vigorous group of Christians worshipping in Er-Shr-Pu.

Economic recovery is painfully slow. The people exist on a health-sapping low level of living. There are, nevertheless, hopeful signs. The people are not satisfied with their present condition. They are calling upon their government to take more decisive steps to terminate the war. They have forced a currency reform which is being rigorously carried out. The army is improving its pay system. No longer will a general receive a lump sum of money to give out to his troops as he sees fit. Each soldier is to draw his own pay from the bank.

These are hopeful signs, but the most hopeful is that the people are realizing their need of a spiritual re-birth. Christianity is being breathed across this spiritually bleak and desolate land. Human beings are becoming living souls. Chinese are coming to Christ from all classes. Individuals, families, and even entire villages are accepting his way of life. And, as they come each bears this testimony: there is hope for the Soul of China."

- Adsit, Glyn B., "Precious Package," *World Call*, January, 1949, p. 39 (Re-printed by permission, White, Cyrus N., President and Publisher, Christian Board of Publications, 1221 Locust Street, Suite 1200, St. Louis, MO 63103).

"Precious Package. To give birth to a son is the greatest desire of a typical Chinese woman. In a society where the family is still the very important unit, giving birth to sons is very necessary. The parents, when they grow old, must depend upon their sons for economic security. In China, there are no old age pensions, old folks homes, or social securities. It is a small wonder then, that when a son is born he is called a 'Precious Package'; within him is enfolded all the hopes of past and future generations.

About one half of all Chinese babies die in the first year of life. The mother jealously guards her son during these dangerous months. She prays that diphtheria, small-pox, whooping cough, and typhoid fever will pass him by. If he is fortunate enough to reach his first birthday, a gala party is given in his honor. A big feast is prepared and all those who sent him presents at his birth are invited.

Belief in evil spirits have led the Chinese to pretend that their boy babies are girl babies. They put jewelry on his wrists and ankles. A silver necklace is hung around his neck. They dress him in colorful clothing and do eve-rything they can to deceive the spirits. They love their Precious Package and do not want the gods to take him away.

The bundle you see Lewis Smythe, professor in Nanking University, China, carrying is a 'precious pack-age.' In it are hundreds of millions of dollars in Chinese national currency. Lewis was heard to remark, 'The money in this bag will last our family for about one week.' He was not joking since the money is next to worthless.

Fortunately the Chinese government has inaugurated a new currency reform. We are happy about this for now [as of September, 1948] we can carry a month's salary in our billfolds. We no longer need to carry a basket. One American dollar is worth four Chinese dollars. Once again, we can almost live on our salaries. We are wonder-ing if the money will remain stable."

• "Missionaries Back From China," Beth Prim, *The Daily Oklahoman,* Oklahoma City, Oklahoma, Sunday, January 30, 1949.

"Reporters get wary, sometimes, and with good reason. The celebrities and foreign diplomats and refugees and authorities who come to town for interviews sometimes seem to have axes to grind or special interests to plead for their countries or their causes. Sometimes, too, someone spends a few weeks or months in a foreign land and because of their positions, become authorities.

Consequently, it happens that facts that come out in interviews about such areas as China sometimes lack persuasiveness, even though the visitor has the best of intentions.

When, however, a well-educated missionary and his wife who have just come out of a controversial area such as central China, arrive in town, they are well-worth seeing.

Missionaries deal with people, all classes of them, and their problems. They perhaps get better acquainted with the people of the country than any other group.

And they generally know more about the situations in their mission field than anyone there other than natives or nationals, as the missionaries usually call them.

Glyn B. Adsit, his wife and baby son have just come out of central China after repeated warnings from the United States government, the United Christian Missionary Alliance, and finally from a Chinese Christian general who was a member of his church at Hofei in Anhwei province, central China.

Glyn and Jean Adsit went to Phillips University at Enid, then to Cornell and later to Yale where they studied Chinese for a year. They arrived in China in August, 1947, while the civil war flowed around them they began to work in rural areas around Hofei. The Disciples of Christ denomination (called the Christian church here) was the only one in Hofei. The center there included a hospital, a school, a rural center and the church. It has taken 50 years to build up the work there and the missionary doctor at the Christian hospital took care of unbelievable cases.

Mrs. Adsit helped in the 'get well-baby clinic' where babies three and four months old who had never had baths were brought in to be bathed in the clinic's little wooden tubs.

Almost two years after they arrived they were told by the Chinese Christian general in their church that, 'If you want to get out, now is the time.'

Permission had been granted for use of the hospital's operating room. A battle with the communists was expected within two weeks, the general told them, and it did actually occur. It was the battle of Pengpu.

So the Adsits prepared to move—quickly. All they took of their household furnishings and personal belongings, they had to carry on the rickety bus which was their only way out. Their library and many other valuables had to be left.

They hurried toward Nanking, passing the bodies of hundreds of dead soldiers and pushing through the mass of confusion. They reached the coast after incredible hardships and got passage on a U.S.-bound steamer.

They barely made it home by Christmas.

This week they are in Oklahoma City visiting the Lincoln Terrace Christian church here which supports them.

Adsit concedes communists have won China. They have strict military discipline. Communist deserters are shot without formality when they are captured. The nationalists merely try to persuade their deserters to come back to the army. Also, the wives and children of the nationalist army often go along to live near the battle lines.

None of this is true in the communist army. Adsit says, 'He considers Chiang-Kai-Shek a Christian gentlemen, but not always fortunate in the men he places in leadership.'

The big force which helps the communists is that they have 'an ideology which holds them together.' A strong central force dominates their thinking.

The missionary points out that there are three distinct branches of communism in China.

First, is the pro-Russian group, which has only a few in number, 'but dominates the army.'

Second, is the pro-Chinese communist group which promote the land reform idea.

And third, is the anti-national group which is not necessarily communist, but is seeking to get rid of the present Chiang-Kai-Shek set up.

Any communistic rule will be difficult for Protestant churches in China unless the system changes radically, he concludes.

He said his family wants to get back as soon as possible, however.

They believe in the potentialities of their mission field."

• "Thinks China Going Red," *The Parsons Kansas Sun,* Wednesday, February 23, 1949, p. 2. (An unsigned news story and photo.)

"Thinks China Going Red. In a radio talk over KLKC today, Glyn B. Adsit, a former missionary to China, said he believed that all of China will be communistic within three months.

Adsit who returned from his mission work in Hofei in the province of Anhwei only two months ago, is a native of Topeka and is now on a speaking tour which includes a large number of Christian churches in the mid-west area.

In explaining his statement that all of China will soon be Communist, the religious speaker pointed to the extreme zeal of Communist soldiers, the discontent of certain classes in the country and the strong tie of certain Communist groups with Russia.

Chiangs Defended

In his radio address, he also devoted considerable time to a discussion of Chiang-Kai-Shek, Madame Chaing and the nationalist government.

'I believe the Chiang-Kai-Sheks are good, conscientious Christians. There is a campaign that has been going on for several years to defame them and I fear this criticism is communistic in its origin,' the missionary asserted.

In an interview later the former Topekan again affirmed his faith in the Chiangs, but also stated his belief the nationalists government headed by Chiang was corrupt. However, he did not feel that this corruption was in any large part the general's responsibility.

He pointed to the fact that the Chiangs have remained in China fighting one war or another for 30 years. He also told of orphanages they have established and of other benevolent acts.

Christians Doomed

Adsit also believes that the Chinese Communists will sooner or later eliminate Christians now in that country. Asked if he believed this conflict between the political leaders and church officials was necessary, Adsit said he believed it definitely was.

'Christianity cannot compromise with the present form of militant Communism,' he stated. However, the missionary added his great hope is that someday the two philosophies could work together.

After being graduated from high school in Topeka, Adsit went to Phillips University in Enid, Oklahoma, where he received an A.B. degree. From Phillips he went to Cornell and was graduated with a master's degree. He also studied the Chinese language at Yale for a year, in addition to doing other graduate work at that school.

Accompanied to China by his wife, a child was born to the couple while they were in that country. They were in China for nearly two years."

- "Missionary Society Sets Tempe Meet," Unsigned newspaper article, unknown reporter. Public, Phoenix, Arizona, March 13, 1949.

"Missionary Society Sets Tempe Meet. Tempe, March 13. Glyn B. Adsit will be guest speaker for the advance planning conference of the Arizona Christian Missionary Society in the Lyceum lounge at Arizona State College here Wednesday.

Adsit who will make a number of talks during the meeting was forced to return to the United States from China by the civil war. He and his wife were sent as missionaries to Hofei, China, by the Disciples of Christ church.

Registration will open at 9:00 a.m. Wednesday.

Speakers will include Mrs. M.F. Lyweia, on Missionary Education; the Rev. Earl Fox and the Rev. Milford Pribble on Christian Education on the campus. Louis Mayo, state secretary evangelist, will talk on state work and Mrs. Louise Moseley, national World Call secretary, will talk on the church magazine.

At the afternoon meeting, a panel discussion is scheduled on Evangelism, Christian Education, and Stewardship led by the rev. W.P. Ford and Mayo. The pastors will discuss church building programs and at night, in addition to the guest speakers, George Heiskell, Phoenix, will talk for the Laymen's League and Kenneth Sawyer, Tucson, on the camp ground. The Arizona Christian Missionary Society state board will hold a luncheon at the Casa Loma Hotel.

Luncheon for others attending will be served at the college dining hall and a dinner at the grammar school cafeteria by the women of the Tempe Community Christian Church."

- "Missionary Speaks Out—War Lords, Not Chiang, Blamed for Reverses," Thomas Turner, Central Texas Bureau of the News, *The Dallas Morning News*, Dallas, Texas, Thursday, April 28, 1949, p. 20, Section II.

"A young Christian Church missionary just back from China said in Waco Wednesday that he doubted if one half of the nearly three billion dollars worth of American aid goods ever reached the Chinese people.

Glyn Adsit, speaking at the sixty-second annual state convention of Christian churches, defended China's long-time leader, Chiang Kai-shek, however.

Chiang, he said, is an able, Christian man who did the best he could despite a corrupt government.

'Chiang is like Truman, he didn't rise to his position by himself,' commented Adsit, who returned four months ago after year and a half in China.

'I hear people say that Chiang and his family are fabulously wealthy. He has donated hundreds of acres to the church, given herds of registered cattle and homes. He has never had to stay in China. He could have fled to safer nations,' said Adsit.

Somebody in the United States is trying to drag Chiang's name through the mud, and he wouldn't be surprised to see the hands of the Communists behind the idea, the missionary snapped.

'Don't ever believe that the Chinese Communists are any different than Communists anywhere in the world,' he declared. 'Kai-shek never had an army, he had a group of warlords banded together with their individual private armies,' Adsit said. Rach of the warlords, he explained, was always looking out for himself first, 'even if it meant going over to the Communist side.'

'More American arms and ammunition was handed to the Communists than was ever taken by force,' he said.

Chiang was ousted recently because the Chinese people are sick of war, and crave peace no matter who brings it, the missionary theorized.

Wednesday was the third day of the 4-day meeting. Nearly 800 delegates from 435 Texas churches had registered, and delegates from Dallas and other towns were still arriving.

A noted California pastor, Dr. Cleveland Kleinhauer, delivers the featured address nightly.

Dr. C.F. Cheverton of Texas Christian University presides over a Bible lecture session each morning. A different prominent churchman preaches daily."

- "Missionary Work Interrupted by War—Amarillo Visitor and Family Forced From China by Advancing Red Army,"

Interview of Jean Adsit by Henry Matthews, Staff Writer, *Times*, Amarillo, Texas, late April, 1949.

"Few people in the United States realize the threat and power of the Communist armies in China more than Mr. and Mrs. Glyn Adsit. The Adsit family was, in fact, chased from China by the advancing Red army.

The Adsits were doing missionary work at Hofei, Anhwei Province, but were forced to give up their work and return to this country, rather than face horrible existence under the Chinese Communist government.

Mrs. Adsit, the former Miss Jean Dowd of Amarillo, and her son, Timothy Lee, are visiting with her sister, Mrs. J.E. Ethridge, 4244 West Tenth, while her husband is attending the Texas State convention of the Christian church at Waco.

Mrs. Adsit is a graduate of Amarillo High school and attended Amarillo College. After her junior college studies she attended Phillips University at Enid, Oklahoma where she met her husband, Glyn Adsit of Topeka, Kansas.

Both Mr. and Mrs. Adsit graduated from Phillips and went together to Cornell University and then to Yale where they studied foreign languages.

After leaving Yale they joined the missionary work of the Christian church and were sent to the rural center of Hofei, China. Adsit's work there consisted mostly of teaching agriculture and horticulture to the Chinese. His students would then return to their own villages and teach what they had learned to others.

Timothy Lee Adsit who celebrated his first birthday Tuesday, was born in Hofei.

The Adsits went to China in August of 1947 and returned to the U.S. last December, after repeated warnings from the United States government of the danger of the approaching Red army.

Hofei is about 75 miles northwest of Nanking, which only recently fell into Communist hands.

Since their return from the Far East the Adsits have been visiting relatives in Kansas.

The family did not come into actual face-to-face contact with the invaders, but heard many weird and ugly stories from their friends behind Communist lines. At one time while bicycling to a neighboring village Mr. Adsit and his party were shot at twice by an unidentified gunman.

An investigation by the province governor's office could not find any trace of the gunman. The area was near a cemetery, where the dead were laid on top of the ground. It was presumed that the gunman had hidden behind one of the grave mounds, and had escaped unseen.

A friend of the Adsits, O.J. Goulter, another American missionary, told the Adsits of the conditions behind the Red lines. He said that after his town had fallen the red soldiers would delve and investigate into every home, searching every room. He said that one day soon after the Reds had come, there were a large number of them roaming through his house. His wife, in an attempt to draw their attention from their property, began singing in her English tongue.

The soldiers stopped snooping to listen. For several days after that the soldiers would return to the Goulter residence, not to loot, but to listen to the 'foreign lady' sing.

The Goulters, who do not have any children, remained in China, behind the Communist 'Iron Curtain' to continue their missionary work.

The first warning to Americans in the Hofei area came from the United States government in November of last year [1948]. They said the Reds were nearing that sector and advised all Americans to return home.

Several other warnings came before the missionary groups from all churches in that area held a meeting and decided that all couples with children and certain others should return home.

The Adsits were reluctant to leave the work they had started in China, but, considering the future of their son and the conditions which would be forced upon them by the Communists, decided it would be best to return home.

[The] present plan of the Adsits is to return to Phillips University for advanced study. Both, Mr. and Mrs. Adsit, are enthusiastic about returning to China as soon as conditions warrant, even though they feel it may be several years before it is safe.

One of the greatest thrills Mrs. Adsit had while in China occurred while on a visit to Kuling, the summer capital. Mr. and Mrs. Adsit were walking about the city and happened to meet Generalissimo and Madame Chiang Kai-Shek.

'I was absolutely stunned,' said Mrs. Adsit, 'somehow my husband managed to say Good Morning and the Madame returned with an English Good Morning in a very nice tongue.'

Mrs. Adsit later listened to a speech by Madame Chiang Kai Shek at a meeting of the International Women's club in Nanking. She was impressed with the fluency of Madame's English."

- "Communism World Issue-Second Missionary In Warning of Spread," *World-Herald*, Omaha, Nebraska, May 1949.

"A second warning against communism's strides in China was sounded by another missionary here Thursday.

The statements of Glyn Adsit, recently returned Disciples of Christ missionary from the Nanking area, followed those of Sten Lindberg, Baptist missionary.

'Communism is not a Chinese problem, but a world-wide one,' he said. 'Like Christians, Communists want to see a world-wide spread of their beliefs.'

Further comparing Christianity to Communism, Mr. Adsit said that Stalin is 'like God' to Communists.

Mr. Adsit said any country with strong military and scientific power needs Christianity as a 'moral brake.'

He and his wife and baby left China before the communists entered the third stage of infiltration.

'The first stage was a nod of the communists head… go ahead with your work, we won't bother you, they said. The second stage was a shake of the head…you can't teach religion anymore. We didn't wait for the third stage…off with your heads,' the missionary said.

The missionary is in Omaha to speak at the annual convention of the Nebraska Christian Churches."

- "Predicts China's Fall to Reds Within a Month." Unsigned news article, *Des Moines Tribune*, Des Moines, Iowa, Monday, May 23, 1949, p. 6.

"Missionary speaks here. All China will be in Communist hands within another month.

That was predicted here Monday by a Christian church missionary who with his family left Hofei in Anhwei province, two weeks before the Red armies came in.

At Convention. The missionary, Glyn Adsit, addressed convention delegates of the Christian church of Iowa (Disciples of Christ) meeting at Central Christian church, Ninth and Pleasant streets.

Adsit declared the Nationalist government is 'corrupt to the core.' But he defended Generalissimo Chiang Kai-Shek and his wife, saying they were 'the most misunderstood people on earth' today.

'I know the Chiangs personally,' Adsit said. 'He is a sincere Christian gentleman and has done all that is humanly possible. I happened to know they have used much of their own money and resources for the development of China.'

Many Difficulties. But Chiang had been beset by many difficulties, Adsit said. Eighty-five per cent of the people could not read nor write, he said. Chiang had been 'hand tied' by men who had helped him become president.

'Many of these have become rich and powerful at the expense of the United States and China,' he said. 'but the Chiangs are not guilty.'

'Though the Chinese people love and trust Chiang, they have given up his government because it failed to keep promises of food, peace and jobs for all.

'The Communists will find it hard to keep many of the promises they are making. The masses do not know or care anything about Communism. They are happy for a change, and if peace comes, they will be satisfied for a while.'

Short-Lived. Adsit believes this satisfaction will be short-lived. He told a Chinese story, heard from refugees fleeing the Communists armies. 'They say Communist policy comes in three stages,' he said, 'the affirmative nod of the head, the negative nod of the head, and the cutting off of the head. Our stations have been in the first stage, and are entering into the second.'

'The greatest desire of the Chinese is for peace. They have known none for 30 years. They have not enough food, not enough doctors, and have no real opportunity for education. Because of their suffering they have a peculiar strength not found in any other people.'

Adsit and his wife were at the Christian church station in Hofei (150 miles northwest of Nanking) a year and eight months, he said. Their 13-month-old son was born there.

100-Bed Hospital. The station includes a 100-bed hospital (supplied largely by United States navy surplus, he said), a school and a church with 600 Christian Chinese members.

A second speaker at the Monday morning general session was C.O. Hawley of Indianapolis, Indiana who told of the Christian church program in advancing mission work.

Mrs. Milton Hines of Des Moines and Homer Watkins of Sioux City discussed children's work and church school enlargement in the state, and the Rev. James K. Hemstead of Ames delivered the morning sermon.

Nearly 2,000 laymen, women and ministers from all parts of the state are expected to attend the convention during its four-day program."

- "Iowa Disciples Launch 1949 Convention," *The Challenger,* Drake University, Des Moines, Iowa, Vol. 1 No. 5, May 23, 1949, p. 1.

"Youth Session Introduces 103rd Annual State Meet. With the theme 'The Church Calls and We Answer,' the youth session of the 1949 Convention of the Christian Churches in Iowa was held at Central Christian Church, convention headquarters, Sunday afternoon.

The session was the opening meeting of the annual convention. The main speaker was Dr. Henry G. Harmon, president of Drake University. He spoke on the subject 'Means and Meaning of Life,' urging youth to seek purpose in life and find real meaning.

The young people were afforded the opportunity of viewing some different aspects of Christian service. This was implemented by four speakers in various fields, each speaking on the subject 'Why I Chose to Invest My Life in...' The speakers were Frank Gardner, professor of church history and Christian thought at Drake Bible College; Glyn Adsit, convention missionary from Hofei, China (Mr. Adsit went to China as a missionary in 1947 but was forced to return this year because of the Civil War); William Brizendine, Drake student preparing for the pastoral ministry; and Miss Verna Evelyn Johnson, Director of Student Work at the Ames Christian Church..."

- "Rev. Glyn Adsit to Preach at Carmen," Unsigned news article, paper unnamed, no page given, Oklahoma, June 13, 1949.

"Carmen. June 13. Special. Rev. Glyn B. Adsit has accepted the call to the Carmen Christian church. He succeeds Rev. Arthur Buhler who resigned several weeks ago. Rev. Adsit recently returned from missionary service in China, and is still connected with mission service. He will begin his duties in Carmen June 19, 1949."

- Goulter, Oswald J., Missionary and Field Director, Kiangsu-Anhwei Christian Rural Service Mission, Chuhsien, Anhwei, China, In the Midst of Revolution—"The Year's Work of the Kiangsu-Anhwei Christian Rural Service Mission," June 30, 1949, Letter to Mr. and Mrs. Glyn B. Adsit.

"Introduction: The Union was organized by seven missions and five large mission institutions in the Nanking area, for the purpose of developing an adequate program for the rural churches in this area. The year has been one of extreme unrest and even danger as the service Center at Chuhsien was directly in the path of the warring armies. Nevertheless the year has been one of continuous activity and development by the Union. The activities up to June 30, 1949 are as follows:

The Farmer's Winter Institute: Because of the war, it was not possible to hold the Winter Institute during the spring of 1949, but the one held the previous spring was a good demonstration. It was held for five weeks with 27 delegates from five missions. It gave training in agriculture, animal husbandry, crop diseases, tree culture, arithmetic and religious education to both Christians and inquirers from rural churches. The teaching and lecture staff consisted of 20 specialists and pastors, from five colleges and institutions.

The Pastor's Institute: Planned for June each year, it will not be held until the fall this year. Last year, there were 24 pastors and church leaders from 7 missions and institutions. This is the most important single feature of the year's program. It seeks to give direct help to the rural leaders and acquaint them with the facilities afforded by the Union. Many subjects are studied and plans are made for the year.

Farmer's Short-time Institutes: Due to the war, only one was held at the Service Center during the past year.

It was held in September with 152 farmers in attendance. Its popularity was evidenced by the fact that each session showed a large increase in attendance of neighbors invited by the delegates. The season has been noted for a loss of fifty per cent in some grain crops due to pests. The group were instructed in pest control, crop improvement, and many other topics. When visiting demonstration farms in the district, delegates were given samples of improved seed to take home.

Nursery School: A nursery school was opened at the center as a demonstration for rural churches. Children from 4-6 years were cared for mornings only. A simple nursery school could be opened at any rural church, especially where mothers have to work in the fields at certain times of the year. The school was attended by children from the homes of the new officers and officials and has been given unqualified praise by parents who were astonished at the progress of their own children. We plan on a training institute for girls and women from rural churches who wish to open a similar nursery school.

The Anti-blind Clinic: Dr. Lee Ruh-ling came to Chuhsien twice with his "Anti-blind Clinic." He treated over a thousand cases, performing modern miracles by restoring sight to people who had been blind for as long as 15 years.

Emergency Clinic at Chusien: Because of the extreme urgency due to war and the absence of all medical service, we opened a temporary clinic at the Center. By treating over thirty patients a day, it has helped to establish the Union in this community. We hope to develop it into a travelling clinic.

Public Health Education: Dr. Clara Nutting joined the Union Staff in June 1948, but left for West China in November. She made a good start in public health education for rural churches, beginning in the Wuhu district. She met with thirty different groups connected with four different missions.

Mother's Club: Mrs. Chu-Hsao-tan, who is in charge of the Christian Homes Dept., of the Union has organized a Mother's club at the Service Center. In this club, the mothers of the Nursery School children meet once a month to study problems connected with child care.

Temporary Clinics: Dr. T'an opened a temporary clinic among the refugees camped near Chuhsien Railway Station. He visited the center three days a week. The chief difficulty faced was due to the fact that the greatest need was for food rather than for medicine among his patients.

Handwork Classes for Girls: During the period of extreme unrest all schools were closed and every institution in the city closed its doors except for the Christian institutions. Seeking to afford help to any group in distress, the Union opened a class for young women. The Union supplied wool for a knitting class, and the girls were allowed to keep one pair of socks for every four pairs knitted. The remainder are to be sold to buy wool to continue the project. Forty girls joined this group.

Demonstration Gardens: The six mow of land available to the Service Center has been planted to vegetables, fruit trees and crops for demonstration and teaching purposes. Here the farmers can see and evaluate crops of improved cotton, wheat, sweet-corn, beans, etc. Thirty kinds of wheat growing side by side, and cotton plants with many times the amount of cotton that could be found on any local plants form an object lesson that has to be seen to be believed. Fitting in with the new government drive for increased agricultural production we prepared thirty thousand tomato plants for distribution. They were welcomed by many institutions including government and military, as well as by hundreds of gardeners and farmers. Every day visitors come to see the demonstration plots. Most rural churches could duplicate such a project.

Tree-planting Relief Project: Quite an extensive tree-planting project was carried out in the spring of last year. Work relief was given to 250 refugees. A total of 124,100 trees were planted on 780 mow of land, and the project has continued until the present time. Other relief projects were planned but were stopped by inflation and war.

Rural Church Materials: A start has been made in the preparation of materials for general church work and religious education in the Rural Churches. Over ten kinds of hymn-sheets, pamphlets, family membership forms, etc. have been printed, and many others gathered. Samples may be distributed free and larger quantities for the cost of printing. These and other things will be distributed to pastors in attendance at the Pastor's Institutes when it is possible to hold them.

Relief Clothing: One hundred bales of old clothing from the American Advisory Committee were distributed to 1,000 families for use by their 3,000 individual members, chiefly refugees. Other relief has been given to refugees and to soldiers returning home from battlefields. The latter returning from as far away as Manchuria and going to Szechuan, were given food and medical care while they rested in some deserted house, then were provided with the means for making the next stage of their journey. Probably no more pathetic group could be found in a world where the common man has been but trash hurled about by the hurricanes of war. Wounded, hungry, shoeless, half-naked, wet with rain, snow, sweat, and blood, they start out sometimes on crutches on their thousand mile journey.

Handwork Projects for Money: An attempt has been made to find work women can do in their homes by means of which they can eke out a living during these disturbed times. Material for shoemaking is given to all who wish it. Every second pair is returned to be sold so more material can be purchased. Dress-making and other projects are also under way.

Better Homes Institute: From February 21 to 24, a four-day Better Homes Institute was held at the Service Center. Each day a large increase in attendance attested to the eager interest shown by delegates. The first day was given over to instruction and demonstrations in vegetable gardening and the external improvement of the home; the second day to religion for the family; the third day, to health and hygiene; the fourth day to child-training and clothes making. Nets for baby beds were given to those couples having tiny babies, and the use of many other cheap and useful articles was demonstrated. Opportunity was given to delegates to join a group of cooperating families for the development of model homes.

Literacy Classes: Cooperation in a literacy program is now possible for every rural church in our area. The Union provides half-time salary for the person in charge of the school, also readers, chalk and other items. At present the following schools are under way: Friends Mission, 3 classes; Christian Advent, 2; Christian, 6; Methodist, 4. Our plan calls for at least one literacy class in every rural church of every cooperating mission if called for. In four places classes were not possible, so home literacy programs were initiated. A small group of students gathers in each of half-a-dozen homes each day and are visited by the teacher regularly. The Union is also prepared to finance this type of literacy program. We believe that this method can be used even where literacy classes and other Christian work are stopped.

Union Primary School: Since the liberation took place, we have up to date, for the first time been allowed to use our buildings without interference by military. To fill an urgent need we started out to conduct a day-time literacy class for children, it promptly grew into a primary school. As running a primary school is not a part of the permanent program of the Union, it will be transferred to the local Christian Church at the end of the first term of this year. The term has been very successful with 130 pupils.

Reading and Game Room: One of the most successful projects has been the reading and recreation room. Newspapers and other literature, checkers, chess, ping-pong, etc., are available. It is a boon to soldiers, students, and the general public, and is open from 9:00 a.m. to 11:30 a.m., and 1:00 to 6:30 p.m. The walls are decorated with charts, pictures and exhibits.

General Purpose and Plans: We have sought to demonstrate the projects that can be carried out during these difficult times. We believe that the approach to the rural community illustrated by these projects is not only the essential Christian approach of unselfish service, but that it will win for the church in a society where the theological or preaching approach is under very serious criticism by friend and foe alike. We have prepared an outline of "Rural Church Service-Program Plans" in Chinese and English. The rural churches may select from this the activities they wish to carry out in cooperation with the Union. These "Plans" will be sent on request. In the absence of Dean Chang, Dr. Luther Shao is Chairman of the Standing Committee. He may be addressed at 74 Pao Tai Chai, Nanking. Mr. Goulter, or Pastor Chu Hsao-tan may be addressed at 21 Tzui Wen T'ing Rd., Chuhsien, Anhwei, (China). O.J. Goulter, Field Director."

- Yocum, C.M., Division of Foreign Missions, The United Christian Missionary Society, Indianapolis, Indiana, Letter to Mr. And Mrs. Glyn B. Adsit, July 5, 1949.

"My Dear Glyn, at the last meeting, I informed our board of trustees that you had decided that it was best for you folk not to return to your work in China. They asked me to say to you that of course they accept your decision, but they do it with regret and that they sincerely trust that whatever work you undertake you will be imminently successful and happy. Your salaries and allowances will be discontinued as of July 1, your pension fund certificate is in your hands so that you may continue it in whatever field connection you may make.

Since you folk were not on the field for a period of at least fifteen years, you are not eligible to continue your missionary benefit agreement.

Again may we say to you that we deeply appreciate your services in China and that our prayers and best wishes go with you into whatever service you enter. Anything that we can do for you at any time, kindly let us know. Cordially yours, C.M. Yocum."

- Omer, Lois, Secretarial Assistant to Spencer P. Austin, Executive Secretary, Department of Resources, The United Christian Mission Society, Indianapolis, Indiana, Letter to Mr. Glyn B. Adsit, July 27, 1949.

"Dear Mr. Adsit, thank you very much for your letter of July 23 with the record of your additional expense account of $79.90 and the check you enclosed for $57.52 to cover the balance due The United Christian Missionary Society. I have passed the check and expense account on to the treasury department.

All of us here at the office will continue to remember the amazing number of field appointments (speaking engagements) you have served since January 1949. Thank you again for your help in all of this and for the very prompt responses you have made from time to time to our regular and emergency calls. I hope you will have time at home with Jean and the baby during the remainder of the summer and before you begin a school schedule in September. With best wishes to each of you, Sincerely, Lois Omer, Secretarial Assistant, Spencer P. Austin."

Sly, Virgil A., Executive Secretary, Acting Secretary for China, Division of Foreign Missions, The United Christian Missionary Society, Indianapolis, Indiana, "China Bulletin," Extracts of recent Mail from China including warning from John M. Cabot, American Consul General, to Friends of China, September 7, 1949.

"China Bulletin. Dear Friends of China: Following this brief letter you will find extracts of recent mail from China. I need not comment concerning the story they tell. When you read them you will know as much as we do.

We are hopeful Miss Margaret Lawrence has left for Japan where she will work until she can enter China. We will send three China women candidates to Japan this fall who will also await entry. Yet we must be prepared for anything, because anything can happen.

One of the most serious is that of taxes. The new government may make our work impossible by severe taxation. Other factors may develop; at present considerable freedom exists.

We cannot get any mail into China either by plane or boat. I have been able to get some cables through. Be assured that I will keep in touch with you as the situation develops. Sincerely Virgil A. Sly, China Secretary." [Enclosed to this letter were the following letters.]

- McCallum, James H., Nanking, China, Confidential Letter to Dr. C.Y. Yocum, Foreign Division, United Christian Missionary Society, April 17, 1949, pp.1-3 (Copy to Glyn B. Adsit, received July 12, 1949 at Missions Building, Indianapolis, Indiana).

"Dear Cy, at least part of this letter I should like to be confidential for reasons I shall explain. We want you to know what is going on and yet we do not want to have published facts which might have an adverse effect associated with the names or stations in Communist areas. It is already noted by them that we have means of communication and fortunately all the reports have been favorable. The situation is too tense to add any embarrassment. We will have to consider carefully just what we should report especially in the newsletter for it is time that we balance our optimism with a little realism.

Interruption, I am listening in to the Hollywood Bowl Easter Sunrise meeting at 9:00 p.m. Sunday night.

In the past month there has been a gradual change in the situation north of the river. People who come out, farmers, merchants and professional people have little encouraging to say. On the contrary they almost all show nervousness and a reluctance to answer questions. The atmosphere is gloomy and full of fear and suspicion.

Factually, we have this information, from one of our very trusted workers who came out on account of his wife's illness. Mr. Goulter has not been permitted to return to Chushien from Hofei. George and Irene report that Oswald, Wenona, and Verla are confined to the same residence building where he was confined by the Japanese. We need to confirm this before we fully accept it. George and Irene are virtually confined to their residences and the church, since their visit to other places would be looked on with suspicion. George and Irene's passports have been taken up as well as their residence certificates. I have George's signature to this statement. It is also reported that the passports of the other three are also being retained but I have no proof of this.

The process of visitation and questioning continues to go on. This is true of everyone, Chinese and missionaries. But special attention seems to be given to the mission group. Day after day and hour after hour the friendly, curious or the official visitor or the investigator [spy] take up most of the time of the missionaries and our leading workers. They are not sure of the import of it all for it is unnecessarily repetitious. Some of the questions certainly put us on the spot. What is the objective of Christianity and of a missionary? Is it necessary that you, one missionary, occupy a big house when people are sleeping in the open? How many meals do you eat and what do you eat? Do you have meat? Sugar? Would it not be better to eat two meals and share one with the hungry? How many pair of shoes have you? How many this and that-chairs, cups, kettles, etc. But particular attention is paid to the source and amount of income. It does not seem possible to avoid this constant visitation which becomes wearing and wearying.

There is a saying among the Chinese describing the three stages of Communist occupation. First, there is the *tien tieo* (affirmative nod of the head). Then, there is the *yao t'eo* (negative shake of the head). Finally, there is the *k'an teo* (cutting off of the head). This is the common talk and expectation of most Chinese.

Then there is the technique that they use in spreading their propaganda and getting what they want. There are meetings every day which representatives of each household are supposed to attend. Meetings, meetings, meetings, they say. At certain times they seem to have quota of supplies to secure for the army. With the skill of certain evangelists or church dedicators, I might mention they get it out of the people voluntarily by the process of priming and hand raising and hand clapping. And the people find it hard to meet the pledges they make in a moment of enthusiasm or generosity. And increasingly they skip out and the society is so organized that those who are left behind have to suffer for every deflection. And this goes on and on.

There is practically no business and no crops are being planted this spring. The able bodied who have not fled have been drafted either into the army or for labor.

Every household has to furnish either a soldier or this labor or pay for the same. In the case of the missionary, the amount is made four times the average on account of the house and number of possessions. When people have sold off all their things, they see the end of something ahead. I understand that George has to furnish twenty-four quarts of rice every time they come around to collect.

Four of our best young men whom we have trained for rural work in the Hofei area have gone into Communist training schools we presume to continue in Communist service afterward.

Our preachers are beginning to realize that they may have to find some occupation to support themselves. None of us in evangelistic work are counted as productive units in a communist society and so are not entitled to a share in the things that are produced, yet we are supposed to bear our share of the cost. We have not come to the point where we know what this will bring us to and we hope we can get along with what we have long enough to see.

I cannot entirely understand and so I cannot truly convey to you what I sense. There is something in the heavy, oppressive air that surrounds these people that effects them very quickly. When this man came out he was afraid to talk even when in a very small, intimate mission group. He continually looked around to be sure no one was looking and was very nervous. Others whom we do not know well, but who are business men, who transfer money for us to our people in Chuhsien in return for cash here to do business, have shown the same attitude. We hope this is something that will change and that we can weather it all right.

We have had considerable correspondence followed by a series of cables with the families in the Philippines regarding their return. Our attitude toward the situation has changed a good deal since last November. There are so many reasons pro and con for going or coming at this point that it would be useless to try to mention them. We have had to decide on the most important ones and we seem to be unanimous in opinion. We are in favor of uniting families as far as we can and it seemed best to try to do this before a turnover, whatever form it may take for there are apt to be many difficulties and delays and complications. A number of families with children have returned to Nanking including some in the American embassy staff. So we gave our families in the Philippines a chance to make the choice and we had expected the move to have been made before this. Letters and cables have been flying back and forth and last night we had what we expect to be final word that Mrs. Reynolds and the children will board the President Wilson in Manila on April 20 and will arrive in Shanghai on the twenty-sixth. We hope nothing will prevent them from coming to Nanking and we expect they will stay here in Nanking until a political change takes place when they will go on to Wuhu or Hubert will come here. George Cherryhomes requested his family to remain in the Philippines, though Margaret was rather anxious to come also.

You may wonder why I make the confidential report above and at the same time, consent to people coming back. The confidential report is not much different from what we had expected. It is just closer and more personalized. And, we feel we must hold on to every person we can as long as we can especially among our younger staff members. We think the tense periods will not last and if we can just weather them, that something more favorable will work out.

Yesterday was Easter, a gloomy day from the weather standpoint, but a good day from the Christian standpoint. I baptized forty-four, half of them in the morning at South Gate and the others at the Drum tower in the afternoon. The daughter of Luther Shao and the son of pastor Wang Yoh-tung were among them and students from Ginling, Nanking University and Central University including the son of Chen-Keh-ching (William) of the Park Avenue church in New York.

Everything is going on without interruption. We are living under a sort of perpetual crisis and find that we have to go ahead and plan ahead without regard to what we read or hear over the radio and when we are stopped, we will just do something else. We have not been hearing much from Indianapolis and we hope you do not think we are negligent. I find the picture changing so often and so quickly that anything I might try to say might be misleading. I have tried to report every change in personnel or decisions that we make. We will have an administrative committee meeting on the twenty-first and you will be hearing shortly. I will ask Reynolds to wire you when they reach Shanghai and then you will know they are actually there, and we will try to let you know when they reach Nanking. Very Sincerely, James H. McCallum."

• McCallum, J.H., 45 Pao T'ai Chieh, Nanking, China, Letters to no heading dated April 27, 1949; May 11,

1949, and May 28, 1949 respectively, but sent to United Christian Missionary Society arriving at the Missions Building on July 12, 1949, pp.1-3.

"April 27, 1949. We are among the 'liberated' of China. It all came so quickly that we had little time to get any word out and there was nothing to say. Saturday the twenty-third was a day of confusion and tension. There was no authority left in the city, not even a police system, so there was looting. But a group got together to maintain order and a ragtag police force got on the job, which helped a lot. On Sunday morning we were well covered and went to our churches a lot. On Sunday morning we were well covered and went to our churches as usual.

Here in Nanking are Mr. and Mrs. Lewis Smythe, Mrs. Searle Bates, Mrs. Edna Gish, Mrs. McCallum and I. Hubert Reynolds came in on the twenty-second to go to Shanghai to meet his family. He got the night train, but did not proceed more than thirty miles where he spent the day Saturday and the train finally brought him back. He went out with the last remnants of one army and came in with the first of the other. Mr. Bates and Mr. Haskell had made hurried trips to Shanghai and were on the night train coming back to Nanking on the twenty-second. They reached Chinkiang just as it was being liberated and went to the Methodist Girl's School there, where they have been since. We have had two telephone calls made by others for them and we are sending special letters to help them get a pass or required permission to travel to Nanking. As yet there are no trains on this line. Mr. Reynolds made three attempts to reach Wuhu, as he would rather be there since he cannot reach Shanghai, and since he has not returned and we have no further word from him, we assume he is on his way and will reach Wuhu today.

We expect now that we will have better contact with the other stations though free communications may be a little slow in getting reestablished. Nanking is a big place to take over and though we seem to be free here to get around, and the P.O. will take out letters, it is with no assurance that permanent arrangements are yet made for freer communications. There is already an improvement in our electricity.

Joe Smith is in Wuhu; Wenona Wilkinson, Verla Elliot and Oswald Goulter in Hofei, Irene Goulter and George Cherryhomes in Chuhsien, Lyrel Teagarden and Pauline Starn in Nantung. All the Chinese are in their usual places and work is continuing though in the schools, they are giving a good deal of their time to meetings and activities in connection with the new regime…May 11, 1949. Within the past two days, I have heard from every missionary in the mission except Harriet Reynolds who we presume is in touch with you. We are all okay. Safe, in good spirits, and well. When Verla, Wenona and Oswald went to Hofei over a month ago, they were put under arrest and house detention and were just released without explanation on May 6. Oswald is promised a military escort back to Chuhsien and may be there by now. Irene and George are all right in Chuhsien and the work goes on there very well. They have freedom within the city as all of us do now in every station. Hubert and Joe are in their usual places in Wuhu and carrying on as usual.

It was the most orderly and peaceful takeover we have had in Nanking and I have been through five of them. Searle Bates had scheduled an address in Shanghai on Thursday and he did some business for us that day that made it necessary for Walter Haskell to rush to Shanghai. Actually we had a chance to pick up about seven thousand cash which we needed very much. They lost out by about thirty minutes in the opportunity to get through, but reached Chinkiang where they stopped over in the Methodist Mission and it took them until yesterday to get permission to come on through to Nanking.

Lyrel and Pauline are okay and in good spirits though still having to borrow to live. We have resources on the way which we have not been able to get through for over three months. Now that we are on the same side of the line, we will work everything out satisfactorily. Mrs. Gish, Mr. and Mrs. Bates, Mr. and Mrs. Lewis Smythe and Eva and I are in our usual homes and our work is going along without interruption.

Hofei has been the most affected by the new regime. Only the south residence formerly occupied by the Goulters and the hospital are under our complete control. The hospital carries on under financial difficulty. The Coe Middle School has been closed and only a primary school remains. We have use of one-fifth of the property, the rest being used for a teacher's training institute. Since April 1 the church has been used as residences and worship has been forbidden. We hope this will be changed since one of the announced planks is freedom of worship and freedom to criticize religion. The residence used by the Adsits is used as a medical and operating center. The rural center is occupied by soldiers though our man there is left in charge of agricultural work. The women's center is used for head-quarters for a bureau of education.

Elsewhere in the mission, we do not have any interference though I cannot say that we do not have difficulties, internal as well as external. We have the means now to get on for several months and by that time we are sure that something will be worked out for our continuation. As I can get word out I will try.

What are some of our reflections to date? I asked a non-Christian businessman, head of a bus line, who came and reported to us the details we have from Hofei, what the people on the street say. This is a summary of his comments.

Hofei in appearance is a poor community. All those big buildings, institutions, and residences stand out as representing wealth and comfort that the ordinary people do not enjoy. Many of the Christians also dress in foreign clothing and appear to be of a privileged class (even though a lot of this foreign clothing is relief clothing).

Right in the midst of very heavy troop movements toward the Yangtze, here appear three foreigners who might easily be spies. The whole thing caused a reaction which was more than it would normally have been.

Every one of us is confronted with the question of living in a fine house and having what the poor consider a great abundance. How can we reconcile this with the idea of Christian sacrifice and care for the poor and needy? People who never saw any of the ordinary things which we have in our homes are amazed at it all. If we and the church can adjust to all this then we will be on a really better basis than a wealthy and subsidized foreign movement. All churches in Nanking are working together more than at any time. If we can just avoid open friction until we work something out...May 28, 1949. Letters which we tried to get out before Shanghai was liberated have returned to us and it was not possible to get through. Now we do not know what communications are possible. Every so often we will write and someday mail will start again.

Everyone is getting on very well. Adjustments are being made by all of us to a new set of principles and regulations and even a new vocabulary. However, changes are being made very slowly in a place like Nanking. Schools are the first to be affected and there the work of education and 'reorientation' goes on rapidly. A great many extra meetings and outside activities have been added. Our public utilities have been fully restored and electricity and water are improved much over the past. The railway is reopened both to the north and to Wuhu and we hope soon will be to Shanghai.

As of today: Oswald and Irene Goulter and George Cherryhomes are in Chuhsien, Verla Elliot and Wenona Wilkinson in Hofei, Joseph Smith and Hubert Reynolds in Wuhu; Lyrel Teagarden and Pauline Starn in Nantung; Mrs. Reynolds and children in Shanghai in Presbyterian mission compound; Dr. and Mrs. M.S. Bates, Dr. and Mrs. Lewis Smythe, Walter W. Haskell, Mrs. Gish, and

Mr. and Mrs. McCallum in Nanking. Joan Smythe is in Shanghai American School. We are all in our own homes and carrying on our daily work as usual.

We still have news facilities without newspapers which normally come from Shanghai and may be resumed in a limited way. It has been some time since we have had mail or outside communications. We hope there is mail stacked in Shanghai that has not been destroyed and will eventually reach us. We postponed our convention and hope to have it in the fall or whenever it is possible to travel conveniently. J.H. McCallum."

- McCallum, J.H., 45 Pao T'ai Chieh, Nanking, China, Letter to no heading dated June 19, 1949 but sent to United Christian Missionary Society, Indianapolis, Indiana arriving at the Missions Building on July 20, 1949.

"Yesterday I sent a cable 'Lawrence Cherryhomes Haskell New Missionaries come first opportunity (stop) Teagarden desires information cousins welfare (stop) Situation Encouraging All well—McCallum.' There have been a couple of letters of inquiry about Miss Lawrence and the new missionaries. I have replied twice by mail and assume from the lateness of Cy Yocum's airmail [both copies of which reached me—the original first] that you might not have had our answer. This wire also will indicate that we want the return of anyone who is able to come, and of new missionaries. I presume thought that we will have to take them as individual cases. I did not mention Winifred Smith. This was not an oversight but I have not had a chance to confer with Joseph Smith and he has not answered my inquiry on that point. The procedures for passes, visa's and other arrangements have not been worked out by the new government. Some are being allowed to leave and we hope Mrs. Gish may sail in July. This wire is to let you know that as far as we are concerned all is clear.

I should add that there is a small group among our missionaries who feel that it is so important to try to get new missionaries out that we should urge you to send an additional number if that is possible, even before they have finished their training. One of the reasons for this is the assumption that it will be easier at first than later to get in. You may get such an expression of opinion. We will consider this proposal in our committee and make our recommendation but we are not likely to change our present arrangement unless we have some further loss. We are reminding you though that the Nanking Theological Seminary and the university hospital are reminding us of our vacancies there and a doctor is always on the list, at the head of the list any time.

We have had reports this week from all stations and we are very much encouraged. Schools are finishing with the usual baccalaureate and commencement exercises and we have been busy all week with attendance at such functions and at board meetings. We are a little disturbed that Luther Shao in a poll canvass of the Seminary constituency is the high man for nomination for the presidency of Nanking Theological Seminary. Plans are under way for a Union Young People's summer conference in Nanking and a brief retreat following for all of our young people. Daily Vacation Bible plans are under way in almost every station. Church attendance and interest keeps up everywhere. There has been a good recovery at Hofei. We are able to cash drafts, which relieves our financial tension greatly. Communications are improving except for foreign mail. Prices tend a bit downward in comparison to American dollars though there are irregularities, and shortages of goods from abroad makes them higher. There have been some gains in the struggle against inflation after an early slump. None of us are even considering vacations and it is unlikely that we will be able to move about much until a civil government is established" (J.H. McCallum).

- Reynolds, Harriet Robertson, Shanghai, China, Letter to no heading dated July 1, 1949 but sent to United Christian

Missionary Society, Indianapolis, Indiana arriving at the Missions Building on August 24, 1949.

"There seems to be no general agreement on just what mail conditions are now. At least the P.O. is still accepting out-going mail, and I'm writing this on the chance that Mr. Mills can again get it through for me to the Presbyterian office in Hong Kong to be sent on airmail to the US. When it is convenient for you to do it, I hope UCMS will officially, in whatever way you do these things, thank the Presbyterian Headquarters in USA (Northern Pres.) and in Shanghai (c/o Miss Margaret Frame or Plummer Mills, 169 Yuen Ming Yuen Road), and the Associated Mission Treasurers, c/o Mr. Roy Lanning, 169 Yuen Ming Yuen Road, for their kindness and generous help to the children and me here in Shanghai.

It seems fairly certain that we will be here through August. It is still impossible for foreigners to get passes to leave Shanghai. Dr. Lewis Smythe and Mr. Andy Roy came from Nanking this week and were able to take their high school daughter and son home with them by getting their names added to the passes issued in Nanking. They left on the night train last night. Night travel is considered safer now because of the occasional Nationalists bombings. I understand Hubert has a pass to come to Shanghai and return, and Lewis Smythe thinks that would be all that is necessary. However, since it would be pretty serious if he got here and couldn't return very quickly, he probably won't come until after August 12 when he could plan to stay a little while and take us back with him. For the next week, he and Joe with Chinese leaders are conducting a youth conference on the Wuhu Academy campus. Then for the next month, these young people and leaders will have thirteen or more DVBS (Daily Vacation Bible School) in Wuhu and surrounding areas. Mr. Wan, the Academy principal and chairman of our Wuhu church board, was in Shanghai this week and visited us. He is very enthusiastic about the projected conference and DVBS program. He told me a good deal about the problems the Academy has faced but he gave the same reaction that Hubert has given in his letters: things are better and more hopeful now than they were a month ago. In fact, he is quite hopeful regarding the whole economic and political picture here and its effect on the schools. He feels that the new regime is sincere in its desire to work out a coalition government, and that the schools will have a good future. Dr. Smythe spoke in a similar vein. Only seventy out of eight hundred University of Nanking students left before school closed in response to urgent pleas for them to volunteer for special Communist jobs or training. A good many high school students did leave, including some seniors who would have graduated within a week. Mr. Wan spoke highly of the great influence even a brief period, as little as a week, had had on some of the students. While he is definitely not going to run our school on such a basis, he says that in character development, indoctrination, and development of poise and purpose, he has been astonished by the effects on some of his former students. He says one very excellent result is the elimination of 'squeeze.' It is quite generally reported that the new officials are not susceptible to bribing, and are trying to be very fair in their treatment of all people. In matters which they cannot handle effectively as yet, they withhold legislation until they do feel able to carry it out.

This blockade, recognized or not, and the nuisance bombing (with senseless but serious results when bombs fall in residence quarters, cemeteries, etc.) have delayed the recovery of business. Prices have risen a great deal in the past two weeks. While exchange has remained the same, process on rice and all commodities have increased almost double. That will mean that our American dollars, as deposited according to law by June 25, won't last as long as we had hoped to make them. Prices inland are lower; exchange is also a little lower, but anything we buy, especially imported things such as canned goods, milk powder, toilet articles will probably be pretty high for awhile.

Our life goes on quite normally. We wish we could get that idea through to you as we visualize you listening to 'Voice of America' with its stories of the bombing, the harbor situation, and the other matters, or reading pretty 'one-sided' views in the newspapers. There are tensions and various kinds of small annoyances, and will probably continue to be, but we're living pretty normal, happy lives.

When I asked Mr. Wan about the church work at Wuhu, he smiled a big smile and said, 'It grows all the time.'

Since I found I was to stay longer in Shanghai, I began to push for a DVBS in the community church and found a number of other interested people. We are scheduled to open our three weeks school on July 5. We are attempting to reach as many children as possible of American, German, Chinese, and other nationalities. Our enrollment won't be large, but we expect to have a good school. Tomorrow we are to go to a picnic honoring the choirs, but given by all the families in the church. I have contacted all our Chinese pastors in Shanghai, and visited three of the churches (there are five groups meeting here). Only one pastor is a paid worker, the others being lay pastors, but they carry on an active program. I'd like to be able to do more with them, if they would care for it, but because of the distance, the use of Shanghai dialect, and the difficulty of leaving the children, I've had to be content with just making friendly contacts. I hope Hubert can visit these groups when he comes. Several of us who have been working with the community church have been endeavoring to make it more Chinese-conscious, especially to the extent of providing something for the Chinese children of English speaking parents who don't speak English.

At the close of the youth conference in Wuhu, Mary Chao, the Chinese who lived with us last year, plans to come to us here in Shanghai. She has gone through a difficult period of making her choice of staying in the academy or accepting tempting offers to enter one of the indoctrination schools. We will be glad to have her in our family again. We've been enjoying Miss Hsu, the Ginling graduate and former Yenching teacher, who has been staying with us, giving us Mandarin and piano lessons.

We're going to celebrate the Fourth of July on Monday by having a picnic on our compound lawn given by the Americans for the Chinese and German families who live in the compound. There will be about forty of us.

Today, Virginia celebrated her eighth birthday (really on July 3) by inviting several little American, Chinese, and Filipino friends to a 'Three Lands' party. We used ideas from all three countries in invitations, entertainment, and refreshments. As you see, we have many opportunities for friendly social life. It is necessarily fairly simple and inexpensive, but it does much to keep the children happy, and all of us enjoy such companionship. Two of our guests today (and they have been here frequently enough to be really good friends now) were Miss Lin, acting principal of our Nantung School who was caught here in Jan. when Nantung was liberated, and her little nephew the age of Douglas. It is finally possible to send money and supplies through to Lyrel and Polly and others at Nantung, and she and I have been working together from this angle on it with the Nanking office and the letters and messengers from Nantung. Six months is a long time to be cut off from letters, money, and other supplies as has been the case with this station.

On the compound we have a Presbyterian missionary who came in from Wusih a couple of weeks ago. He still hasn't been able to get word whether his wife and son are in Hong Kong; have gone to US or made other plans. When he came, he did not know they had left Shanghai. While mail with you outside is difficult, we are getting excellent service within the liberated areas. Hubert and I get letters in one or two days. Newspapers get through, and he received a Christian Literature society order I had sent to him in record time. One has to do ordering and paying for things through friends or messengers because it is difficult, if not impossible, to transmit money from one section to another.

Lewis thinks we may have to cash some drafts to keep from getting caught short if drafts or checks should not be acceptable here. I asked Mr. Lanning. He said for the present, drafts were much in demand. He felt this was apt to continue" (Harriet Robertson Reynolds).

• Smythe, Lewis S.C., Nanking, China, Letter to no heading dated July 13, 1949 but sent to United Christian Missionary Society, Indianapolis, Indiana arriving at the Missions Building on August 18, 1949.

"The general political outlook discourages Searle (Bates), but we are all so thankful that Christian work can be continued that we are willing to let the future take care of itself, especially as no one can predict, because what we do will partly determine that future! I had a long talk with Cora Teng of YMCA this morning and she is hopeful after attending the preparatory conference in Peiping. She confirmed what I had learned in Shanghai about prospects for the incops as described in 'Sparks.' Y.T. Wu and T.L. Shen were also there and bring very much the same story. Christian work, especially Protestant, will have a fair chance. If we don't make good, it will be our own fault. That is the present policy anyway.

A personal friend opened up this chance for us to send one letter to Peg. So we are putting in what we can. But, I did not feel that I could spread it to many others and Macis in Shanghai. At our meeting at Haskell's Sunday night, we discussed Margaret's coming. The consensus was that unless you wanted her to do some special work in Japan for a few months, she had better wait in the USA until we can cable that free entry into Shanghai is possible. Blockade is only hindrance because the new regime has passenger entry on the slate when that started. While in Shanghai at this NTS meeting, Edna will look further into ships. I checked two weeks ago and APL was booking people but making no promises! We now get the North-China Daily News and all boat and plane companies continue to carry ads, but give no dates! JMP exchange is 1850 to US $1.00 on drafts and Shanghai Commercial and Savings Bank here collects on UCMS daft in Shanghai for one-half of one percent. Rice higher than other commodities now. MOE index on July 4 was up 5.56 times May 2 when Jen Min Piao started. US dollar exchange has about tripled in that time. So we probably face the old scissors action of exchange and prices under present exchange controls. When trade opens up it will tend to break that scissors action. (Searle probably is getting mail into the same opportunity, so look for something from him.)

I saw Harriett and the children while in Shanghai. She is very happy that she came on because she has letters in two days from Hubert in Wuhu. He could go to Shanghai to see her but has summer conferences through August 10. Will go then and probably stay with her at Winling Compound until September 1 and then take them back to Wuhu on his pass, as I did Joan. She is active in DVBS, etc. and is a source of strength to Chinese workers from Tungchow and other places" (Smythe, Lewis S.C).

- McCallum, J.H., 45 Pao T'ai Chieh, Nanking, China, Letter to no heading dated July 31, 1949 but sent to United Christian Missionary Society, Indianapolis, Indiana arriving at the Missions Building on August 10, 1949.

"We have received your cables and will probably be sending one to you within a day. As long as we are cut off by mail, we will try to radio to you around the first of every month. Should necessity require, I still can reach you by phone from Shanghai.

Entrance and Exit Permits. We have been trying to get an official answer to your query about Margaret Lawrence entering China. Until a civil government is established and procedures are worked out it is very uncertain that people may be permitted to enter China from America. I was told this morning that it would have to wait until the new government is established and recognized by the United States. At the same time, the local authorities in Shanghai or Teintsin have authority to allow people to come in to those ports. We have been hoping that Mrs. Gish could go home on furlough by going through the port of Tientsin for permits are being given there. This morning I was told that Nanking does not have authority to grant a travel permit from here to Tientsin. They will give a permit to Shanghai and to exit from this area via Shanghai. I was refused permission to go to Wuhu. It is understood that when the civil government is established that we may have freedom to travel around within liberated areas. So far it is only possible to move to and from Shanghai. It is reported that the new civil government will be set up on the double ten, Oct. 10, holiday. In case there is an evacuation or escorted ship from Shanghai, Mrs. Gish will attempt to go on furlough and we started her application for an exit permit today.

Optimism. We continue to report that all are safe and well and busy on the job. A cool summer so far has been a blessing. Church attendance has kept up well for the summer period and the youth groups have been especially active. We have had DVB schools in every station and some kind of Young People's Conference was built around the DVBS program and they prepared to conduct eleven schools, then of them in rural villages. The high water, which is especially high in the Wuhu area has flooded out three or four of them but the teachers have doubled up in the remaining. At Nanking we held a splendid Union Young People's Summer Conference including the youth of all major missions and institutions such as Ginling College and Nanking University and the YM and YWCA organizations. There were over a hundred and fifty in attendance and formed a local all city youth group. The full week of conference was held in Chuhsien and Wuhu and the shorter period retreats were held in Hofei and Nantung and will be added to the Nanking schedule. We have large numbers of inquirers in Chuhsien and Hofei. We have taken back some of the Hofei property and more is promised. The Coe Memorial Middle School may reopen in the fall. The primary school started in Chuhsien may continue. There are no restrictions to our holding our religious services. No property has been destroyed though war has swept over all our stations, and no lives were lost through local fighting. Taxes so far are very light as far as we are affected.

Pessimism. Some have complained that our reports have been too optimistic. These are tough times for everyone. The average Mr. Man is near desperation. It is not easy to make an economic adjustment to the first stages of a Communist regime. There is no more food or resources to go around. The worst flood in, say fifty years, does not help the outlook. The American dollar is shrinking and with the blockade on there is danger that there will be no demand for it. There is an intense anti-American campaign on everywhere daily through papers, over radio, through posters and political and reorientation meetings. So far, only occasional incidents have occurred as a result of this, generally as a squeeze or sort of extortion from business firms. But schools and hospitals and other institutions are full of explosive material. It is more the atmosphere and the future possibilities that cause fear rather than actualities. One must have the utmost patience and preserve good humor under the most trying conditions and so sometimes we our down as well as up. For the first time in mission history, we have a leader in Luther Shao who is capable of going around among the missionaries and helping to cheer them up. He is doing a wonderful job in these months. But sometimes he gets discouraged. Big institutions like the university and hospital seem to have an almost impossible job to carry on and they are really struggling with their problems every day. Our load is heavy but far from impossible. It is useless for us to worry over what we cannot prevent or to speculate over the international situation, though it affects us very vitally" (J.H. McCallum).

- "Youth Rally is Underway," Unsigned newspaper article, paper name, page number not identified, University Place Christian Church, Enid, Oklahoma, September 17-22, 1949.

  "A former missionary, a teaching fellow, President of the Ministerial Association and Student Council President are among the ones chosen to speak at the 8th annual youth revival. It will be held at University Place Christian Church, September 17-22 (1949).

  Adsit Opened Revival. Glyn Adsit opened the week's revival services speaking Sunday evening on the subject, 'Disappointed in the Morning, Confident by Noon.' Glyn is a graduate student and teaching fellow from Topeka, Kansas. He is a former missionary to China under the United Christian Missionary Society and is now student pastor at Carmen, Oklahoma…"

- Unsigned announcement, "Missionaries Resign," *The Christian-Evangelist*, September 28, 1949, p. 970 (Re-printed by permission, White, Cyrus N., President and Publisher, Christian Board of Publications, 1221 Locust Street, Suite 1200, St. Louis, MO 63103).

  "Mr. and Mrs. Glyn Adsit have resigned as missionaries to the China field. Their future plans have not been announced."

- Goulter, Oswald J., Field Director, The Kiangsu-Anhwei Christian Rural Service Union, Chuhsien, Anhwei, China, Letter to Glyn and Jean Adsit, October 25, 1949.

  "Dear Glyn and Jean, I have been intending to write you for a long time, but the mails have been quite irregular. There is promise of more regular service now that the stupid Nationalist blockade and bombing seems likely to be broken up. A few days ago one of their planes flew over

Nanking with landing lights on. I wanted to come down and surrender. When the people down below caught on they stopped firing on it and let it come in.

Irene and I are on our first trip out since liberation, are spending two weeks in Nanking, it is like visiting another world. They have had no particular change here, everything goes on just as usual around the new capital at Peking. I think you have read of Irene's and my adventures. It was trying at times, but we have made rapid progress in developing the rural center for the union, more rapid than we would have if the old regime had continued because we have not been able to travel. The old house you once planned on using at Chuhsien has proven to be the nicest home we have ever had. The windmill I brought out is working very well so we have running water for house and garden, flush toilets, etc., for the first time in China. The fruit trees from Hofei and US are growing like magic; no one will believe we planted them as tiny trees when we came from Hofei. They are as big as ordinary full-grown trees already.

The service center is repaired and we use the large building now. The downstairs is all used by the primary school and it swarms with pupils. I am sending a photo to World Call that you will see shortly. (The Kiangsu-Anhwei Christian Rural Service Union was made up of twelve missions and colleges cooperating in an integrated program built around the needs of the Chinese villagers on the concept of helping them to help themselves.)

One thing that reminded me of you folks was the prospective use of your house at Hofei. When I was there it was used by a unit who seemed to have quite a different idea about fixing it up. They considered that no doors were necessary, and as I saw gaping holes that used to be doors, I thought of the trouble you went to go to make the new doors, even the front gate was gone. Now it is rented, and I have been told that it is being prepared for the Russian advisors. I took Wenona and Verla back, and we did not get the very nicest welcome. They seemed to think in some quarters that I had beaten it because they were coming. Things are picking up now that the new People's Government of China has taken a liberal attitude toward religion, so we hope this attitude will seep down even to Hofei.

I think I told you that we sent back for the sugar that you left with Corprons, it proved to be a real blessing during the subsequent months. However, I left some funds with you for a couple of the boys at the rural center for board. I don't remember the exact amount, nor the value of the sugar, so I thought we might let the two count as balanced.

George is well and looking forward to Marge's return before long as folk are beginning to seep back. The Bible training school at Chuhsien is going ahead with fifteen young men and young women now.

We have three of your old Hofei acquaintances there still, but two dropped out this term. Tong-Chi-Chieh got into some trouble at San Ho, so is out at least temporarily. He is not too well balanced, gets all worked up at times over some personal things such as a bit of teasing by other boys. I hope he may come back later as he is an intense personality with deep convictions. I don't know just what has happened to the boy you helped so much who worked at your place part time, but I will follow him up and get him into our school if he has made sufficient progress to make the grade. We have some young men with much higher education just beginning their training. They remind me of a group of young Phillips ministerial students more and more as they get further training. This group is the hope of our evangelistic program. Two are already out at work, and are building up some of the country churches destroyed under the Japanese occupation. Five of them will be ready to go out next spring, so I hope one will be engaged by the San Ho Church and another by Liang Yuen as pastor-evangelists. I hope to get upwards of a hundred trained before we come home on furlough. I have financed the Bible Training School entirely with specials up to date, but we have a plan for getting the Chinese church and some Chinese friends who have money, to support it in part as time goes on.

The situation at Chuhsien is improving just now. The new People's Government of China allows representatives of religious interests on its national consultative committee, and the same thing is true of similar committees for local areas. They asked the Christians to appoint a representative, so Mr. Chu Hsao-tan was selected. As he is one of the smartest men I know I was not surprised when they appointed him in charge of one of the three divisions of the committee as chairman. This gives the Christians a place in the community and may lead to a settled situation. Of course one always has to put the qualifying phrase 'up to date' to all such hopes.

Let us know where you are located. I often think of our San Ho trip and the swarming people, curious to know what we had come for. It's still that way, but I think people are making much more progress in understanding the Christian purpose. We have had three larger groups baptized at Chuhsien this year, and have a still larger group of some hundred or more inquirers. We had a Christian rally and then had to hold an inquirers rally, there were more inquirers than Christians. San Ho, Liang Yuen, and Shi Tan Chiao, have all made wonderful progress during the past year. Luther Shao plans to go to Shi Tan Chiao for a large baptism service before Christmas. Many of those young men at Liang Yuen will be baptized at the same time. At one of the small places near San Ho there were thirty-five baptized, and still another which has not had one Christian, now has eighteen waiting for baptism.

I hope you folks can stir people up to increased support as this is the great period of church building for China. If we do not go ahead now, things may settle down to an attitude of opposition. But this is the great day of decision when China is deciding her attitude which may last for centuries.

Folks from my living link church at California, and other friends have written of attending your meetings or hearing your talks at conventions. I am sure you can do a great deal to serve China from the home side and help establish the Christian faith as an accepted part of the amazing new society which is being built here. The people seem to want to get what is good from all sources, hence their interest in Communism as well as in other things from the West. Pray for us that we may have the spirit of God as a moving power in this crisis. With all good wishes and our prayers for your work, Oswald J. Goulter [Field Director]."

- Yoau, Kas Ho, Friend and Christian Convert in Hofei, China, Letter to Mrs. and Mr. Adsit, October 21, 1950

"Dear Mr. and Mrs. Adsit, after you left Hofei, the Liberation Army quickly occupied the city, and your house also was occupied by them. Since I was not the owner of that house, I left it by their order. But all your belongings, I have sent to the hospital and told them to take care of them, as you told me to do in case I have to leave.

I am now still out of a job. I hope to open a small shop for selling cooked beef. I hope the proceeds will be enough to keep my family, but in order to do this, I will need a considerable amount of money and a big pressure cooker.

If you will kindly let me have the use of your pressure cooker, please write a note to Misses Li and Wei. Because it is in their hands. Also money for a little start; this money could be remitted to my brother who is in Nanking living at Mr. McCallums house. He will see that this money reaches me okay.

Give my best regards to your family. Thank you in advance, yours respectfully, Kao Ho-Yoau."

- Elliot, Verla, Missionary, Berkeley, California, Letter to Jean and Glyn Adsit, Enid, Oklahoma, November 10, 1951.

"Dear Jean, Glyn and Timmy, yours was one of the loveliest letters I ever received. Your poetic quotations and prayers were so appropriate for me, my heart dissolved in tears. This is a letter that I will not tear up and throw in the basket upon having answered it.

I attended the area assembly in Fresno and stayed with Polly in her hotel. She left the Seattle assembly early and came down to Berkeley to see the Cherryhomes and me and her own sister here. The Polly and I went together on down to Fresno in the Wesley Ford's car.

Grace Young was there, and of course the Ploppers live there. She attended a missionary dinner with all of us one evening, but Mr. Plopper took her home immediately afterward and put her to bed. I'm talking about Alma of course, not Grace! Mac and Eva were there and George Cherryhomes. I met Mr. and Mrs. Brady, formerly of China and also met Marge's parents, Mr. and Mrs. Paul Kennedy for the first time. Royal Dye of Africa, Goldie Allenbaugh and Faith McCracken of Africa, and a Mr. and Mrs. Beardly, formerly of India, were the other missionaries present. We met that evening with the new president, Dale Fyers, Jessie Trout, and Virgil Sly. I made public and final my decision to go to India, principally because Jessie was trying to get me to do state secretary work. I was flattered that she thought I could do it, but am not ready yet to leave the foreign field. All in all it was a good convention.

It was a treat to hear Mossie Wiker and Perry Gresham speak for the first time.

Saturday evening, Dorothy Mitchel Shockley and I returned to San Francisco to have Japanese food with Grace and Doug Corpron down from Yakima for a heart convention. It was good to see them again. It was the first time I's seen Grace since 1949 when Wenona and I said good-bye to them after we made the evacuation from Hofei. I remember we all crossed the Yangtze together, or rather came from Wuhu to Nanking by boat. We got off at Hsia Gwan and ate a bowl of hot noodles at one of those little stands and they waved good-bye and went right onto a navy ship for Shanghai and we went on into Nanking to the McCallums.

Grace and Doug are both looking real well, neither too thin nor too fat. Doug has a good practice built up again and is working more to keep his income down than up so his income tax won't be too high. They were disappointed because I did not decide to return to White Swan Indian Mission to work with the Normants.

I don't believe I had my sailing date when I wrote you last, did I? Well, it is to be December 29 from New York on the *Queen Elizabeth*, three days to South Hampton, and we, Mary Pollard and I, plan to stay eight to ten days in England and Scotland before taking a British ship on to Bombay. We hope and Don West hopes, that we will arrive in Jubbalpore in time for the India Convention, which is to be held there February 5 on. I don't know how many days. Don West will be there then. I have had letters of welcome to India already from Ethel Shreve, Ray and Merle T. Rice and from Ken Potee, the India foreign secretary.

Mary and I went to S.F. day before yesterday to start our immunization shots and yesterday, I spent all day in bed completely knocked out with yellow fever, cholera, plague, typhus, tetanus, and typhoid. Next week, we go back for seconds on all these and our smallpox vaccinations. I was scheduled to speak for a CWF in Sacramento First Christian last night, and George insisted at the last minute, actually after my cab had arrived to take me to the bus station, ongoing in my place. It is a good thing he did for I would have been one sad sack if I'd gone. Dorothy wanted me to come to Hayward this weekend to meet her husband, John Shockley, and her eight-year-old son. I guess I'll feel like going by tomorrow morning.

Leaving here November 29 and will be arriving December 2 in Salt Lake City and Ogden for women's day speeches. Colorado Springs on the fourth, then Thanksgiving dinner, delayed, with my sisters the fifth or sixth. From the seventh to sixteenth of December, I'll be speaking in Loveland, Greeley, Manzanola, Ardway, rocky Ford, Las Animas and then, LaJunta for a youth meet and women's day. Then I'll have from then on with my family to get packed for India, and I'll try to reserve the last Sunday for Fort Collins. I may have to fly to NY if I stay in Colorado for Christmas.

Well, I hope everything is going okay with you and you are all well. On the tenth of October, I mailed some books to Glyn. Did you get them? There will be another surprise package coming one of these days soon.

Take care, and do keep writing please. Love, Verla [Elliot]. [Now Verla Sutton] P.S. The Cherryhomes baby is due next weekend. Marge is feeling fine."

- Elliot, Verla, Missionary, Berthoud, Colorado, Christmas Letter to Glyn and Jean Adsit, December 2, 1951.

"Christmas 1951. 'Unnoticed as a snowflake, white innocence made itself at home in a common stable. And hope was born, hard by the migrants' road, beneath a tumult of oppression, of feasting and tax-gathering. The new regime from Heaven, takes it's rise in the strangest corners of earth. Christian Church Hofei, Anhwei, China, 50th Anniversary, 1949. O Heavenly Father, bless to us at this Christmas season the drama of the Holy Family, and help us each to find his happy role in it: Mary-tender and gentle, treasuring her Offspring for God. Joseph-steward and sojourner, guarding his scared trust. The Child-serene and fearless—the Hope of a despairing world for its Promised Peace. A happy holy Christmas to you. Verla Elliot.' P.S. My farewell to Hofei, China. Sailing date still February 8 on Queen Mary. Christmas dinner at Bernice and Forrests this year. Spending this week with sister, Hermie and Del Grunwood (married this last summer)."

"According to a *New York Times* dispatch of May 1956, the Communists have virtually completed the liquidation of a century and a half and more of foreign missionary work in China. Confiscated were the hundreds of schools, colleges, hospitals, orphanages, libraries, and countless other Christian institutions that long had bencfited China. Gone, too, were the millions that had been spent annually on healing, schooling, preaching, and counseling. But most seriously, gone was the spirit of Christ that had been the hope of the future of China." (Janss, Edmund W., *Yankee Si!*, William Morrow and Company, 1961, p.67).

Chapter 4

Speaker for the United Christian Missionary Society, 1951

Upon Glyn and Jean's return from China, the United Christian Missionary Society (UCMS) contacted Glyn and asked him to travel among the churches and tell the story of the Disciples mission work in China. Glyn agreed to do that for one year. The UCMS paid Glyn a livable salary for one year as he spoke on behalf of missions work. Glyn spoke at the Disciples large international convention and in many state conventions and dozens of local churches and women's missionary groups. All that year, Jean and Tim stayed with Jean's sister, Billie Wilson, who, with her husband, Phil, was operating a hotel in Lakin, Kansas, that was owned by her father, E.M. Dowd.

After the year was up, Glyn and Jean had to decide what they were going to do from then on. Glyn was approached by the head of the Christian Church's United Promotion Division of the United Christian Missionary Society, Mr. C.O. Hawley. Mr. Hawley wanted Glyn to join the United Promotion staff and help write materials, develop programs, and speak to Disciples of Christ churches to help raise money for their home and foreign missions work. Jean and Glyn talked it over and prayed about it, and finally, Glyn decided that he would not accept the offer, mainly because he was only thirty-three years old at the time and Jean was thirty-one, and they wanted to have more children, and Glyn did not want to be gone three fourths of the time from Jean and son, Tim. Concerning this time period, Glyn writes:

> We decided that I would return to Phillips University to continue graduate studies, and after graduating from that three-year program, that I would go into serving local congregations as a minister. I had already spent seven years in college and university work, and had received two degrees, the BA and masters. We knew it would be a hard row to hoe, but Jean encouraged me to go ahead. We had no furniture at that time, having lost all our worldly possessions in China. The Christian Church in Stratford, Texas, was Jean's supporting church while we were in China. She had lived in Stratford before moving to Amarillo. They invited us to the church and asked Jean to preach the morning sermon…After the morning service, an old-time rich rancher, R.C. Buckles, said, 'Folks, our Jeanie, and her husband, lost all their furniture in China, everything they had. I'm going to pass my hat around and whatever is in there I will match it, and we'll get them set up with some furniture.' He passed the hat and the money received was enough for us to go to a used furniture store the next day and buy the furniture. That furniture not only lasted the three years we were in graduate school, but we took most of it to our first local church. And now, some forty-two years later, we still have some of that furniture. (Yes, I mentioned Jean is Scotch and Irish.)
>
> —Adsit, Glyn B. and Adsit, Alice Jean, Unpublished manuscript information written by Glyn as dictated by Jean to be used at her graveside and memorial service upon her death, Bend, Oregon, March 13, 1991, p.3.

(Incidentally, for the record, the author, still has some of that same furniture in his home today, and some was given to Glyn and Jean's grandkids. My wife calls it, "early parsonage.")

Phillips University, 1950-52—Honing the Edge, the Finishing Touches

Concerning this time period, Glyn writes:

> It was Walter Hargraves that said to me, "Glyn, don't stop until you get that Bachelor of Divinity, you won't ever know how ignorant you are until after you have completed it." At that time, I had just returned from China and had traveled for the United Christian Missionary Society for some seven months and had a flattering offer from Mr. C.O. Hawley to take a position in his department. Walter was trying to show me that I was needed in the preaching ministry, rather than in promotional work. I am glad I stayed in school. I know what Walter meant. It is in the graduate ministry (this term means the accepted type of ministerial work). The undergraduate work is merely a beginning. I have achieved a synthesis of my Christian beliefs these past three years. I have not lost any of my enthusiasm.
>
> I still pray to God and feel that He hears and answers me. I feel that I am ready to go out to the field and start to work. My spiritual pilgrimage has been an interesting one to me at least. I am surprised how much influence my mother has had on my life. I did not realize that before. This growth that I have made has come as a result of influence exerted by Sunday school teachers; ministers in churches; teachers in college; friends; and most of all, from God. I have found that I have prayed most of my life. The content and meaning of prayer has changed for me. I do not ask for things so much anymore, but I pray that I might know God's will for me in this world today. I have found that prayer works for me. I have been conscious of

God's presence in my life since my 'sudden' experience in 1941. I do not feel any different from any other young man called to the ministry. But I have felt, and do feel, that God called me for a purpose and has to some extent revealed that purpose to me. I still feel the necessity to keep in daily touch with Him for further guidance. I am convinced that I have touched the real meaning of life in my thinking and praying. It is my prayer that my spiritual pilgrimage will continue to be toward the fulfillment of God's purpose set for me.

—Adsit, Glyn B., "My Spiritual Pilgrimage"
Unpublished paper written in partial fulfillment of the
course requirements for the course entitled, Psychology
of Religion, Dr. W.E. Powell, Professor, Phillips
University, Enid, Oklahoma, January 2, 1952, pp. 21-22.

Thus, while at Phillips for the second time, Glyn continued his studies, and Jean took care of Tim and kept encouraging Glyn. She did not work outside the home during this time. Glyn took the necessary courses and also preached at a student church in Carmen, Oklahoma, on weekends. He also taught two New Testament Greek and Bible classes for two years. Jean made many friends during this three-year period.

As time for graduation approached, Glyn and Jean had to decide what they were going to do. Glyn was offered the opportunity to stay at Phillips University as a professor or accept a local church pastorate. They decided for local church work and began to put out feelers to determine which churches were open. Glyn writes,

The President of Phillips, Doctor Briggs, called me into his office and asked if I would be interested in accepting the Orange, California church. Jean and I, talked it over, and said yes. I had worked in California in the 1930s and knew something about the state. The church called me on the phone, and I told them I could not go anywhere until after graduation in late May of 1952. They said they would be sending a round-trip train ticket to come out and look them over and to see the church on a Sunday morning and asked me to preach at that time. I did that, and they called me to be their pastor effective June 1, 1952. This was our first church full-time in the United States. It had almost six hundred members, so we began our ministries with churches in California, Oklahoma, Oregon, and Texas…

—Adsit, Glyn B. and Adsit, Alice Jean, Unpublished manuscript information written by Glyn as dictated by Jean to be used at her graveside and memorial service upon her death, Bend, Oregon, March 13, 1991, p.3-4.

After leaving the China mission field in 1949, Glyn and Jean served as pastors in various churches in America for the next forty-two years. They always held a fondness for China in their hearts, and the churches they served all actively supported missions work throughout the world.

Chapter 5
Brief Summary

Whatever is happening in and to the Christian Church, Disciples of Christ in China since 1951, today, we know that the church is still there. We know that there are local Chinese pastors who minister to their people during the week and on Sunday morning preach the gospel from their pulpits or in living rooms and dens. We do not know what temptations and trials have come to those through these years when the bamboo curtain has prevented communication, but we do know that things began to open up to the West again when President Nixon visited China and that some religious freedoms have been restored. We also know that God has never left China and that Christians have drawn strength and hope from the certainty of his presence.

We remember with gratification the fact that very early in the history of the Disciples of Christ mission work in China we began to turn over to Chinese leadership the administration of the work of the churches as was documented in Glyn and Jean's memoirs. The churches, the institutions under their direction, had been under local Chinese supervision for a good many years when the American missionaries were forced to leave the country. Whatever they suffered has been in spite of and not because the Chinese were not able to administer the work.

Now that a few chinks of light are hinting that perhaps the bamboo curtain is not impregnable, we see some private ownership and entrepreneurism returning, and we are beginning to hope that the time will come again soon when we can have unrestricted and open fellowship with our Christian friends on mainland China. We are beginning to wonder whether perhaps someday soon, it might not be possible once again for us to reach out a hand to the church in China offering personnel and financial help. That day has not fully come yet, but when it does, we must be ready to help fulfill the Great Commission: "Go therefore and make disciples of all nations, baptizing them in the name of the Father and the of the Son and of the Holy Spirit, teaching them to observe all that I have commanded you and lo, I am with you always, to the close of the age" (Matthew 28:19-20, KJV). Prophetic signs and careful study indicates to this author that the end time harvest is underway and close at hand. No one knows the exact day or hour of Christ's return, but as Christians, we are to continue to walk the Christian walk, share the gospel, and strengthen our own faith and understanding through prayer and reading the Bible and by helping to fulfill the Great Commission. I challenge you to be a beacon for the coming of His light and to plant seeds of change wherever the door opens to do so.

Appendix

Map of China showing Hofei, Anhwei, Province, China

Missionaries getting ready to board the S.S. Marine Adder as they head to China in 1947.

Glyn and Jean Adsit on board the S.S. Marine Adder as they sailed for China in 1947.

Pedi–Cab/Rickshaw in the streets of Shanghai, China, in 1947.

Open air market in narrow streets of Shanghai, China, in 1947.

Eight-room stone house located in Hofei, China, where Glyn, Jean, and Tim Adsit, and Lyrel Teagarden lived. The buildings beyond the wall around the house are part of the rural center consisting of a church, school, a 150-bed hospital and farming areas.

Chinese boys hauling drinking and bathing water on their shoulders from the well to the 8 room house in Hofei, China, in 1947. Glyn used to share his sense of humor and say, "We had running water in China, we ran from the well and back to the house."

Typical rural Chinese farmhouse outside Hofei, China, in 1947.
Notice the narrow mud and gravel foot and bicycle paths.

Country Chinese women grinding wheat with 16lb. hammers.
They do this in rhythm and in unison all day long.

Nationalist Chinese Soldiers inspecting Doctor Douglas Corpron's pass. This military compound was located directly behind the rural center which consisted of a church, school, 150-bed hospital, and farming area in Hofei, China, in 1947. These are some of the same soldiers who used to practice bugling at 4:00 a.m. according to Glyn Adsit.

Missionaries Jean Adsit, Nurse Grace Young, and Mrs. Corporon near the gated south entrance and ancient wall surrounding Hofei, China, on September 15, 1947.

Narrow gravel street and pagoda in Hofei, China, in 1947.

Serving Chinese children soup out of tin cups at the rural center grade school in Hofei, China, in 1947.

Chinese boy with harrow and water buffalo in a rice paddy in a rural area 10 li from Hofei, China, on December 7, 1947.

Glyn Adsit traveling home to Hofei from San Ho in a sudan chair after he, Oswald Goulter, and Pastor Wang got snowed in and their bicycles would not work in the snow and mud. Glyn suffered frostbitten toes on this trip in December 1947, and he felt humiliated at having to be carried by another human being.

Chinese boy taking a pig to market in 1947.

A missionary, Verla Elliot, teaching an adolescent age Sunday school class at the rural center in 1947.

Eighty-seven-year-old Chinese woman flaying wheat. She beats the grain out then sweeps it up and winnows it. Notice her bound feet. This custom is not in practice much anymore in China.

*Graves of those shot for stealing by the Nationalist Chinese
soldiers in December of 1947. This picture was taken by looking
just over the wall that surrounded the house where Glyn, Jean,
and Tim Adsit and Lyrel Teagarden lived in Hofei, China.*

*Grass fired kitchen stove in a typical rural Chinese
family home around Hofei, China, in 1947.*

*Pastor Wang and friends in front of a church school
under construction at the rural center in 1947.*

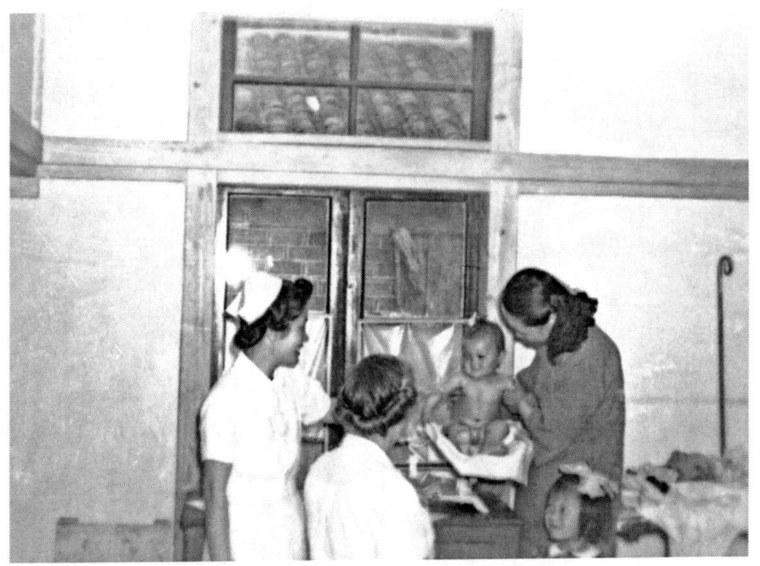

Well baby clinic in the rural center hospital in Hofei, China, in 1947 where Jean Adsit worked while serving on the mission field.

Glyn B. Adsit holding a basket of red hard boiled eggs, a Chinese custom to announce the birth of a son, this author, on April 26, 1948. Glyn describes how these eggs were distributed elsewhere in the text.

Glyn and Jean Adsit holding their new born son, Tim, while on vacation in Kuling, China in the summer of 1948.

Missionaries attending a planning retreat while in Kuling, China, in July/August 1948.

Riding bicycles on the road to ErShrPu where Glyn Adsit, Verla Elliot, Miss Shr, and Mr. Fang were shot at.

Straw hut belonging to a poor Chinese family living just outside Glyn and Jean's front gate in Hofei, China, in 1947. Glyn and Jean used to share some food from their own yard and garden with this family.

A rare photograph of Chiang-Kai-Shek and Madame Chiang-Kai-Shek taken in early September 1948 while they were walking to attend a Community Christian Church in Kuling, Kiangsi, China.

Chiang-Kai-Shek, President of Nationalist China and Madame Chiang-Kai-Shek on their way to a Community Christian Church in Kuling, China, in early September 1948.

*Glyn and Jean Adsit traveling home from China on
December 11, 1948, while aboard the USS General HW
Butner. The ship docked in San Francisco, California.*

Never before published and historically-significant photos of Chiang Kai-shek and Madame Chiang Kai-shek, then President of Nationalist free China taken by my father, Glyn Adsit in September 1948, while they were walking to church in Kuling, China.

Three missionaries who were shot at while traveling the road and bicycle path from Hofei to ErShrPu. Caption: Riding bicycles on the road to ErShrPu from Hofei where Glyn Adsit, Verla Elliot, Miss Shr, and Mr. Fang were shot at.

Endnotes

Preface

Chen, Angie. (June 2002). The Stand-A Journal of Christian Thought at UCSD. Online at (*http://www.thestandjournal.org/ successful-evangelism-requires-political-and-cultural-sensitivity pp.2-3*).

Chapter 1

My Spiritual Pilgrimage, an unpublished paper, written in partial fulfillment for the course entitled Psychology of Religion, January 2, 1952, pp. 9-11.

Journal Entry, In the District Court of Shawnee County, Kansas, Third Division, Case No. 55866, filed April 3, 1939 and finalized six months after October 30, 1939.

My Spiritual Pilgrimage, an unpublished paper, written in partial fulfillment for the course entitled Psychology of Religion, January 2, 1952, p.11.

Ibid, p.11.

Ibid, p.11-12.

Ruth 1:16-17, KJV

Unpublished manuscript information written by Glyn Adsit as dictated by Jean Adsit on March 13, 1991, to be used at her graveside and memorial service upon her death, p. 1.

My Spiritual Pilgrimage, an unpublished paper written in partial fulfillment for the course entitled Psychology of Religion, January 2, 1952, pp.12-13.

Ibid., pp. 13-16.

Chapter 2

My Spiritual Pilgrimage, pp.16-17, 1952.

Ibid., pp. 16-19.

Unpublished manuscript information written by Glyn Adsit as dictated by Jean Adsit on March 13, 1991, to be used at her graveside and memorial service upon her death, p. 1.

Adsit, Glyn B. and Adsit, Alice Jean, Letter of application sent to the United Christian Missionary Society, written on stationary from the Westside Christian Church, Tulsa, Oklahoma, 1943, pp. 1-2.

Ibid., pp.1-2.

Chapter 3

My Spiritual Pilgrimage, an unpublished paper, written in partial fulfillment for the course entitled, Psychology of Religion, Phillips University, Enid, Oklahoma, January 2, 1952, pp. 19-20.

Unpublished manuscript information written by Glyn Adsit as dictated by Jean Adsit on March 13, 1991, to be used at her graveside and memorial service upon her death, p. 1.

Hill, Marilynne, *Letter and Manuscript of Study Guide,* Director of Adult work, The United Christian Missionary Society, to Mrs. Glyn Adsit, September 1, 1961, p.1.

Ely, Lois Anna, *Lest We Forget China Sixty-Five Years of Ups and Downs*, Christian Women's fellowship Group Study Packet, January to June 1962, pp. 1-28.

Unpublished manuscript information written by Glyn Adsit as dictated by Jean Adsit on March 13, 1991, to be used at her graveside and memorial service upon her death, p. 2.

Ibid., p. 1.

Adsit, Glyn B. (1945-49). *Adsit Diary.* Unpublished Materials Collection. In possession of Tim L. Adsit, TLAW, Inc. ©, 20730 Barton Crossing Way, Bend, OR 97701-7711.

Glyn Bemister Carter Adsit, Amarillo, Texas, July 25, 1941, Letter of resignation to Mize, F.V., Manager, "A" Telegraph Office, Santa Fe Railroad, Amarillo, Texas.

Mize, F.V., Manager, "A" Telegraph Office, Santa Fe Railroad, Amarillo, Texas. Personal letter accepting resignation sent to Mr. G.B. Adsit, July 26, 1941.

Davis, John L., Editor, "Classroom and Campus," *World Call*, February, 1945. p. 24.

Author unknown. "Bible College Students Ordained," *Christian Evangelist*, July 4, 1945, p. 655.

Adsit, Glyn B., Graduate Student in Sociology and Rural Education, Cornell University, Ithaca, New York, Letter and picture to Editor, World Call Magazine, Indianapolis, Indiana, October 11, 1945.

Goulter, Oswald J., "You in Heaven"—Democracy Can Win in China, If—, *The Christian-Evangelist*, July 10, 1946, pp. 679-680. Article sent to Glyn B. Adsit.

"China Mission Descriptive Report," From the United Christian Missionary Society, Indianapolis, Indiana, 1946, pp.1-3. Report contained in a letter to Glyn and Jean Adsit.

Higdon, Dr. E.K.. Foreign Division Application Packet, "How to Become a Foreign Missionary—Qualifications, Preparation and Procedure, The United Christian Missionary Society, Indianapolis, Indiana, Letter to Glyn and Jean Adsit, 1947.

Higdon, E.K., Dr., Executive Secretary, Department of Oriental Missions, The United Christian Missionary Society (UCMS), Indianapolis, Indiana, Letter to Whom It May Concern, April 10, 1947 Re: Certification of Ordination as Ministers for Mr. And Mrs. Glyn B. Adsit and Appointment as Missionaries of the UCMS.

Adsit, Glyn B., Minister, Graduate Student, Yale University, New Haven, Connecticut, Letter to Dr. E.K. Higdon, April 15, 1947.

Adsit, Glyn B., Minister, Graduate Student, Yale University, New Haven, Connecticut, Letter to Mr. C.A. Weesner, April 15, 1947.

"Lincoln Terrace Assigned Glyn B. Adsit," Unsigned news article, name, specific date, page number not available, May 1947.

Doan, Mrs. Mary Lediard, Presiding, Commissioning Service Bulletin for Glyn and Jean Adsit et al, June 25, 1947.

McCormick, H.B., President, Payne, Hazel Scott, Secretary, United Christian Missionary Society, Indianapolis, Indiana, to Glyn and Jean Adsit, Letters/Certificates of Appointment As Missionaries of the Society to China, Missions Building, Indianapolis, Indiana, June 25, 1947.

McCormick, H.B., President, The United Christian Missionary Society, Indianapolis, Indiana, Letter to Mr. And Mrs. Glyn Adsit, July 21, 1947.

Garcia, George and Marie, Minister, Filipino United Church, Honolulu, Hawaii, Letter to Glyn and Jean Adsit, July 25, 1947.

Adsit, Glyn., Minister and Missionary, *SS Marine Adder*, On the Ocean Voyage to China, Letter to Mrs. R.L. Adsit and Mr. and Mrs. Duane Adsit (Mother, Duane, and Pat), August 13, 1947.

Higdon, E.K., Dr., Executive Secretary, Department of Oriental Missions, The United Christian Missionary Society, Indianapolis, Indiana, "Some Comments On Rural Work With Special Reference To The Hofei District In China", Copy of letter to Mr. Glyn B. Adsit, August 18, 1947.

Adsit, Glyn and Jean, Ministers and Missionaries, *SS Marine Adder*, Day and one half out of Japan on the ocean heading to China, Letter to Mother, Duane, and Pat, August 21, 1947.

Adsit, Glyn and Jean, Ministers and Missionaries, Shanghai, China, Letter to Mother (R.L. Adsit), Duane, and Pat Adsit, August 26, 1947.

Turley, Hollis Lee, "The High Calling," *World Call*, September 1947, pp. 21-22 (Re-printed by permission, White, Cyrus N., President and Publisher, Christian Board of Publications, 1221 Locust Street, Suite 1200, St. Louis, MO 63103).

Adsit, Glyn and Jean, Ministers and Missionaries, Lutheran Center, Shanghai, China, Letter to Mother, Duane, and Pat, September 1, 1947.

Adsit, Glyn B., Minister and Missionary, Shanghai, China, to Mother, Reecie Adsit, undated note, circa September 1947.

McCormick, H.B., President, The United Christian Missionary Society, Indianapolis, Indiana, Letter to Mr. And Mrs. Glyn Adsit, September 11, 1947.

Adsit, Glyn B., Minister and Missionary, Nanking, China, to Mother and family, September 15, 1947.

Adsit, Glyn B., Minister and Missionary, Chuhsien, Anhwei, China, to Mother and Family, September 23, 1947.

Adsit, Glyn B., Minister and Missionary, Chuhsien, Anhwei, China, to Mother and Home Folks, October 1, 1947.

Adsit, Jean, Minister and Missionary, location Nanking, China, Letter to Mother, Reecie Adsit, October 4, 1947.

Adsit, Glyn B. and Jean, Ministers and Missionaries, Nanking, China, to Mr. Edwin Marx, October 18, 1947.

Adsit, Glyn B. and Jean, Ministers and Missionaries, Nanking, China, to Mr. Edwin Marx, October 18, 1947.

Marx, Edwin, Office of the Secretary-Treasurer, United Christian Missionary Society, China, Mission, Nanking, KU, Letter to Glyn B. Adsit, October 24, 1947.

Adsit, Glyn B., Minister and Missionary, Hofei, China, Letter to Mother (R.L. Adsit), November 20, 1947.

Buckner, George Walker, Jr., Editor, *World Call International Magazine* of Disciples of Christ, Indianapolis, Indiana, Letter to Glyn B. Adsit, November 24, 1947.

Adsit, Glyn B., Minister and Missionary, *Luchowfu Christian Hospital, Hofei, Anhwei, China,* Letter to Mother (R.L. Adsit), December 4, 1947.

Adsit, Glyn B., Minister and Missionary, Luchowfu Christian Hospital, Hofei, Anhwei, China, Christmas Letter to Friends in America, December 7, 1947.

Higdon, E.K., Executive Secretary, Department of Oriental Missions, The United Christian Missionary Society, Indianapolis, Indiana, Letter to Mr. And Mrs. Glyn B. Adsit, December 18, 1947.

Adsit, Glyn B. and Jean, Ministers and Missionaries, Luchowfu Christian Hospital, Hofei, Anhwei, China, Letter to Mother, Duane, Pat, and Mike Adsit, December 21, 1947.

Adsit, Glyn B., Minister and Missionary, Hofei, Anhwei, China, Letter to Mother and All the Rest, Christmas 1947.

Adsit, Jean (and Glyn), Minister and Missionary, Hofei, Anhwei, China, Letter to Mother, December 26, 1947.

Adsit, Glyn B., "A Prodigal Son Returns-A Story of Wang Yun Ting, Elder at Chuhsien," *World Call*, January, 1948, pp. 17-18 (Re-printed by permission, White, Cyrus N., President and Publisher, Christian Board of Publications, 1221 Locust Street, Suite 1200, St. Louis, MO 63103).

Adsit, Glyn B., Minister and Missionary, Hofei, Anhwei, China, letter to Mother and all brothers, sisters, nephews and dogs, January 4, 1948.

Adsit, Glyn B., Minister and Missionary, The Christian Mission, Hofei, Anhwei, China, Letter to Folks, January 17, 1948.

Niedermeyer, Mabel, Missionary Education, The United Christian Missionary Society. Indianapolis, Indiana, Letter to Mr. and Mrs., Glyn B. Adsit, January 20, 1948.

Adsit, Glyn B. and Jean, Ministers and Missionaries, The Christian Mission, Hofei, Anhwei, China, Letter to Family, February 1, 1948.

Adsit, Glyn B. and Jean, Ministers and Missionaries, Hofei, China, Letter to Mr. Edwin Marx, February 4, 1948.

Adsit, Glyn and Jean, Ministers and Missionaries, Hofei, Anhwei, China, Letter to Mother and all the family, February 6, 1948.

Adsit, Jean, Minister and Missionary, Hofei, China, Letter to Mom (Reecie Adsit), February 17, 1948.

Adsit, Glyn and Jean, Ministers and Missionaries, Hofei, China, Letter to Homefolks, February 26, 1948.

Adsit, Glyn and Jean, Minister and Missionaries, Hofei, Anhwei, China, Letter to Dr. E.K. Higdon, March 1, 1948.

Adsit, Glyn B., Minister and Missionary, Hofei, Anhwei, China, article entitled, "Hofei Christian Hospital—Mission of Mercy," submitted to George Walker Buckner, Jr., Editor, *World Call*, International Magazine of Disciples of Christ, March 1, 1948.

Adsit, Glyn and Jean, Ministers and Missionaries, Hofei, Anhwei, China, Letter to Central Christian Church, Enid, Oklahoma, and Lincoln Terrace Christian Church, Oklahoma City, Oklahoma, March 4, 1948.

"China: You Shall Never Yield," *Time Magazine*, copyright Time, Inc. 1948, reprinted with permission in *Front Rank*, A magazine of Christian Living for Adults and Older Young People, Volume 58, No. 10, Christian Board of Publications, Saint Louis, Mo., March 6, 1948, pp. 6-7, 10-11.

Adsit, Glyn and Jean, Ministers and Missionaries, Hofei, Anhwei, China, Letter to Mother, Pat, Duane, Hurshel, and Bessie and all the rest, March 22, 1948.

Adsit, Glyn and Jean, Ministers and Missionaries, Hofei, Anhwei, China, Letter to Family, March 29, 1948

Adsit, Glyn and Jean, Ministers and Missionaries, Hofei, Anhwei, China, Letter to Loved Ones, April 4, 1948.

Higdon, E.K., Executive Secretary, Department of Oriental Missions, The United Christian Missionary Society, Indianapolis, Indiana, Letter to Mr. and Mrs. Glyn B. Adsit, April 5, 1948.

Adsit, Jean, Minister and Missionary, Hofei, China, Letter to Mother (Reecie Adsit), April 10, 1948.

Adsit, Glyn B., Minister and Missionary, Hofei, Anhwei, China, Letter to Home Folks, April 19, 1948.

Adsit, Glyn B., Minister and Missionary, Hofei, Anhwei, China, Articles sent in a letter to George Walker Buckner, Jr., Editor, *World Call* , International Magazine of the Disciples of Christ entitled, "China's Sorrow," "I Baptize Thee," and "Easter in Hofei," April 25, 1948.

Adsit, Glyn B., Minister and Missionary, Hofei, China, Letter to Grandma, Uncle and Aunts, May 1, 1948.

Adsit, Jean and Glyn and newborn son Timothy Lee, Minister and Missionary, Hofei, China, Letter to Grandma, Uncles, Aunts, and Cousins, May 1, 1948.

Adsit, Glyn B., Minister and Missionary, Hofei, Anhwei, China, Letter and Pictures to Mabel Niedermeyer, Missionary Education, The United Christian Missionary Society. Indianapolis, Indiana, May 7, 1948.

Adsit, Glyn, Minister and Missionary, Hofei, China, Letter to Robins, May 10, 1948.

Adsit, Jean, Minister and Missionary, Hofei, China, Letter to First Christian Church, Amarillo, Texas, Reprinted in their church newsletter, May 16, 1948.

Adsit, Glyn B., Minister and Missionary, Hofei, Anhwei, China, Letter to Home Folks, May 26, 1948.

Adsit, Glyn B., "Hofei Hospital—Mission of Mercy," *World Call*, June, 1948, pp. 16-18. (Re-printed by permission, White, Cyrus N., President and Publisher, Christian Board of Publications, 1221 Locust Street, Suite 1200, St. Louis, MO 63103.

Adsit, Glyn, Minister and Missionary, Nanking, China, to Mother and Home Folks, June 9, 1948.

Adsit, Glyn B., Minister and Missionary, *Lot 15-B, Kuling, Kiangsi, China*, Letter to Mother and Family, June 30, 1948.

Adsit, Glyn B., Minister and Missionary, Lot 15-B, Kuling, Kiangsi, China, Letter to Home Folks, July 17, 1948.

Adsit, Jean, Minister and Missionary, Lot 15 B, Kuling, Kiangsi, China, Letter to Mother (R.L. Adsit), July 21, 1948.

Adsit, Glyn B., "China's Sorrow," *World Call*, July-August, 1948, p. 27. (Re-printed by permission, White, Cyrus N., President and

Publisher, Christian Board of Publications, 1221 Locust Street, Suite 1200, St. Louis, MO 63103).

Adsit, Glyn B., "Easter in Hofei, China," *World Call*, July-August, 1948, p. 41. (Re-printed by permission, White, Cyrus N., President and Publisher, Christian Board of Publications, 1221 Locust Street, Suite 1200, St. Louis, MO 63103).

Adsit, Glyn B., Minister and Missionary, Lot 15-B, Kuling, Kiangsi, China, Letter to Mom and Folks, August 13, 1948.

Adsit, Glyn B., Minister and Missionary, Lot 15-B, Kuling, Kiangsi, China, Letter to Home Folks, August 23, 1948 documenting never before published pictures of President Chiang Kai Shek and Madame Chiang Kai Shek.

Adsit, Glyn B., "I Baptize Thee," World Call, September, 1948, p. 47. (Re-printed by permission, White, Cyrus N., President and Publisher, Christian Board of Publications, 1221 Locust Street, Suite 1200, St. Louis, MO 63103).

Adsit, Glyn and Jean, Ministers and Missionaries, Hofei, Anhwei, China, Letter to Mom and Folks, September 12, 1948.

Adsit, Glyn B., Minister and Missionary, Hofei, Anhwei, China, Letter to James McCallum, September 22, 1948.

Adsit, Glyn., Minister and Missionary, Hofei, Anhwei, China, Letter to Mr. Walter Haskell, Treasurer, UCMS in China, Nanking, China, September 22, 1948.

Adsit, Glyn B., Treasurer, Hofei Station, Anhwei, China, Letter to Mr. Wang, September 24, 1948.

Adsit, Glyn B., Minister and Missionary, Hofei, Anhwei, China, Letter to Joy Snow, September 24, 1948.

Adsit, Glyn B., Minister and Missionary, Hofei, Anhwei, China, Letter to Administrative Council, United Christian Missionary Society, Nanking, China, September 24, 1948.

Adsit, Glyn B., Minister and Missionary and Treasurer, Hofei Station, Hofei, Anhwei, China, Letter to Administrative Council, United Christian Missionary Society, Nanking, China, September 24, 1948.

McCallum, J.H., United Christian Missionary Society, China Mission, Nanking, China, Letter to Glyn Adsit, September 29, 1948.

Adsit, Jean., Minister and Missionary, Hofei, China, Letter to Mom, September 29, 1948.

Adsit, Glyn B., Minister and Missionary, Hofei, China, Letter and article sent entitled, "Precious Package," to George Walker Buckner, Jr., Editor, *World Call*, International Magazine of Disciples of Christ, September 29, 1948.

Adsit, Glyn B., Minister and Missionary, Hofei, Anhwei, China, Letter to Mac (James McCallum) and on the back of the first letter, Letter to Walter (Haskell), October 11, 1948.

McCallum, J.H., Letter to Glyn B. Adsit, October 14, 1948.

Adsit, Glyn B., Minister and Missionary, Hofei, Anhwei, China, Letter to James McCallum and Luther Shao, October 23, 1948.

Adsit, Glyn B., Minister and Missionary, Hofei, Anhwei, China, Letter to James McCallum and Luther Shao, October 23, 1948.

Adsit, Jean, Minister and Missionary, Hofei, Anhwei, China, Letter to Clinton P. Campbell, October 26, 1948.

Adsit, Glyn B., Minister and Missionary, Hofei, Anhwei, China, Open Letter to Dear Friends, no address or name given, but sent to all Living Link Churches, documenting an incident where Glyn and others got shot at, October 26, 1948.

Adsit, Glyn B., Minister and Missionary, Hofei, China, Letter to Mother and Home Folks. Also enclosed article entitled, "Hope For the Soul of China," to be sent to George Walker Buckner,

Jr., Editor, *World Call*, International Magazine of Disciples of Christ, October 27, 1948.

Adsit, Glyn B., "The Bible Has a Message for Today," sermon preached in Hofei, China, October 10, 1948, pp.1-3.

Adsit, Glyn B., Minister and Missionary, Hofei, Anhwei, China, Letter to James McCallum and Luther Shao, November 6, 1948.

Cabot, John M., American Consul General, Letter to All American Nationals Residing in the Provinces of Kiangsu and Anhwei, Circa November 1948 (No date given but found attached to a letter from Glyn to Hofei Friends dated November 15, 1948 mentioned below this message).

Adsit, Glyn B., Minister and Missionary, Puko, China, letter to Hofei Friends, November 15, 1948.

McCallum, James, Office of the Secretary-Treasurer, United Christian Missionary Society, China Mission, Nanking, KU, China, State of the Mission Letter to Mr. Virgil Sly, November 18, 1948.

Pickens, Reverend H.B., Editor, The Butner Bulletin, Vol. 9, No. 35, USS General H.W. Butner, December 11, 1948.

Adsit, Jean, Minister and Missionary, Story Outline Jean Wrote About the Trip Leaving China, Aboard USS General W.H. Butler, December 11, 1948.

"Son of Topekan Heads Home From Warlands of China With Wife, Baby," Clipping found in scrap book, unsigned news article, name of paper, specific date, and page number not identified, Topeka, Kansas, December 1948.

Author unknown, "Missionary Personnel in China," *World Call*, January, 1948, p. 14 (Re-printed by permission, White, Cyrus N., President and Publisher, Christian Board of Publications, 1221 Locust Street, Suite 1200, St. Louis, MO 63103).

Adsit, Glyn B., "Hope for the Soul of China," *World Call*, January, 1949, pp. 27, 29 (Re-printed by permission, White, Cyrus N., President and Publisher, Christian Board of Publications, 1221 Locust Street, Suite 1200, St. Louis, MO 63103).

Adsit, Glyn B., "Precious Package," *World Call*, January, 1949, p. 39 (Re-printed by permission, White, Cyrus N., President and Publisher, Christian Board of Publications, 1221 Locust Street, Suite 1200, St. Louis, MO 63103).

"Missionaries Back From China," Beth Prim, *The Daily Oklahoman*, Oklahoma City, Oklahoma, Sunday, January 30, 1949.

"Thinks China Going Red," *The Parsons Kansas Sun*, Wednesday, February 23, 1949, p. 2. (An unsigned news story and photo).

"Missionary Society Sets Tempe Meet," Unsigned newspaper article, _________Public, Phoenix, Arizona, March 13, 1949.

"Missionary Speaks Out—War Lords, Not Chiang, Blamed for Reverses," Thomas Turner, Central Texas Bureau of the News, *The Dallas Morning News*, Dallas, Texas, Thursday, April 28, 1949, p. 20, Section II.

'Missionary Work Interrupted by War—Amarillo Visitor and Family Forced From China by Advancing Red Army," Interview of Jean Adsit by Henry Matthews, Staff Writer, *Times*, Amarillo, Texas, late April, 1949.

"Communism World Issue-Second Missionary In Warning of Spread," *World-Herald*, Omaha, Nebraska, May 1949.

"Predicts China's Fall to Reds Within a Month." Unsigned news article, *Des Moines Tribune*, Des Moines, Iowa, Monday, May 23, 1949, p. 6.

"Iowa Disciples Launch 1949 Convention," *The Challenger*, Drake University, Des Moines, Iowa, Vol. 1 No. 5, May 23, 1949, p. 1.

"Rev. Glyn Adsit to Preach at Carmen," Unsigned news article, paper unnamed, no page given, Oklahoma, June 13, 1949.

Goulter, Oswald J., Missionary and Field Director, Kiangsu-Anhwei Christian Rural Service Mission, Chuhsien, Anhwei, China, In the Midst of Revolution—"The Year's Work of the Kiangsu-Anhwei Christian Rural Service Mission," June 30, 1949, Letter to Mr. and Mrs. Glyn B. Adsit.

Yocum, C.M., Division of Foreign Missions, The United Christian Missionary Society, Indianapolis, Indiana, Letter to Mr. And Mrs. Glyn B. Adsit, July 5, 1949.

Omer, Lois, Secretarial Assistant to Spencer P. Austin, Executive Secretary, Department of Resources, The United Christian Mission Society, Indianapolis, Indiana, Letter to Mr. Glyn B. Adsit, July 27, 1949.

Sly, Virgil A., Executive Secretary, Acting Secretary for China, Division of Foreign Missions, The United Christian Missionary Society, Indianapolis, Indiana, "China Bulletin," Extracts of recent Mail from China including warning from John M. Cabot, American Consul General, to Friends of China, September 7, 1949.

McCallum, James H., Nanking, China, Confidential Letter to Dr. C.Y. Yocum, Foreign Division, United Christian Missionary Society, April 17, 1949, pp.1-3 (Copy to Glyn B. Adsit, received July 12, 1949 at Missions Building, Indianapolis, Indiana).

McCallum, J.H., 45 Pao T'ai Chieh, Nanking, China, Letters to no heading dated April 27, 1949; May 11, 1949, and May 28, 1949 respectively, but sent to United Christian Missionary Society arriving at the Missions Building on July 12, 1949, pp.1-3.

McCallum, J.H., 45 Pao T'ai Chieh, Nanking, China, Letter to no heading dated June 19, 1949 but sent to United Christian

Missionary Society, Indianapolis, Indiana arriving at the Missions Building on July 20, 1949.

Reynolds, Harriet Robertson, Shanghai, China, Letter to no heading dated July 1, 1949 but sent to United Christian Missionary Society, Indianapolis, Indiana arriving at the Missions Building on August 24, 1949.

Smythe, Lewis S.C., Nanking, China, Letter to no heading dated July 13, 1949 but sent to United Christian Missionary Society, Indianapolis, Indiana arriving at the Missions Building on August 18, 1949.

McCallum, J.H., 45 Pao T'ai Chieh, Nanking, China, Letter to no heading dated July 31, 1949 but sent to United Christian Missionary Society, Indianapolis, Indiana arriving at the Missions Building on August 10, 1949.

"Youth Rally is Underway," Unsigned newspaper article, paper name, page number not identified, University Place Christian Church, Enid, Oklahoma, September 17-22, 1949.

Unsigned announcement, "Missionaries Resign," *The Christian-Evangelist*, September 28, 1949, p. 970 (Re-printed by permission, White, Cyrus N., President and Publisher, Christian Board of Publications, 1221 Locust Street, Suite 1200, St. Louis, MO 63103).

Goulter, Oswald J., Field Director, The Kiangsu-Anhwei Christian Rural Service Union, Chuhsien, Anhwei, China, Letter to Glyn and Jean Adsit, October 25, 1949.

Elliot, Verla, Missionary, Berkeley, California, Letter to Jean and Glyn Adsit, Enid, Oklahoma, November 10, 1951.

Elliot, Verla, Missionary, Berthoud, Colorado, Christmas Letter to Glyn and Jean Adsit, December 2, 1951.

Janss, Edmund W., *Yankee Si!*, William Morrow and Company, 1961, p.67.

Chapter 4

Adsit, Glyn B. and Adsit, Alice Jean, Unpublished manuscript information written by Glyn as dictated by Jean to be used at her graveside and memorial service upon her death, Bend, Oregon, March 13, 1991, p.3.

Adsit, Glyn B., "My Spiritual Pilgrimage" Unpublished paper written in partial fulfillment of the course requirements for the course entitled, Psychology of Religion, Dr. W.E. Powell, Professor, Phillips University, Enid, Oklahoma, January 2, 1952, pp. 21-22

Adsit, Glyn B. and Adsit, Alice Jean, Unpublished manuscript information written by Glyn as dictated by Jean to be used at her graveside and memorial service upon her death, Bend, Oregon, March 13, 1991, p.3-4.)

Chapter 5

Mathew 28: 19-20 (KJV)

Bibliography

Adsit, Glyn B. (1945-49). *Adsit Diary*. Unpublished Materials Collection. In possession of Adsit, Tim L.,TLAW, Inc. ©, 20730 Barton Crossing Way, Bend, OR 97701-7711.

Adsit, Glyn B., *Letter of resignation to Mize, F.V., Manager, "A" Telegraph Office, Santa Fe Railroad,* Amarillo, Texas, July 25, 1941.

Adsit, Glyn B., Graduate Student in Sociology and Rural Education, Cornell University, Ithaca, New York, Letter and picture to Editor, *World Call Magazine*, Indianapolis, Indiana, October 11, 1945.

Adsit, Glyn B., Minister, Graduate Student, Yale University, New Haven, Connecticut, Letter to Dr. E.K. Higdon, April 15, 1947.

Adsit, Glyn B., Minister, Graduate Student, Yale University, New Haven, Connecticut, Letter to Mr. C.A. Weesner, April 15, 1947.

Adsit, Glyn., Minister and Missionary, SS Marine Adder, On the Ocean Voyage to China, Letter to Mrs. R.L. Adsit and Mr. and Mrs. Duane Adsit (Mother, Duane, and Pat), August 13, 1947.

Adsit, Glyn B., Minister and Missionary, Shanghai, China, to Mother, Reecie Adsit, undated note, circa September 1947.

Adsit, Glyn B., Minister and Missionary, Nanking, China, to Mother and family, September 15, 1947.

Adsit, Glyn B., Minister and Missionary, Chuhsien, Anhwei, China, to Mother and Family, September 23, 1947.

Adsit, Glyn B., Minister and Missionary, Chuhsien, Anhwei, China, to Mother and Home Folks, October 1, 1947.

Adsit, Glyn B., Minister and Missionary, Hofei, China, Letter to Mother(R.L. Adsit), November 20, 1947.

Adsit, Glyn B., Minister and Missionary, *Luchowfu Christian Hospital, Hofei, Anhwei, China,* Letter to Mother (R.L. Adsit), December 4, 1947.

Adsit, Glyn B., Minister and Missionary, Luchowfu Christian Hospital, Hofei, Anhwei, China, Christmas Letter to Friends in America, December 7, 1947.

Adsit, Glyn B. and Jean, Ministers and Missionaries, Luchowfu Christian Hospital, Hofei, Anhwei, China, Letter to Mother, Duane, Pat, and Mike Adsit, December 21, 1947.

Adsit, Glyn B., Minister and Missionary, Hofei, Anhwei, China, Letter to Mother and All the Rest, Christmas 1947.

Adsit, Glyn B., "A Prodigal Son Returns-A Story of Wang Yun Ting, Elder at Chuhsien," *World Call,* January, 1948, pp. 17-18 (Re-printed by permission, White, Cyrus N., President and Publisher, Christian Board of Publications, 1221 Locust Street, Suite 1200, St. Louis, MO 63103).

Adsit, Glyn B., Minister and Missionary, Hofei, Anhwei, China, letter to Mother and all brothers, sisters, nephews and dogs, January 4, 1948.

Adsit, Glyn B., Minister and Missionary, The Christian Mission, Hofei, Anhwei, China, Letter to Folks, January 17, 1948.

Adsit, Glyn B., Minister and Missionary, Hofei, Anhwei, China, article entitled, "Hofei Christian Hospital—Mission of Mercy," submitted to George Walker Buckner, Jr., Editor, *World Call*, International Magazine of Disciples of Christ, March 1, 1948.

Adsit, Glyn B., Minister and Missionary, Hofei, Anhwei, China, Letter to Home Folks, April 19, 1948.

Adsit, Glyn B., Minister and Missionary, Hofei, Anhwei, China, Articles sent in a letter to George Walker Buckner, Jr., Editor, *World Call* , International Magazine of the Disciples of Christ entitled, "China's Sorrow", "I Baptize Thee", and "Easter in Hofei," April 25, 1948.

Adsit, Glyn B., Minister and Missionary, Hofei, China, Letter to Grandma, Uncle and Aunts, May 1, 1948.

Adsit, Glyn B., Minister and Missionary, Hofei, Anhwei, China, Letter and Pictures to Mabel Niedermeyer, Missionary Education, The United Christian Missionary Society. Indianapolis, Indiana, May 7, 1948.

Adsit, Glyn, Minister and Missionary, Hofei, China, Letter to Robins, May 10, 1948.

Adsit, Glyn B., Minister and Missionary, Hofei, Anhwei, China, Letter to Home Folks, May 26, 1948.

Adsit, Glyn B., "Hofei Hospital—Mission of Mercy," *World Call*, June, 1948, pp. 16-18. (Re-printed by permission, White, Cyrus N., President and Publisher, Christian Board of Publications, 1221 Locust Street, Suite 1200, St. Louis, MO 63103.

Adsit, Glyn, Minister and Missionary, Nanking, China, to Mother and Home Folks, June 9, 1948.

Adsit, Glyn B., Minister and Missionary, *Lot 15-B, Kuling, Kiangsi, China*, Letter to Mother and Family, June 30, 1948.

Adsit, Glyn B., Minister and Missionary, Lot 15-B, Kuling, Kiangsi, China, Letter to Home Folks, July 17, 1948.

Adsit, Glyn B., "China's Sorrow," *World Call*, July-August, 1948, p. 27. (Re-printed by permission, White, Cyrus N., President and Publisher, Christian Board of Publications, 1221 Locust Street, Suite 1200, St. Louis, MO 63103).

Adsit, Glyn B., "Easter in Hofei, China," *World Call*, July-August, 1948, p. 41. (Re-printed by permission, White, Cyrus N., President and Publisher, Christian Board of Publications, 1221 Locust Street, Suite 1200, St. Louis, MO 63103).

Adsit, Glyn B., Minister and Missionary, Lot 15-B, Kuling, Kiangsi, China, Letter to Mom and Folks, August 13, 1948.

Adsit, Glyn B., Minister and Missionary, Lot 15-B, Kuling, Kiangsi, China, Letter to Home Folks, August 23, 1948 documenting never before published pictures of President, Chiang Kai Shek and Madame Chiang Kai Shek.

Adsit, Glyn B., "I Baptize Thee," *World Call*, September, 1948, p. 47. (Re-printed by permission, White, Cyrus N., President and Publisher, Christian Board of Publications, 1221 Locust Street, Suite 1200, St. Louis, MO 63103).

Adsit, Glyn B., Minister and Missionary, Hofei, Anhwei, China, Letter to James McCallum, September 22, 1948.

Adsit, Glyn., Minister and Missionary, Hofei, Anhwei, China, Letter to Mr. Walter Haskell, Treasurer, UCMS in China, Nanking, China, September 22, 1948.

Adsit, Glyn B., Treasurer, Hofei Station, Anhwei, China, Letter to Mr. Wang, September 24, 1948.

Adsit, Glyn B., Minister and Missionary, Hofei, Anhwei, China, Letter to Joy Snow, September 24, 1948.

Adsit, Glyn B., Minister and Missionary, Hofei, Anhwei, China, Letter to Administrative Council, United Christian Missionary Society, Nanking, China, September 24, 1948.

Adsit, Glyn B., Minister and Missionary and Treasurer, Hofei Station, Hofei, Anhwei, China, Letter to Administrative Council, United Christian Missionary Society, Nanking, China, September 24, 1948.

Adsit, Glyn B., Minister and Missionary, Hofei, China, Letter and article sent entitled, "Precious Package," to George Walker Buckner, Jr., Editor, *World Call,* International Magazine of Disciples of Christ, September 29, 1948.

Adsit, Glyn B., Minister and Missionary, Hofei, Anhwei, China, Letter to Mac (James McCallum) and on the back of the first letter, Letter to Walter (Haskell), October 11, 1948.

Adsit, Glyn B., Minister and Missionary, Hofei, Anhwei, China, Letter to James McCallum and Luther Shao, October 23, 1948.

Adsit, Glyn B., Minister and Missionary, Hofei, Anhwei, China, Open Letter to Dear Friends, no address or name given, but sent to all Living Link Churches, documenting an incident where Glyn and others got shot at, October 26, 1948.

Adsit, Glyn B., Minister and Missionary, Hofei, China, Letter to Mother and Home Folks. Also enclosed article entitled, "Hope For the Soul of China," to be sent to George Walker Buckner, Jr., Editor, *World Call,* International Magazine of Disciples of Christ, October 27, 1948.

Adsit, Glyn B., "The Bible Has a Message for Today," Sermon preached in Hofei, China, October 10, 1948, pp.1-3.

Adsit, Glyn B., Minister and Missionary, Hofci, Anhwei, China, Letter to James McCallum and Luther Shao, November 6, 1948.

Adsit, Glyn B., Minister and Missionary, Puko, China, Letter to Hofei Friends, November 15, 1948.

Adsit, Glyn B., "Hope for the Soul of China," *World Call*, January, 1949, pp. 27, 29 (Re-printed by permission, White, Cyrus N., President and Publisher, Christian Board of Publications, 1221 Locust Street, Suite 1200, St. Louis, MO 63103).

Adsit, Glyn B., "Precious Package," *World Call,* January, 1949, p. 39 (Re-printed by permission, White, Cyrus N., President and Publisher, Christian Board of Publications, 1221 Locust Street, Suite 1200, St. Louis, MO 63103).

Adsit, Glyn B. *My Spiritual Pilgrimage*, an unpublished paper, written in partial fulfillment for the course entitled, Psychology of Religion, Dr. W.E. Powell, Professor, Phillips University, Enid, Oklahoma, January 2, 1952.

Adsit, Glyn B. and Adsit, Alice J., Letter of application sent to the United Christian Missionary Society, Indianapolis, Indiana, written on stationary from the Westside Christian Church, Tulsa, Oklahoma, 1943.

Adsit, Glyn and Jean, Ministers and Missionaries, SS Marine Adder, Day and one half out of Japan on the Pacific Ocean heading to China, Letter to Mother, Duane, and Pat, August 21, 1947.

Adsit, Glyn and Jean, Ministers and Missionaries, Shanghai, China, Letter to Mother (R.L. Adsit), Duane and Pat Adsit, August 26, 1947.

Adsit, Glyn and Jean, Ministers and Missionaries, Lutheran Center, Shanghai, China, Letter to Mother, Duane, and Pat, September 1, 1947.

Adsit, Glyn B. and Jean, Ministers and Missionaries, Nanking, China, to Mr. Edwin Marx, October 18, 1947.

Adsit, Jean (and Glyn), Minister and Missionary, Hofei, Anhwei, China, Letter to Mother, December 26, 1947.

Adsit, Glyn B. and Jean, Ministers and Missionaries, The Christian Mission, Hofei, Anhwei, China, Letter to Family, February 1, 1948.

Adsit, Glyn B. and Jean, Ministers and Missionaries, Hofei, China, Letter to Mr. Edwin Marx, February 4, 1948.

Adsit, Glyn and Jean, Ministers and Missionaries, Hofei, Anhwei, China, Letter to Mother and all the family, February 6, 1948.

Adsit, Glyn and Jean, Ministers and Missionaries, Hofei, China, Letter to Homefolks, February 26, 1948.

Adsit, Glyn and Jean, Minister and Missionaries, Hofei, Anhwei, China, Letter to Dr. E.K. Higdon, March 1, 1948.

Adsit, Glyn and Jean, Ministers and Missionaries, Hofei, Anhwei, China, Letter to Central Christian Church, Enid, Oklahoma, and Lincoln Terrace Christian Church, Oklahoma City, Oklahoma, March 4, 1948.

Adsit, Glyn and Jean, Ministers and Missionaries, Hofei, Anhwei, China, Letter to Mother, Pat, Duane, Hurshel, and Bessie and all the rest, March 22, 1948.

Adsit, Glyn and Jean, Ministers and Missionaries, Hofei, Anhwei, China, Letter to Family, March 29, 1948.

Adsit, Glyn and Jean, Ministers and Missionaries, Hofei, Anhwei, China, Letter to Loved Ones, April 4, 1948.

Adsit, Jean and Glyn and newborn son Timothy Lee, Minister and Missionary, Hofei, China, Letter to Grandma, Uncles, Aunts, and Cousins, May 1, 1948.

Adsit, Glyn and Jean, Ministers and Missionaries, Hofei, Anhwei, China, Letter to Mom and Folks, September 12, 1948.

Adsit, Jean, Minister and Missionary, location Nanking, China, Letter to Mother, Reecie Adsit, October 4, 1947.

Adsit, Jean, Minister and Missionary, Hofei, China, Letter to Mom (Reecie Adsit), February 17, 1948.

Adsit, Jean, Minister and Missionary, Hofei, China, Letter to Mother (Reecie Adsit), April 10, 1948.

Adsit, Jean, Minister and Missionary, Hofei, China, Letter to First Christian Church, Amarillo, Texas, Reprinted in their church newsletter, May 16, 1948.

Adsit, Jean, Minister and Missionary, Lot 15-B, Kuling, Kiangsi, China, Letter to Mother (R.L. Adsit), July 21, 1948.

Adsit, Jean., Minister and Missionary, Hofei, China, Letter to Mom, September 29, 1948.

Adsit, Jean, Minister and Missionary, Hofei, Anhwei, China, Letter to Clinton P. Campbell, October 26, 1948.

Adsit, Jean, Minister and Missionary, Story Outline Jean Wrote About The Trip Leaving China, Aboard *USS General W.H. Butler*, December 11, 1948.

Adsit, Glyn B. as dictated by Adsit, Alice J. (March 13, 1991). *Unpublished manuscript* to be used at her graveside and memorial service upon her death, Bend, Oregon.

Author unknown. "Bible College Students Ordained," *Christian Evangelist*, July 4, 1945.

Author unknown, "Missionary Personnel in China," *World Call*, January, 1948, p. 14 (Re-printed by permission, White, Cyrus N., President and Publisher, Christian Board of Publications, 1221 Locust Street, Suite 1200, St. Louis, MO 63103).

Buckner, George Walker, Jr., Editor, *World Call International Magazine* of Disciples of Christ, Indianapolis, Indiana, Letter to Glyn B. Adsit, November 24, 1947.

Cabot, John M., American Consul General, Letter to All American Nationals Residing in the Provinces of Kiangsu and Anhwei, Circa November 1948 (No date given but found attached to a Letter from Glyn to Hofei Friends dated November 15, 1948 mentioned below this message).

Chen, Angie. The Stand-A Journal of Christian Thought At UCSD. (June 2002). Online at (http://www.thestandjournal. org/successful-evangelism-requires-political-and-cultural-sensitivity pp.2-3).

"China Mission Descriptive Report," From the United Christian Missionary Society, Indianapolis, Indiana, 1946. Report contained in a letter to Glyn and Jean Adsit.

"China: You Shall Never Yield," *Time Magazine*, Copyright Time, Inc. 1948, reprinted with permission in *Front Rank*, A magazine of Christian Living for Adults and Older Young People, Volume 58, No. 10, Christian Board of Publications, Saint Louis, Mo., March 6, 1948, pp. 6-7, 10-11.

"Communism World Issue-Second Missionary In Warning of Spread," *World-Herald*, Omaha, Nebraska, May 1949.

Davis, John L., Editor, "Classroom and Campus," *World Call*, February, 1945.

Doan, Mrs. Mary Lediard, Presiding, Commissioning Service Bulletin for Glyn and Jean Adsit et al, June 25, 1947.

Elliot, Verla, Missionary, Berkeley, California, Letter to Jean and Glyn Adsit, Enid, Oklahoma, November 10, 1951.

Elliot, Verla, Missionary, Berthoud, Colorado, Christmas Letter to Glyn and Jean Adsit, December 2, 1951.

Ely, Lois Anna, *Lest We Forget China Sixty-Five Years of Ups and Downs,* Christian Women's fellowship Group Study Packet, January to June 1962.

Garcia, George and Marie, Minister, Filipino United Church, Honolulu, Hawaii, Letter to Glyn and Jean Adsit, July 25, 1947.

Goulter, Oswald J., "You in Heaven"—Democracy Can Win in China, If—, *The Christian-Evangelist,* July 10, 1946. Article mailed to Glyn B. Adsit.

Goulter, Oswald J., Missionary and Field Director, Kiangsu-Anhwei Christian Rural Service Mission, Chuhsien, Anhwei, China, In the Midst of Revolution—"The Year's Work of the Kiangsu-Anhwei Christian Rural Service Mission," June 30, 1949, Letter to Mr. and Mrs. Glyn B. Adsit.

Goulter, Oswald J., Field Director, The Kiangsu-Anhwei Christian Rural Service Union, Chuhsien, Anhwei, China, Letter to Glyn and Jean Adsit, October 25, 1949.

Higdon, Dr. E.K.. Foreign Division Application Packet, "How to Become a Foreign Missionary-Qualifications, Preparation and Procedure, The United Christian Missionary Society, Indianapolis, Indiana, Letter to Glyn and Jean Adsit, 1947.

Higdon, E.K., Dr., Executive Secretary, Department of Oriental Missions, The United Christian Missionary Society (UCMS), Indianapolis, Indiana, Letter to Whom It May Concern, April 10, 1947 Re: Certification of Ordination as Ministers for Mr. And Mrs. Glyn B. Adsit and Appointment as Missionaries of the UCMS.

Higdon, E.K., Dr., Executive Secretary, Department of Oriental Missions, The United Christian Missionary Society, Indianapolis, Indiana, "Some Comments On Rural Work With Special Reference To The Hofei District In China", Copy of letter to Mr. Glyn B. Adsit, August 18, 1947

Higdon, E.K., Executive Secretary, Department of Oriental Missions, The United Christian Missionary Society, Indianapolis, Indiana, Letter to Mr. And Mrs. Glyn B. Adsit, December 18, 1947.

Higdon, E.K., Executive Secretary, Department of Oriental Missions, The United Christian Missionary Society, Indianapolis, Indiana, Letter to Mr. and Mrs. Glyn B. Adsit, April 5, 1948.

Hill, Marilynne, *Letter and Manuscript of Study Guide,* Director of Adult work, The United Christian Missionary Society, Indianapolis, Indiana, to Mrs. Glyn Adsit, September 1, 1961

Holy Bible. Ruth 1:16-17, (KJV). London and New York, Collins Clear Type Press, 1957.

___ Mathew 28: 19-20 (KJV). London and New York, Collins Clear Type Press, 1957.

"Iowa Disciples Launch 1949 Convention," *The Challenger,* Drake University, Des Moines, Iowa, Vol. 1 No. 5, May 23, 1949, p. 1.

Janss, Edmund W., *Yankee Si!,* William Morrow and Company, 1961.

"Lincoln Terrace Assigned Glyn B. Adsit," Unsigned news article, name, specific date, page number not available, May 1947.

Marx, Edwin, Office of the Secretary-Treasurer, United Christian Missionary Society, China, Mission, Nanking, KU, Letter to Glyn B. Adsit, October 24, 1947.

Matthews, Henry. 'Missionary Work Interrupted by War—Amarillo Visitor and Family Forced From China by Advancing Red Army," Interview of Jean Adsit , Staff Writer, *Times,* Amarillo, Texas, late April, 1949.

McCallum, J.H., United Christian Missionary Society, China Mission, Nanking, China, Letter to Glyn Adsit, September 29, 1948.

McCallum, J.H., Letter to Glyn B. Adsit, October 14, 1948.

McCallum, James, Office of the Secretary-Treasurer, United Christian Missionary Society, China Mission, Nanking, KU,

China, State of the Mission Letter to Mr. Virgil Sly, November 18, 1948.

McCallum, James H., Nanking, China, Confidential Letter to Dr. C.Y. Yocum, Foreign Division, United Christian Missionary Society, April 17, 1949, pp.1-3 (Copy to Glyn B. Adsit, received July 12, 1949 at Missions Building, Indianapolis, Indiana).

McCallum, J.H., 45 Pao T'ai Chieh, Nanking, China, Letters to no heading dated April 27, 1949; May 11, 1949, and May 28, 1949 respectively, but sent to United Christian Missionary Society arriving at the Missions Building on July 12, 1949, pp.1-3.

McCallum, J.H., 45 Pao T'ai Chieh, Nanking, China, Letter to no heading dated June 19, 1949 but sent to United Christian Missionary Society, Indianapolis, Indiana arriving at the Missions Building on July 20, 1949.

McCallum, J.H., 45 Pao T'ai Chieh, Nanking, China, Letter to no heading dated July 31, 1949 but sent to United Christian Missionary Society, Indianapolis, Indiana arriving at the Missions Building on August 10, 1949.

McCormick, H.B., President, Payne, Hazel Scott, Secretary, United Christian Missionary Society, Indianapolis, Indiana, to Glyn and Jean Adsit, Letters/Certificates of Appointment As Missionaries of the Society to China, Missions Building, Indianapolis, Indiana, June 25, 1947.

McCormick, H.B., President, The United Christian Missionary Society, Indianapolis, Indiana, Letter to Mr. And Mrs. Glyn Adsit, July 21, 1947.

McCormick, H.B., President, The United Christian Missionary Society, Indianapolis, Indiana, Letter to Mr. And Mrs. Glyn Adsit, September 11, 1947.

"Missionary Society Sets Tempe Meet," Unsigned newspaper article, _________Public, Phoenix, Arizona, March 13, 1949.

Mize, F.V., Manager, "A" Telegraph Office, Santa Fe Railroad, Amarillo, Texas. Personal letter accepting resignation sent to Mr. G.B. Adsit, July 26, 1941.

Niedermeyer, Mabel, Missionary Education, The United Christian Missionary Society. Indianapolis, Indiana, Letter to Mr. and Mrs., Glyn B. Adsit, January 20, 1948.

Omer, Lois, Secretarial Assistant to Spencer P. Austin, Executive Secretary, Department of Resources, The United Christian Mission Society, Indianapolis, Indiana, Letter to Mr. Glyn B. Adsit, July 27, 1949.

Pickens, Reverend H.B., Editor, The Butner Bulletin, Vol. 9, No. 35, *USS General H.W. Butner*, December 11, 1948.

"Predicts China's Fall to Reds Within a Month." Unsigned news article, *Des Moines Tribune*, Des Moines, Iowa, Monday, May 23, 1949, p. 6.

Prim, Beth. "Missionaries Back From China," *The Daily Oklahoman*, Oklahoma City, Oklahoma, Sunday, January 30, 1949.

"Rev. Glyn Adsit to Preach at Carmen," Unsigned news article, paper unnamed, no page given, Oklahoma, June 13, 1949.

Reynolds, Harriet Robertson, Shanghai, China, Letter to no heading dated July 1st, 1949 but sent to United Christian Missionary Society, Indianapolis, Indiana arriving at the Missions Building on August 24, 1949.

Sly, Virgil A., Executive Secretary, Acting Secretary for China), Division of Foreign Missions, The United Christian Missionary Society, Indianapolis, Indiana, "China Bulletin," Extracts of recent Mail from China including warning from John M. Cabot, American Consul General, to Friends of China, September 7, 1949.

Smythe, Lewis S.C., Nanking, China, Letter to no heading dated July 13, 1949 but sent to United Christian Missionary Society,

Indianapolis, Indiana arriving at the Missions Building on August 18, 1949.

"Son of Topekan Heads Home From Warlands of China With Wife, Baby," Clipping found in scrap book, unsigned news article, name of paper, specific date, and page number not identified, Topeka, Kansas, December 1948.

"Thinks China Going Red," *The Parsons Kansas Sun*, Wednesday, February 23, 1949, p. 2. (An unsigned news story and photo)

Turley, Hollis Lee, "The High Calling," *World Call*, September 1947, pp. 21-22 (Re-printed by permission, White, Cyrus N., President and Publisher, Christian Board of Publications, 1221 Locust Street, Suite 1200, St. Louis, MO 63103)

Turner, Thomas. "Missionary Speaks Out—War Lords, Not Chiang, Blamed for Reverses," Central Texas Bureau of the News, *The Dallas Morning News*, Dallas, Texas, Thursday, April 28, 1949, p. 20, Section II.

Unsigned announcement, "Missionaries Resign," *The Christian-Evangelist*, September 28, 1949, p. 970 (Re-printed by permission, White, Cyrus N., President and Publisher, Christian Board of Publications, 1221 Locust Street, Suite 1200, St. Louis, MO 63103).

Yocum, C.M., Division of Foreign Missions, The United Christian Missionary Society, Indianapolis, Indiana, Letter to Mr. And Mrs. Glyn B. Adsit, July 5, 1949.

"Youth Rally is Underway," Unsigned newspaper article, paper name, page number not identified, University Place Christian Church, Enid, Oklahoma, September 17-22, 1949.

About the Author

Tim Adsit was born to missionary parents in Hofei, China, on April 26, 1948. He is best known as a successful teacher, school administrator, author, business owner, pastor, and outdoorsman. He possesses a doctor of divinity from Cambridge Theological Seminary and advanced degrees and post-graduate study in education and educational administration from Oregon State University and the University of Oregon. He lives in Dallas, Oregon.

In addition to this book, Dr. Adsit has authored several other books, including: *Practical Ideas for Cutting Costs and Ways to Generate Alternative Revenue Sources,* Rowman and Littlefield, 2005; *Cutting Costs and Generating Revenues in Education,* Rowman and Littlefield, 2011; *Small Schools, Education, and the Importance of Community: Pathways to Improvement and a Sustainable Future,* Rowman and Littlefield, May 2011; and *The Stillness of Nature Speaks Louder Than a Choir of Voices: Adsit's Poetry Anthology, Volume I, Thoughts and Inspiration Afield,* iUniverse, 2011.

Dr. Adsit also has authored other books in the final stages of completion, including: *Thrice Ordained: Fishers of Men,* the complete biography of his parents lives as exceptional parents, teachers, missionaries, and ministers; *Success! The Tim Adsit Story* and *Method,* the compelling autobiography of his own life; and *Passport to Your Success: Strategic Planning at the Personal and Professional Level.*

Should you wish to contact the author, you may reach him at: Tim Adsit, 1635 SE Jonathan, Dallas, Oregon, 97338. Phone: 1-503-751-1238.

Note: New contact information Tim Adsit, P.O. Box 463, Prairie City, OR 97869; Phone: cell. 1-503-991-9446; home: 1-541-820-4250; e-mail: timads@bendbroadband.com.